I0335047

اذكار الصّباح والمساء

والمسبعات العشر قبل طلوع الشمس وقبل الغروب

MORNING & EVENING

INVOCATIONS

and

THE TEN SEVENS

before SUNRISE & *before* SUNSET

ARRANGED BY

Sheikh Dr **THAIKA SHU'AIB** *'Alim*

Allah benefit us by him in both abodes, Amin!

MORNING & EVENING INVOCATIONS AND
THE TEN SEVENS BEFORE SUNRISE & BEFORE SUNSET

First Print Edition, 2022
ISBN: 978-1-952306-35-8 (paperback)

Jointly Published by:

IMAM GHAZALI PUBLISHING (USA) | **THE NOBLE ARK** (SINGAPORE)

Production Team
Hafiz THAIKA MUHAMMAD SADAQAH *Jalali*
MUHAMMAD IDRIS *Jalali*
MUHAMMAD ADNAAN SATTAUR *Abu Faris*

Acknowledgements
The Production Team's gratitude is due to a large group of beautiful souls. Allah ﷻ reward them, as it befits Him, for as long as this work is in circulation and put in practice by the beloved loving seekers of the Divine Countenance.

Bulk Ordering Information
Special discounts are available on quantity purchases. For details, please contact the distributors at info@sattaurpublishing.com or www.sattaurpublishing.com.

Proudly printed in the United States of America.

CONTENTS

PREFACE 7

THE BASIS 17

MORNING & EVENING INVOCATIONS
[adhkar as-sabah wa l-masa']

1. INVOCATION **ONE** 22
Sayyiduna **ABU SA'ID AL-KHUDRI'S** ﵁ INDISPENSIBLE *isti'adha*

2. INVOCATION **TWO** 22
Sayyiduna **SULAIMAN'S** ﵇ TREMENDOUS *tasmiya*

3. INVOCATION **THREE** 23
Sayyiduna **ZAID B. THABIT'S** ﵁ VERSES OF SUPREME PROTECTION

4. INVOCATION **FOUR** 26
Sayyiduna **ABU AD-DARDA'S** ﵁ VERSE OF SUPREME SUFFICIENCY

5. INVOCATION **FIVE** 26
Sayyiduna **MA'RUF AL-KARKHI'S** ﵁ TEN WORDS FOR THIS WORLD & THE NEXT

6. INVOCATION **SIX** 28
Sayyiduna **'ABD ALLAH B. 'ABBAS'** ﵁ VERSES OF COMPLETE SUFFICIENCY

7. INVOCATION **SEVEN** 29
Sayyidatuna **JUWAIRIYA'S** ﵁ EXPRESSION OF DIVINE GLORIFICATION

8. INVOCATION **EIGHT** 30
Sayyiduna **ABU HANIFA'S** ﵁ SALVATION AT RESURRECTION & PRESERVATION OF FAITH

9. INVOCATION **NINE** 32
Sayyiduna **QABISA B. AL- MUKHARIQ'S** ﵁ LITANY FOR THIS WORLD & THE NEXT

10. INVOCATION **TEN** 33
Sayyiduna **ABU BAKRA'S** ﵁ LITANY FOR WELL-BEING & SEEKING REFUGE

11. INVOCATION **ELEVEN** 34
Sayyiduna **ANAS B. MALIK'S** ﵁ EMANCIPATION FROM THE INFERNO

12. INVOCATION **TWELVE** 35
Sayyiduna **ABU HURAIRA'S** ﷺ EXPRESSION OF SUBMISSION

13. INVOCATION **THIRTEEN** 38
Sayyiduna **'ABD ALLAH B. GHANNAM'S** ﷺ EXPRESSION OF GRATITUDE

14. INVOCATION **FOURTEEN** 39
Sayyidatuna **FATIMA AZ-ZAHRA'S** ﷺ DIVINE EXALTATION & ARDENT ENTREATY

15. INVOCATION **FIFTEEN** (MORNING **ONLY**) 40
Sayyiduna **AL-HAKIM AT-TIRMIDHI'S** ﷺ PRESERVATION OF FAITH

16. INVOCATION **FIFTEEN** (EVENING **ONLY**) 42
Sayyiduna **'ABD ALLAH B. 'AMR B. AL-'AS'** ﷺ PRESERVATION OF SELF

17. INVOCATION **SIXTEEN** 43
Sayyiduna **ABU HURAIRA'S** ﷺ SHIELD OF PROTECTION

18. INVOCATION **SEVENTEEN** 46
Sayyiduna **'UTHMAN B. 'AFFAN'S** ﷺ SHIELD OF PROTECTION

19. INVOCATION **EIGHTEEN** 46
Sayyiduna **AL-KHIDR** ﷺ *& Sayyiduna* **ILYAS'** ﷺ GREETING OF DIVINE GLORIFICATION

20. INVOCATION **NINETEEN** 47
Sayyiduna **AS-SUYUTI'S** ﷺ PANACEA FOR EVERY AILMENT

21. INVOCATION **TWENTY** 48
Sayyiduna **'ABD ALLAH B. MAS'UD'S** ﷺ FORTIFICATION OF BLESSINGS

22. INVOCATION **TWENTY-ONE** 49
Sayyiduna **AL-GHAZALI'S** ﷺ EXPRESSION OF CONTENTMENT

23. INVOCATION **TWENTY-TWO** 49
Sayyiduna **'ABD ALLAH B. MAS'UD'S** ﷺ EXPRESSION OF RELIANCE

24. INVOCATION **TWENTY-THREE** 52
Sayyiduna **ABU BAKR AS-SIDDIQ'S** ﷺ PROTECTIVE SUPPLICATION

25. INVOCATION **TWENTY-FOUR** 53
Sayyiduna **ABU UMAMA'S** ﷺ REPELLING OF WORRIES & DISCHARGING OF DEBTS

26. INVOCATION **TWENTY-FIVE** 56
Sayyiduna **SHADDAD B. AWS'** ﷺ *crème de la crème* OF SEEKING FORGIVENESS

27. INVOCATION **TWENTY-SIX** 57
Sayyiduna **ABU AD-DARDA'S** ﷺ EXPRESSION OF COMPLETE RELIANCE

28. INVOCATION **TWENTY-SEVEN** 58
Sayyiduna **ANAS B. MALIK'S** ﷺ SUPPLICATION FOR GOOD SURPRISES

29. INVOCATION **TWENTY-EIGHT** 59
Sayyiduna **'ABD ALLAH B. 'UMAR'S** ﷺ ENCOMPASSING SUPPLICATION

30. INVOCATION **TWENTY-NINE** 60
Sayyidatuna **'AISHA AS- SIDDIQA'S** ﷺ COMPLETE SUPPLICATION

31. INVOCATION **THIRTY** 64
Sayyiduna **MA'QIL B. YASAR'S** ﷺ VERSES TO ELICIT PRAYERS OF 70,000 ANGELS

32. INVOCATION **THIRTY-ONE** 66
Sayyiduna **ABU DHARR AL-GHIFARI'S** ﷺ VERSES TO ELICIT SUFFICIENCY

33. INVOCATION **THIRTY-TWO** 67
Sayyiduna **AL-HASAN AL-BASRI'S** ﷺ VERSES TO REPEL EVIL EYE

34. INVOCATION **THIRTY-THREE** 68
Sayyiduna **MUSA'S** ﷺ VERSE TO REPEL WITCHCRAFT & SORCERY

35. INVOCATION **THIRTY-FOUR** 69
Sayyiduna **KA'B B. AHBAR'S** ﷺ SEVEN VERSES OF PROTECTIVE ADEQUACY

36. INVOCATION **THIRTY-FIVE** 73
Sayyiduna **AL-QUSHAIRI'S** ﷺ SIX VERSES OF HEALING CURE

37. INVOCATION **THIRTY-SIX** 75
Sayyiduna **'ABD AL-QADIR AL-JILANI'S** ﷺ SUBLIME *wazifa*

38. INVOCATION **THIRTY-SEVEN** 78
Sayyiduna **'ABD AL-QADIR AL-JILANI'S** ﷺ SUBTLE *daqa'iq* (**MORN & EVE**)

39. INVOCATION **THIRTY-EIGHT** 81
Sayyiduna **'ABD AL-QADIR AL-JILANI'S** ﷺ SPECIAL *awrad* (**MORN & EVE**)

40. INVOCATION **THIRTY-NINE** 88
Sayyiduna **JABIR B. 'ABD ALLAH'S** ﷺ STUPENDOUS *salawat* (**MORN & EVE**)

41. INVOCATION **FORTY** 98
Sayyiduna **'ALI B. ABI TALIB'S** ﷺ VERSES OF *ikhtitam*

THE TEN SEVENS BEFORE SUNRISE & BEFORE SUNSET

[al-musabba'at al-'ashr qabla tulu' ash-shams wa qabla al-ghurub]

INTRODUCTION 100

1. FIRST **SEVEN** *surat al-fatiha* 105
2. SECOND **SEVEN** *surat an-nass* 106
3. THIRD **SEVEN** *surat al-falaq* 107
4. FOURTH **SEVEN** *surat al-ikhlas* 108

5. FIFTH SEVEN *surat al-kafirun* 109
6. SIXTH SEVEN *ayat al-kursi* 110
7. SEVENTH SEVEN *tasbih, tahmid, tahlil, takbir & hawqala* 111
8. EIGHTH SEVEN *salat 'ala n-nabi* ﷺ 114
9. NINTH SEVEN *istighfar* 115
10. TENTH SEVEN *du'a* 116

BENEFIT

[fa'ida]

SEAL OF **PROPHETHOOD** *[khatam an-nubuwwa]* 119
POSTFACE 121
PUBLISHERS' AFTERWORD 126
BIOGRAPHICAL NOTES 127
OBITUARY: *Shaikh Dr* **THAIKA SHU'AIB** *'Alim* 204

NOTES & REFERENCES 210

مُتَعَوِّذًا مُبَسْمِلًا مُحَمْدِلًا مُصَلِّيًا مُسَلِّمًا

اَللّٰهُمَّ رَبَّنَا اٰتِنَا سَعَادَةَ الدَّارَيْنِ

اَلسَّلَامُ عَلَيْكُمْ وَرَحْمَةُ اللّٰهِ وَبَرَكَاتُهُ

PREFACE

يَا اَيُّهَا الَّذِينَ اٰمَنُوا اذْكُرُوا اللّٰهَ ذِكْرًا كَثِيرًا ۝

وَسَبِّحُوهُ بُكْرَةً وَاَصِيلًا ۝

هُوَ الَّذِي يُصَلِّي عَلَيْكُمْ وَمَلَائِكَتُهُ لِيُخْرِجَكُمْ مِنَ الظُّلُمَاتِ اِلَى النُّورِ
وَكَانَ بِالْمُؤْمِنِينَ رَحِيمًا ۝

تَحِيَّتُهُمْ يَوْمَ يَلْقَوْنَهُ سَلَامٌ وَاَعَدَّ لَهُمْ اَجْرًا كَرِيمًا ۝

AFTER THE LAST THIRD OF THE NIGHT, THE MOST BLESSED, momentous and providential time for remembering Allah and being whelmed in His *rahma*, *baraka* and *'inaya* is the period between *salat al-fajr* and sunrise. This is followed in importance by the evening time which includes two periods: (a) between *'asr* and sunset and (b) between *maghrib* and *isha'*. Many are the Qur'anic verses and Prophetic traditions that single out these time periods for special virtues. They are ordinarily known and so will not be repeated here.[1]

Apart from reciting and reflecting upon the Qur'an, there is a huge corpus of recommended invocations for these time periods that one can avail of from the blessed *ahadith*. Many savants and saints of Islam have been inspired to compile *awrad* and *ahzab* from these Prophetic treasures. Some extraordinary men and women of Allah have also been moved in visions and dreams with beautiful invocations—all for mornings and evenings.

Our Grand-Shaikh, *Imam al-'Arus* Syed Muhammad b. Ahmad Lebbai ؒ (d. 1898)—eponym of the *'Arusiyya* branch of the *Qadiriyya* Sufi order—has collated many such invocations in his multifarious written works. Special mention has to be made of three works in Arwi (Arabic-Tamil): *ghanimatu s-salikin, fathu d-dayyan fi fiqhi khairi l-adyan,* and *maghani mulahi t-tibyan fi sharhi ma'ani fathi d-dayyan*. In them, *Imam al-'Arus* has sieved through volumes of classical Islamic works to extract the kernel with which the Muslims of his time could take benefit from. Being a great-grandson of this luminous personality, I have had the good fortune of benefitting tremendously from these works. It is a sign of his rank with Allah that over a century after his passing, we are still reaping the fruits of his labours of love and piety.

There is a compendium titled *al-munjiyat* wherein some of these invocations—*adhkar, ad'iyya, awrad, ahzab, istighfarat, qasa'id* and *salawat*—have been gathered. Being a hefty, tri-lingual work of almost 500 pages, there was a need for a shorter work comprising invocations for mornings and evenings only,

---

[1] See section titled *The Basis*.

accompanied by translation and transliteration. This is now in your hands.

This compilation began with 23 sets of invocations—symbolically referring to the period of Divine Revelation upon the Prophet ﷺ. It was then expanded to 33 sets of invocations—the age of the people of paradise.[2] It has now been finalised with 40 sets of invocations—the blessed age at which the Prophet ﷺ was bestowed with the office of Prophethood in this world.

Each of the 40 sets of invocations is named after a Divine Envoy *[nabi]*, a Prophetic companion *[sahabi]* or a Muhammadan saint *[wali]*. This is to pay homage to those noble souls through whom these precious treasures have reached us. Seeking a torrent of mercy *[rahma]*,[3] **Biographical Notes** of all the personages are included.

THIS NECKLACE OF INVOCATIONS HAS BEEN STRUNG PRIMARILY with priceless gems and pearls from the Qur'an and the *Sunna*. In addition, a few radiant jewels from some of the Muhammadan *awliya'* or "saints" have been included. As the *proof is in the pudding*, a detailed **Notes & References** section has been appended.

---

2 Mu'adh b. Jabal ؓ said: *The Prophet a said: The people of Paradise will enter Paradise hairless, beardless with their eyes anointed with kohl, aged thirty or thirty-three years.* (Tirmidhi's *Jami'*: 2545) In another *hadith*, Abu Huraira ؓ reports with the words *thirty three years old*, with no doubt. (Ahmad's *Musnad*: 8505)

3 Either Sufyan ath-Thawri g or Sufyan b. 'Uyaina ؓ is reported to have said: *Mercy [rahma] descends when the righteous are mentioned and remembered.* This statement is also attributed to other pious predecessors *[as-salaf as-salihin]*.

DIGRESSION: From the perils that have afflicted a group of the Muhammadan community *[umma muhammadiyya]* is the detrimental treatment of *hadith da'if* (i.e. weak *ahadith* that do not meet the criteria to derive legal rulings) akin to the *mawdudat* (i.e. fabricated and spurious sayings attributed to the Prophet ﷺ). This failure to differentiate between the two has led to their abandonment of a whole corpus of *ahadith*, baseless misgivings *[waswas]* and fuelling of unnecessary conflicts.

Some of the invocations here are from such weak *ahadith*. For the *ahl as-sunna wa l-jama'a* these are valid for devotional purposes. In fact, acting on weak *ahadith* for virtuous deeds is recommended as mentioned in *al-adhkar*. *Imam* an-Nawawi رحمه الله writes:

قال العلماء من المحدثين والفقهاء وغيرهم: يجوز، ويستحب العمل في الفضائل والترغيب والترهيب بالحديث الضعيف، ما لم يكن موضوعاً.

(النووي: مقدمة الأذكار)

The scholars—jurists, traditionists and others—have said that it is permitted, rather recommended, to act on virtuous deeds, on acts of exhortation and warning based on weak hadith, as long as they are not fabricated.

(*Imam* an-Nawawi's *muqaddima* in *al-adhkar*)

Some Muslims also tend to feel ill at ease when it comes to the devotionals of the Muhammadan saints. It has become vogue in some quarters to question the need for and even cast aspersion on *du'a*, *dhikr*, *hizb*, *munajat* and *salat 'ala n-nabi* ﷺ that are not directly from the Qur'an or the *Sunna*. This is most unfortunate.

The Muhammadan saints are the heirs of the Muhammadan legacy and have been elevated by the Muhammadan reality. The Qur'an and the *Sunna*—which define their every waking moment and passing breadth—describe and honour them categorically:

اَنَّ عُمَرَ بْنَ الْخَطَّابِ رَضِيَ اللهُ عَنْهُ قَالَ قَالَ النَّبِيُّ ﷺ:

اِنَّ مِنْ عِبَادِ اللهِ لَأُنَاسًا مَا هُمْ بِاَنْبِيَاءَ وَلَا شُهَدَاءَ يَغْبِطُهُمُ الْاَنْبِيَاءُ وَالشُّهَدَاءُ يَوْمَ الْقِيَامَةِ بِمَكَانِهِمْ مِنَ اللهِ تَعَالٰى ۞ قَالُوْا يَا رَسُوْلَ اللهِ تُخْبِرُنَا مَنْ هُمْ ۞ قَالَ هُمْ قَوْمٌ تَحَابُّوْا بِرُوْحِ اللهِ عَلٰى غَيْرِ اَرْحَامٍ بَيْنَهُمْ وَلَا اَمْوَالٍ يَتَعَاطَوْنَهَا ۞ فَوَاللهِ اِنَّ وُجُوْهَهُمْ لَنُوْرٌ وَاِنَّهُمْ عَلٰى نُوْرٍ لَا يَخَافُوْنَ اِذَا خَافَ النَّاسُ وَلَا يَحْزَنُوْنَ إِذَا حَزِنَ النَّاسُ

۞ وَقَرَاَ هٰذِهِ الْاٰيَةَ ﴿اَلَا اِنَّ اَوْلِيَاءَ اللهِ لَا خَوْفٌ عَلَيْهِمْ وَلَا هُمْ يَحْزَنُوْنَ﴾

سنن أبي داود: (٢٤)كتاب الإجارة: ١١٢

NARRATED 'UMAR B. AL-KHATTAB ﷺ:

The Prophet ﷺ said: There are people from the bondsmen of Allah who are neither prophets nor martyrs; the prophets and martyrs will envy them on the Day of Resurrection for their rank with Allah Most High.

They (the people) asked: Please tell us, O Messenger of Allah, who are they? He ﷺ replied: They are people who love one another for the spirit of Allah, without having any mutual kinship and having no transactions. I swear by Allah, their faces will glow and they will be (sitting) on (pulpits of) light. They will have no fear (on the Day) when the people will have fear, and they will not grieve when the people will grieve.

He ﷺ then recited this Qur'anic verse: ﴾Behold! Verily for the friends of Allah there is no fear, nor shall they grieve.﴿—ABU DAWUD: 3527

While the Muhammadan saints are not *ma'sum,* they are certainly *mahfuz*. Their words and works are characterised by integrity and judiciousness; when they speak, it is not always of their own volition; when they prescribe a devotional, it is inspired by Divine Providence.

Let us be clear: the *highest* ranked saint comes nowhere close to the *lowest* ranked companion of the Prophet ﷺ. Similarly, the most eloquent and skilfully weaved devotional phraseology pales in comparison to the physical beauty and spiritual worth of everything in the Qur'an and the *Sunna*. This is a given.

Let us be *crystal* clear: by incorporating devotionals from the heritage of the Muhammadan saints in our supererogatory worship, we are neither implicitly nor explicitly saying, or even hinting to the slightest, that the Qur'an and the *Sunna* are inadequate. *na'udhu bi Llah!*

Rather, what we are doing is trying to absorb and benefit from the Muhammadan lights that Allah ﷻ has manifest at the hands and on the tongues of *those who turn to Me [in love]*.[4] This is a great blessing. Just as there is no compulsion on any Muslim to adorn themselves with these lights, none has the right to deny those who wish to illuminate themselves with them.

In the end, beyond academic discussions on weak *ahadith* and devotionals of the Muhammadan saints, readers ought to remember this: *awrad* compilations and *ahzab* compositions are not exercises in vainglory. The contents and their order are (a) considered, (b) measured, and, most importantly, (c) inspired. It is the same with the work in your hands.

---

4 al-Qur'an: (*Luqman* 31:15)

THESE INVOCATIONS ARE INTENDED FOR RECITATION EVERY MORNING after *salat al-fajr* and every evening after *salat al-maghrib*. Once fluent, it should take about 15 minutes. When reciting in the morning, it is highly recommended to precede with *surat Yasin*; in the evening, with *surat as-sajda*. The recitations can be done individually as *personal worship* or in a group as *collective worship*.

From the propriety *[adab]* of reciting *awrad* is to be seated at a dedicated place[5] with (a) tranquillity and sincerity of heart *[khushu]* and (b) humility and modesty of limbs *[khudu]*. Anyone who does so with this compilation of forty sets of invocations for forty days will certainly witness tremendous unveilings, *bi idhni Llah*.

DIGRESSION: Forty has unwritten significance in Islam. While an epistle can be penned on this, the following shall suffice for our intent and purpose:

Sayyiduna Musa ﷺ entered a forty day retreat of seclusion on Mount Sinai to prepare for the Audience with Allah ﷻ. *Sayyiduna* 'Isa ﷺ fasted for forty days in the wilderness of the Judean Desert before the start of his ministry. At the age of forty, our beloved Prophet ﷺ spent—according to some, forty—days meditating in the Hira cave on the Mountain of Light *[jabal nur]* whereupon Jibril ﷺ came with the first verse of the final revelation. It has also been reported from the Prophet ﷺ,

5 This can be the mosque for those who pray in congregation or the prayer mat for those who pray at home.

عَنْ مَكْحُوْلٍ قَالَ : قَالَ رَسُوْلُ اللهِ ﷺ :

مَا مِنْ عَبْدٍ يُخْلِصُ الْعِبَادَةَ لِلّٰهِ أَرْبَعِيْنَ يَوْمًا اِلَّا ظَهَرَتْ يَنَابِيْعُ الْحِكْمَةِ مِنْ قَلْبِهِ عَلٰى لِسَانِهِ ۞ (حلية الاولياء ٥:١٨٩| مصنف ابن ابي شيبة ١٣:١٣٢)

NARRATED MAKHUL :

The Messenger of Allah said: Whoever dedicates to God forty days, the wellspring of wisdom shall manifest itself from his heart to his tongue.—Abu Nu'aim, hilyat al-awliya, 5:189. Ibn Abi Shaiba, al-Musannaf, 13:231.

The early Sufi Sahl at-Tustari has also said words to same effect, "Whosoever renounces the world for forty days with sincere devotion, miracles shall emanate from him. If they do not, there is an absence of truthfulness in his renunciation." Imam al-Munawi has said, "*The wisdom in specifying forty days is that this is the time needed to persist in changing or forming basic habits; as is known by experience.*" Allah and His Messenger know best!

IN AN AGE WHERE FULFILLING THE OBLIGATORY IS ENOUGH OF A challenge—especially for those in the daily grind of city life—our advice is to utilise daily commute productively; recite these invocations on your way to work and on your way back home. If reciting them from the book is a challenge (due to driving or other such considerations), listen to the recitation we have prepared. Over time, you will memorise all the invocations herein, *insha' Allah*.

BENEFIT: Ladies can recite these invocations during the days they are not required to pray (due to menses or lochia). When it comes to the verses of the Qur'an, they should be read—depending on the verse—with the intention of remembrance *[dhikr]*, supplication *[du'a]*, praise *[hamd]* or protection *[hifz]*. It is *worship upon worship* for them as refraining from obligatory *salat* is worship and reciting these voluntary *adhkar* is worship.

THE WIDELY KNOWN *AL-MUSABBA'AT AL-'ASHR* OR "THE TEN SEVENS" has also been included. It is a litany gifted by the Messenger of Allah ﷺ to Abu l-'Abbas Balyan b. Malkan al-Khidr عليه السلام. For those of high aspirations and lofty goals, this litany is imperative.

For added *baraka* and manifest *fai'da*, a visual representation of the Seal of Prophethood *[khatam an-nubuwwa]* seals this work.

THIS COMPILATION OF SELECTED INVOCATIONS IS FOR ALL MUSLIMS and not restricted. I beseech Allah Most High to bestow *tawfiq*, *taisir*, *naja*, *falah* & *hidaya* upon all who make this part of their daily routine. We end with this:

راى الجرير الجنيد في المنام فقال له: كيف حالك يا ابا القاسم؟ فقال: طاحت تلك
الاشارات، وذهبت تلك العبارات، وما نفعنا الا تسبيحات كنا نقولها فى الغدوات،

AFTER HIS PASSING, AL-JUNAID WAS SEEN IN A DREAM BY AL-JARIR WHO ASKED *How is your state?* AL-JUNAID REPLIED:

Those subtle signs were lost, those phrases have vanished and nothing benefited us except the invocations we used to make between fajr & sunrise.

Our Lord, accept from us, for You are the All-Hearing, the All-knowing. We ask You for all good—its beginnings and its endings. We take refuge with You from all evil—its beginnings and its endings.

رَبَّنَا تَقَبَّلْ مِنَّاۖ اِنَّكَ اَنْتَ السَّمِيْعُ الْعَلِيْمُ ۞ نَسْأَلُكَ جَوَامِعَ الْخَيْرِ وَفَوَاتِحَهُ وَخَوَاتِمَهُ ۞ وَنَعُوْذُ
بِكَ مِنْ جَوَامِعِ الشَّرِّ وَفَوَاتِحِهِ وَخَوَاتِمِهِ ۞ وَصَلَّى اللّٰهُ عَلٰى سَيِّدِنَا مُحَمَّدٍ وَاٰلِهِ وَصَحْبِهِ وَسَلَّمْ ۞
سُبْحَانَ رَبِّكَ رَبِّ الْعِزَّةِ عَمَّا يَصِفُوْنَ ۞ وَسَلٰمٌ عَلَى الْمُرْسَلِيْنَ ۞ وَالْحَمْدُ لِلّٰهِ رَبِّ الْعٰلَمِيْنَ ۞

THAIKA SHU'AIB
27 *Ramadan* 1441
Kanhangad, INDIA

THE BASIS

From the QUR'AN

يَا أَيُّهَا الَّذِينَ آمَنُوا اذْكُرُوا اللَّهَ ذِكْرًا كَثِيرًا ۞ وَسَبِّحُوهُ بُكْرَةً وَأَصِيلًا ۞

ALLAH MOST HIGH SAYS IN **AL-AHZAB**: 41-42

O you of faith, remember Allah with much remembrance, and glorify him morning & evening

فَسُبْحَانَ اللَّهِ حِينَ تُمْسُونَ وَحِينَ تُصْبِحُونَ ۞
وَلَهُ الْحَمْدُ فِي السَّمَاوَاتِ وَالْأَرْضِ وَعَشِيًّا وَحِينَ تُظْهِرُونَ ۞

ALLAH MOST HIGH SAYS IN **AR-RUM**: 17-18

So, celebrate Allah's glory in the evening & in the morning—praise is due to Him in the heavens and the earth—in the late afternoon & at midday.

وَسَبِّحْ بِحَمْدِ رَبِّكَ قَبْلَ طُلُوعِ الشَّمْسِ وَقَبْلَ غُرُوبِهَا
وَمِنْ آنَاءِ اللَّيْلِ فَسَبِّحْ وَأَطْرَافَ النَّهَارِ لَعَلَّكَ تَرْضَىٰ

ALLAH MOST HIGH SAYS IN **TAHA**: 130

Celebrate the praise of your Lord, before the rising & setting of the sun, celebrate His praise during the night, and at the beginning & end of the day, so that you may find spiritual contentment.

وَاذْكُرْ رَّبَّكَ فِيْ نَفْسِكَ تَضَرُّعًا وَّخِيْفَةً وَّدُوْنَ الْجَهْرِ
مِنَ الْقَوْلِ بِالْغُدُوِّ وَالْاٰصَالِ وَلَا تَكُنْ مِّنَ الْغٰفِلِيْنَ

ALLAH MOST HIGH SAYS IN **AL-A'RAF**: 205

Remember your Lord inwardly, in all humility & awe, without raising your voice, in the mornings & in the evenings—do not be one of the heedless

وَسَبِّحْ بِحَمْدِ رَبِّكَ بِالْعَشِيِّ وَالْاِبْكَارِ

ALLAH MOST HIGH SAYS IN **GHAFIR**: 55

Glorify the praises of your Lord in the time between mid-noon till sunset and in the time between early morning and sunrise till before mid-noon

فِيْ بُيُوْتٍ اَذِنَ اللّٰهُ اَنْ تُرْفَعَ وَيُذْكَرَ فِيْهَا اسْمُهٗ ۙ يُسَبِّحُ لَهٗ فِيْهَا بِالْغُدُوِّ وَالْاٰصَالِ ۞
رِجَالٌ ۙ لَّا تُلْهِيْهِمْ تِجَارَةٌ وَّلَا بَيْعٌ عَنْ ذِكْرِ اللّٰهِ وَاِقَامِ الصَّلٰوةِ وَاِيْتَآءِ الزَّكٰوةِ ۙ يَخَافُوْنَ يَوْمًا
تَتَقَلَّبُ فِيْهِ الْقُلُوْبُ وَالْاَبْصَارُ ۞ لِيَجْزِيَهُمُ اللّٰهُ اَحْسَنَ مَا عَمِلُوْا وَيَزِيْدَهُمْ مِّنْ فَضْلِهٖ ۗ وَاللّٰهُ
يَرْزُقُ مَنْ يَّشَآءُ بِغَيْرِ حِسَابٍ ۞

ALLAH MOST HIGH SAYS IN **NUR**: 36-38

[That light shines] through houses [of worship] which Allah has ordered to be raised, and where His Name is mentioned. He is glorified there morning and evening by men who are not distracted—either by buying or selling—from Allah's remembrance, or performing prayer, or paying alms-tax. They fear a Day when hearts and eyes will tremble, [hoping] that Allah may reward them according to the best of their deeds, and increase them out of His grace. And Allah provides for whoever He wills without limit.

وَلَا تَطْرُدِ الَّذِيْنَ يَدْعُوْنَ رَبَّهُم بِالْغَدٰوةِ وَالْعَشِيِّ يُرِيْدُوْنَ وَجْهَهٗ

ALLAH MOST HIGH SAYS IN **AL-AN'AM**: 52

Do not drive away those who call upon their Lord morning and evening, seeking nothing but His Countenance.

اِنَّا سَخَّرْنَا الْجِبَالَ مَعَهٗ يُسَبِّحْنَ بِالْعَشِيِّ وَالْاِشْرَاقِ

ALLAH MOST HIGH SAYS IN **SAD**: 18

We truly subjected the mountains to hymn [Our praises] along with him in the evening and after sunrise.

From the AHADITH

اَنَّ النَّبِيَّ ﷺ كَانَ اِذَا صَلَّى الْفَجْرَ جَلَسَ فِيْ مُصَلَّاهُ حَتّٰى تَطْلُعَ الشَّمْسُ حَسَنًا

When the Messenger of Allah ﷺ observed the dawn prayer, he sat at the place of worship till the sun had risen enough.

MUSLIM: 670b

قَالَ رَسُوْلُ اللهِ ﷺ: لاَنْ اَقْعُدَ مَعَ قَوْمٍ يَذْكُرُوْنَ اللهَ تَعَالٰى مِنْ صَلَاةِ الْغَدَاةِ حَتّٰى تَطْلُعَ الشَّمْسُ أَحَبُّ اِلَيَّ مِنْ اَنْ اُعْتِقَ اَرْبَعَةً مِنْ وَلَدِ اِسْمَاعِيْلَ ، وَلاَنْ اَقْعُدَ مَعَ قَوْمٍ يَذْكُرُوْنَ اللهَ مِنْ صَلَاةِ الْعَصْرِ اِلٰى اَنْ تَغْرُبَ الشَّمْسُ اَحَبُّ اِلَيَّ مِنْ اَنْ اُعْتِقَ اَرْبَعَةً ،

THE MESSENGER OF ALLAH ﷺ SAID*:*

That I sit in the company of those who remember Allah the Exalted from morning prayer till the sun rises is dearer to me than that I emancipate four slaves from the children of Isma'il, and that I sit with those who remember Allah from afternoon prayer till the sun sets is dearer to me than that I emancipate four slaves.

ABU DAWUD: 3667

قَالَ رَسُوْلُ اللهِ ﷺ: مَنْ صَلَّى الْغَدَاةَ فِيْ جَمَاعَةٍ ثُمَّ قَعَدَ يَذْكُرُ اللهَ
حَتّٰى تَطْلُعَ الشَّمْسُ ثُمَّ صَلَّى رَكْعَتَيْنِ كَانَتْ لَهُ كَأَجْرِ حَجَّةٍ وَعُمْرَةٍ ،
قَالَ قَالَ رَسُوْلُ اللهِ ﷺ تَامَّةٍ تَامَّةٍ تَامَّةٍ،

THE MESSENGER OF ALLAH ﷺ SAID:

Whoever prays fajr in congregation, then sits remembering Allah until the sun has risen, then he prays two rak'a, then for him is the reward like that of a Hajj and 'Umra ... complete, complete, complete.

TIRMIDHI: 586

From the SAINTS

راى الجرير الجنيد في المنام فقال له: كيف حالك يا ابا القاسم؟
فقال: طاحت تلك الاشارات، وذهبت تلك العبارات،
وما نفعنا الا تسبيحات كنا نقولها فى الغدوات،

AFTER HIS PASSING, AL-JUNAID WAS SEEN IN A DREAM BY AL-JARIR WHO ASKED *How is your state?* AL-JUNAID REPLIED:

Those subtle signs were lost, those phrases have vanished and nothing benefited us except the invocations we used to make between fajr & sunrise.

MORNING & EVENING INVOCATIONS

[adhkar as-sabah wa l-masa']

Sayyiduna ABU SA'ID AL-KHUDRI'S
INDISPENSIBLE *isti'adha*

اَعُوذُ بِاللهِ السَّمِيعِ الْعَلِيمِ مِنَ الشَّيْطَانِ الرَّجِيمِ مِنْ هَمْزِهِ وَنَفْخِهِ وَنَفْثِهِ

(١ مرة)

a'ūdhu bi Llāhi s-samī'i l-'alīmi mina sh-shaiṭāni r-rajīmi min hamzihi wa nafkhihi wa nafthihi • (1 time)

I seek refuge with Allah—the All-Hearing, the All-Knowing—from the calumny, conceit and conspiracy of the accursed devil.¹

Sayyiduna SULAIMAN'S
TREMENDOUS *tasmiya*

﴿إِنَّهُ مِنْ سُلَيْمَٰنَ وَإِنَّهُ بِسْمِ اللهِ الرَّحْمَٰنِ الرَّحِيمِ﴾ (١ مرة)

innahū min sulaimāna wa innahū bismi Llāhi r-raḥmāni r-raḥīm • (1 time)

[27:30] *﴾It is from Solomon and it says:*
In the name of Allah, the Universally Merciful,
the Singularly Compassionate﴿[2]

-٣-

Sayyiduna **ZAID B. THABIT'S** ﵁

VERSES OF SUPREME PROTECTION

﴿لَقَدْ جَآءَكُمْ رَسُوْلٌ مِّنْ اَنفُسِكُمْ عَزِيْزٌ عَلَيْهِ مَا عَنِتُّمْ
حَرِيْصٌ عَلَيْكُمْ بِالْمُؤْمِنِيْنَ رَءُوْفٌ رَّحِيْمٌ ۞ فَاِنْ تَوَلَّوْا فَقُلْ
حَسْبِيَ اللّٰهُ ۖ قذ لَآ اِلٰهَ اِلَّا هُوَ ۗ
عَلَيْهِ تَوَكَّلْتُ وَهُوَ رَبُّ الْعَرْشِ الْعَظِيْمِ﴾

(١ مرة)

laqad jā'akum rasūlun min anfusikum 'azīzun 'alaihi mā 'anittum ḥarīṣun 'alaikum bi l-mu'minīna ra'ūfun rahīm • fa-in tawallaw fa-qul ḥasbiya Llāhu lā ilāha illā Huwa 'alaihi tawakkaltu wa Huwa Rabbu l-'arshi l-aẓīm • (1 time)

[9:128-129] *﴾A Messenger has come to you from among yourselves. Your suffering distresses him: he is deeply concerned for you and full of kindness and mercy towards the believers.*

If they turn away, [Prophet], say, "Allah is enough for me, there is no god but Him, in Him I trust, and He is the Lord of the Glorious Throne."﴿ [3]

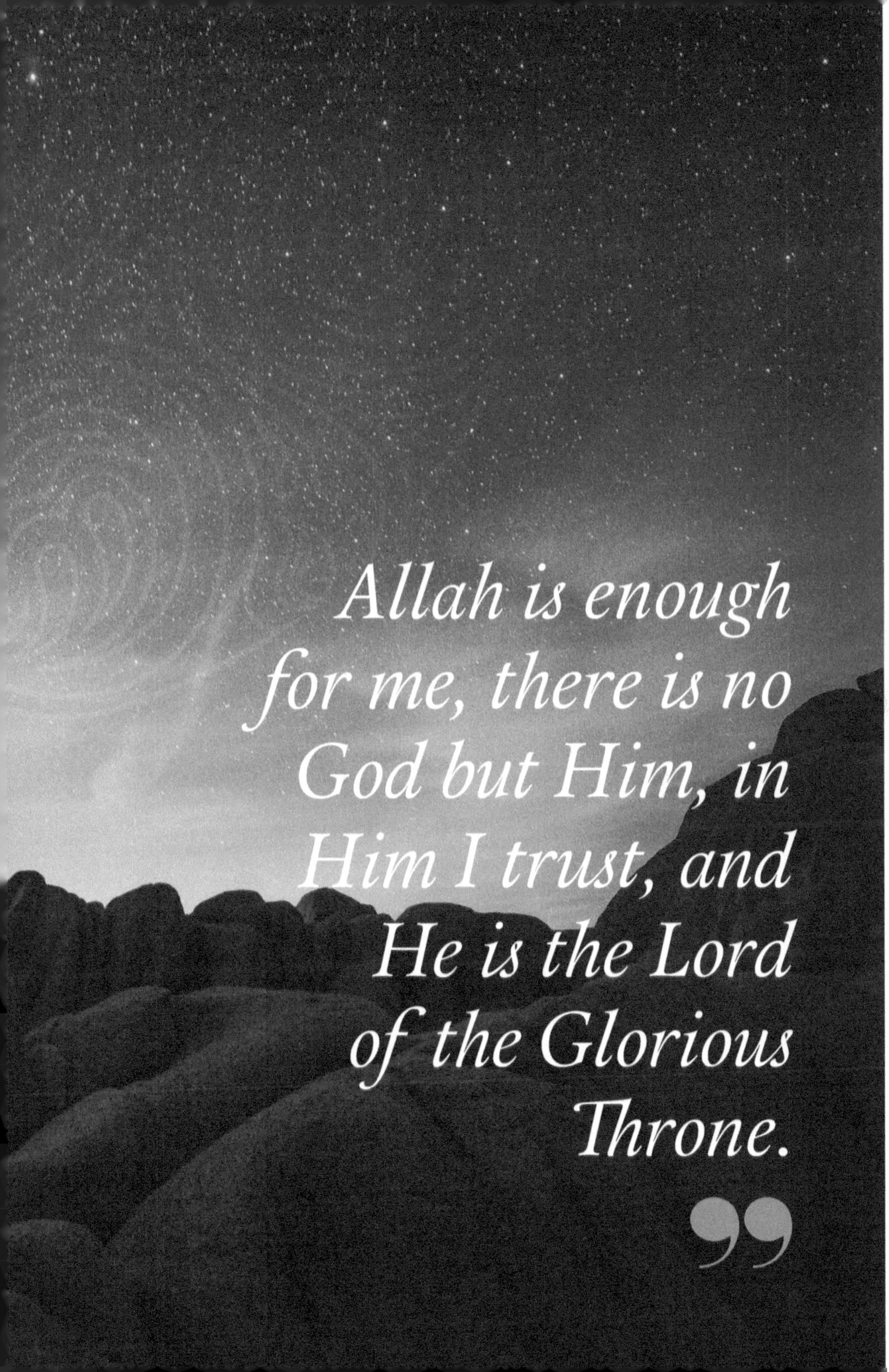
Allah is enough for me, there is no God but Him, in Him I trust, and He is the Lord of the Glorious Throne.

-٤-

Sayyiduna **ABU AD-DARDA'S** ﷺ

VERSE OF SUPREME SUFFICIENCY

﴿حَسْبِيَ اللّٰهُ لَا إِلٰهَ إِلَّا هُوَ عَلَيْهِ تَوَكَّلْتُ وَهُوَ رَبُّ الْعَرْشِ الْعَظِيمِ﴾

(٧ مرات)

ḥasbiya Llāhu lā ilāha illā Huwa 'alaihi tawakkaltu wa Huwa Rabbu l-'arshi l-aẓīm • (7 times)

9:129 ﴾*Allah is enough for me, there is no god but Him; in Him I trust, and He is the Lord of the Glorious Throne.*﴿[4]

-٥-

Sayyiduna **MA'RUF AL-KARKHI'S** ﷺ

TEN WORDS FOR THIS WORLD & THE NEXT

(١) حَسْبِيَ اللّٰهُ لِدِينِي ۞ (٢) حَسْبِيَ اللّٰهُ لِدُنْيَايَ ۞

(٣) حَسْبِيَ اللّٰهُ الْكَرِيمُ لِمَا أَهَمَّنِي ۞

(٤) حَسْبِيَ اللّٰهُ الْحَلِيمُ الْقَوِيُّ لِمَنْ بَغَى عَلَيَّ ۞

(٥) حَسْبِيَ اللّٰهُ الشَّدِيْدُ لِمَنْ كَادَنِيْ بِسُوْءٍ ۞

(٦) حَسْبِيَ اللّٰهُ الرَّحِيْمُ عِنْدَ الْمَوْتِ ۞

(٧) حَسْبِيَ اللّٰهُ الرَّءُوْفُ عِنْدَ الْمَسْأَلَةِ فِي الْقَبْرِ ۞

(٨) حَسْبِيَ اللّٰهُ الْكَرِيْمُ عِنْدَ الْحِسَابِ ۞

(٩) حَسْبِيَ اللّٰهُ اللَّطِيْفُ عِنْدَ الْمِيْزَانِ ۞

(١٠) حَسْبِيَ اللّٰهُ الْقَدِيْرُ عِنْدَ الصِّرَاطِ ۞

حَسْبِيَ اللّٰهُ لَا اِلٰهَ اِلَّا هُوَ عَلَيْهِ تَوَكَّلْتُ وَهُوَ
رَبُّ الْعَرْشِ الْعَظِيْمِ ۞

(١ مرة)

(1) ḥasbiya Llāhu li-dīnī • (2) ḥasbiya Llāhu li-dunyāya • (3) ḥasbiya Llāhu l-karīmu li-mā ahammanī • (4) ḥasbiya Llāhu l-ḥalīmu l-qawiyyu li-man baghā ʿalayya • (5) ḥasbiya Llāhu sh-shadīdu li-man kādanī bi sū'(in) • (6) ḥasbiya Llāhu r-raḥīmu ʿinda l-mawt • (7) ḥasbiya Llāhu r-ra'ūfu ʿinda l-mas'alati fi l-qabr • (8) ḥasbiya Llāhu l-karīmu ʿinda l-ḥisāb • (9) ḥasbiya Llāhu l-laṭīfu ʿinda l-mīzān • (10) ḥasbiya Llāhu l-qadīru ʿinda ṣ-ṣirāṭ • ḥasbiya Llāhu lā ilāha illā huwa ʿalaihi tawakkaltu wa huwa rabbu l-ʿarshi l-ʿaẓīm(i) • (1 time)

(1) *Allah is enough for me in my religion* · (2) *Allah is enough for me in my mundane life* · (3) *Allah, the Generous [al-Karim], is enough for me in what distresses me* · (4) *Allah, the Affectionate [al-Halim], the Strong [al-Qawiyy], is enough for me against him who oppresses me* · (5) *Allah, the Stern [ash-Shadid], is enough for me against him who hurts me by evil* · (6) *Allah, the Compassionate [ar-Rahim], is enough for me at death [mawt]* · (7) *Allah, the Merciful [ar-Ra'uf], is enough for me at the Inquisition in the Grave [qabr]* · (8) *Allah, the Generous [al-Karim], is enough for me at the Reckoning [hisab]* · (9) *Allah, the Beneficent [al-Latif], is enough for me at the Scales [mizan]* · (10) *Allah, the Powerful [al-Qadir], is enough for me at the crossing of the Traverse [sirat]* · *Allah is enough for me, there is no god but He, in Him do I trust, He is the Lord of the Glorious Throne.*[5]

-٦-

Sayyiduna **'ABD ALLAH B. 'ABBAS'** ﵄

VERSES OF COMPLETE SUFFICIENCY

﴿فَسُبْحَٰنَ ٱللَّهِ حِينَ تُمْسُونَ وَحِينَ تُصْبِحُونَ ۝ وَلَهُ ٱلْحَمْدُ فِى
ٱلسَّمَٰوَٰتِ وَٱلْأَرْضِ وَعَشِيًّا وَحِينَ تُظْهِرُونَ ۝ يُخْرِجُ ٱلْحَىَّ
مِنَ ٱلْمَيِّتِ وَيُخْرِجُ ٱلْمَيِّتَ مِنَ ٱلْحَىِّ وَيُحْىِ ٱلْأَرْضَ بَعْدَ مَوْتِهَا
وَكَذَٰلِكَ تُخْرَجُونَ﴾

(١ مرة)

fa-subḥāna Llāhi ḥīna tumsūna wa ḥīna tuṣbiḥūn • wa lahu l-ḥamdu fi s-samāwāti wa l-arḍi wa ʿashiyyan wa ḥīna tuẓhirūn • yukhriju l-ḥayya mina l-mayyiti wa yukhriju l-mayyita mina l-ḥayyi wa yuḥyi l-arḍa baʿda mawtihā wa ka-dhālika tukhrajūn • (1 time)

30:17-19 ❮ *So glory be to Allah when you reach evening & when you rise in the morning · and to Him be praise, in the heavens and on earth, and at eventide and at noontide · He brings out the living from the dead, and brings out the dead from the living; and He gives life to the earth after it is dead; and thus shall you be risen up again [from dust].* ❯[6]

Sayyidatuna **JUWAIRIYA'S**
EXPRESSION OF DIVINE GLORIFICATION

سُبْحَانَ اللهِ وَبِحَمْدِهِ ۞ عَدَدَ خَلْقِهِ ۞ وَرِضَا نَفْسِهِ ۞ وَزِنَةَ عَرْشِهِ ۞ وَمِدَادَ كَلِمَاتِهِ ۞

(٣ مرات)

subḥāna Llāhi wa bi-ḥamdih(i) • ʿadada khalqih(i) • wa riḍā nafsih(i) • wa zinata ʿarshih(i) • wa midāda kalimātih(i) (3 times)

Glory to Allah & Praise to Him · according to the number of His creation · according to the pleasure of His Self · according to the weight of His Throne · according to the ink [used to record] words [for His Praise].[7]

-٨-

Sayyiduna **ABU HANIFA'S** ﷺ

SALVATION AT RESURRECTION & PRESERVATION OF FAITH

سُبْحَانَ الْاَبَدِيِّ الْاَبَدِ ۞ سُبْحَانَ الْوَاحِدِ الْاَحَدِ ۞
سُبْحَانَ الْفَرْدِ الصَّمَدِ ۞ سُبْحَانَ رَافِعِ السَّمَآءِ بِلَا عَمَدٍ ۞
سُبْحَانَ مَنْ بَسَطَ الْاَرْضَ عَلٰى مَاءٍ جَمَدٍ ۞
سُبْحَانَ مَنْ خَلَقَ الْخَلْقَ فَاَحْصَاهُمْ عَدَدًا ۞
سُبْحَانَ مَنْ قَسَمَ الرِّزْقَ وَلَمْ يَنْسَ اَحَدًا ۞
سُبْحَانَ الَّذِيْ لَمْ يَتَّخِذْ صَاحِبَةً وَّلَا وَلَدًا ۞
سُبْحَانَ الَّذِيْ لَمْ يَلِدْ وَلَمْ يُوْلَدْ وَلَمْ يَكُنْ لَّهٗ
كُفُوًا اَحَدٌ ۞ نَجَا مِنْ عَذَابِ يَوْمَ الْقِيَامَةِ ۞ (١ مرة)
اَللّٰهُمَّ اَحْيِنِيْ عَلَى الْكِتَابِ وَالسُّنَّةِ وَتَوَفَّنِيْ مَعَ الْاِيْمَانِ وَالتَّوْبَةِ
۞ اَللّٰهُمَّ صَلِّ عَلٰى رَسُوْلِكَ سَيِّدِنَا مُحَمَّدٍ وَّاٰلِهٖ وَصَحْبِهٖ وَسَلِّمْ ۞
وَافْعَلْ بِنَا ذٰلِكَ وَبِجَمِيْعِ الْمُسْلِمِيْنَ (١ مرة)

subḥāna l-abadiyyi l-abad • subḥāna l-wāḥidi l-aḥad • subḥāna l-fardi ṣ-ṣamad • subḥāna rāfiʿi s-samāʾi bi-lā ʿamad• subḥāna man basaṭa l-arḍa ʿalā māʾin jamud • subḥāna man khalaqa l-khalqa fa aḥṣāhum ʿadada • subḥāna man qasama r-rizqa wa lam yansa aḥada • subḥāna Lladhī lam yattakhidh ṣāḥibatan wa lā walada • subḥāna Lladhī lam yalid wa lam yūlad wa lam yakun la-hu kufuwan aḥad • najā min ʿadhābi yawma l-qiyāmah • (1 time)

Allāhumma aḥyinī ʿala l-kitābi wa s-sunnati wa tawaffanī ʿala l-īmāni wa t-tawbah • Allāhumma ṣalli ʿalā rasūlika sayyidinā Muḥammadin wa ālihi wa ṣaḥbihi wa sallim • wa-fʿal binā dhālika wa bi jamīʿi l-muslimīn • (1 time)

Glorified be He, who is Infinite, Eternal · Glorified be He, who is One, Unequalled · Glorified be He, who is independent of all things · Glorified be He, who has lifted the sky without any pillars · Glorified be He, who has laid out the earth firm on water · Glorified be He, who has created the entire creation and has counted all · Glorified be He, who distributes sustenance without neglecting anyone · Glorified be He, who has neither partner nor son · Glorified be He, who neither begets nor is begotten nor have an equal · [Bestow] salvation from the afflictions of the Day of Resurrection.[8A]

O Allah, keep me alive upon the Book and the Sunna and grant me death in faith and repentance. O Allah whelm salutations upon Your Envoy and our liege Muhammad ﷺ, and his family and companions, and grant them peace. Keep us and all Muslims upon it.[8B]

Sayyiduna QABISA B. AL-MUKHARIQ'S
LITANY FOR THIS WORLD & THE NEXT

سُبْحَانَ اللهِ وَبِحَمْدِهِ ۞ سُبْحَانَ اللهِ الْعَظِيْمِ ۞ لَا حَوْلَ وَلَا قُوَّةَ اِلَّا بِاللهِ الْعَلِيِّ الْعَظِيْمِ ۞

(٣ مرات)

اَللّٰهُمَّ اهْدِنِيْ مِنْ عِنْدِكَ ۞ وَاَفِضْ عَلَيَّ مِنْ فَضْلِكَ ۞ وَانْشُرْ عَلَيَّ مِنْ رَحْمَتِكَ ۞ وَاَنْزِلْ عَلَيَّ مِنْ بَرَكَاتِكَ ۞

(٣ مرات)

subḥāna Llāhi wa bi-ḥamdih(i) • subḥāna Llāhi l-ʿaẓīm(i) • lā ḥawla wa lā quwwata illā bi Llāhi l-ʿaliyyi l-ʿaẓīm(i) • (3 times)

Allāhumma hdinī min ʿindik(a) • wa afiḍ ʿalayya min faḍlik(a) • wa-nshur ʿalayya min raḥmatik(a) • wa anzil ʿalayya min barakātik(a) • (3 times)

Glory to Allah and Praise to Him · Glory to Allah, the Magnificent· There is no power or strength except by Allah, the Most High, the Mighty.

O Allah, guide me from Your part · pour over me Your favour · spread on me Your mercy · and bestow upon me Your blessings.[9]

-١٠-

Sayyiduna ABU BAKRA'S ؓ
LITANY FOR WELL-BEING & SEEKING REFUGE

اَللّٰهُمَّ عَافِنِيْ فِيْ بَدَنِيْ ۞ اَللّٰهُمَّ عَافِنِيْ فِيْ سَمْعِيْ ۞
اَللّٰهُمَّ عَافِنِيْ فِيْ بَصَرِيْ ۞ لَا اِلٰهَ اِلَّا اَنْتَ ۞

(٣ مرات)

اَللّٰهُمَّ اِنِّيْٓ اَعُوْذُ بِكَ مِنَ الْكُفْرِ وَالْفَقْرِ ۞ اَللّٰهُمَّ اِنِّيْٓ
اَعُوْذُ بِكَ مِنْ عَذَابِ الْقَبْرِ ۞ لَا اِلٰهَ اِلَّا اَنْتَ ۞

(٣ مرات)

Allāhumma ʿāfinī fī badanī • Allāhumma ʿāfinī fī samʿī • Allāhumma ʿāfinī fī baṣarī • lā ilāha illā anta • (3 times)

Allāhumma innī aʿūdhu bi-ka mina l-kufri wa l-faqr(i) • Allāhumma innī aʿūdhu bi-ka min ʿadhābi l-qabr(i) • lā ilāha illā anta • (3 times)

O Allah, grant me well-being in my body · O Allah, grant me well-being in my hearing · O Allah, grant me well-being in my sight · there is no god but You.

O Allah, I seek refuge in You from disbelief and poverty · O Allah, I seek refuge in Your from the torment of the grave · there is no god but You.[10]

-١١-

Sayyiduna **ANAS B. MALIKS'S** ﷺ

EMANCIPATION FROM THE INFERNO

اَللّٰهُمَّ اِنِّيٓ اَصْبَحْتُ | اَمْسَيْتُ اُشْهِدُكَ ۞ وَاُشْهِدُ حَمَلَةَ عَرْشِكَ وَمَلٰٓئِكَتَكَ وَجَمِيْعَ خَلْقِكَ

۞ اَنَّكَ اَنْتَ اللّٰهُ ۞ لَا اِلٰهَ اِلَّا اَنْتَ ۞ وَاَنَّ مُحَمَّدًا عَبْدُكَ وَرَسُوْلُكَ ۞ (٤ مرات)

Allāhumma aṣbaḥtu | amsaitu ushhiduk(a) • wa ush-hidu ḥamalata ʿarshika wa malā'ikataka wa jamīʿa khalqik(a) • an-naka anta Llāhu • lā ilāha illā anta • wa anna Muḥammadan ʿabduka wa rasūluk(a) • (4 times)

O Allah, I have entered the morning | evening calling on You to witness · and calling on the bearers of Your Throne and Your angels and all of Your creation to witness · that You are Allah · there is no god but You · and Muhammad is Your [precious] slave and [distinguished] envoy.[11]

-١٢-

Sayyiduna **ABU HURAIRA'S** ؓ

EXPRESSION OF SUBMISSION (**MORNING**)

اَللّٰهُمَّ بِكَ اَصْبَحْنَا وَبِكَ اَمْسَيْنَا ❀ وَبِكَ
نَحْيٰي وَبِكَ نَمُوْتُ ❀ وَاِلَيْكَ النُّشُوْرُ ❀ (١ مرة)

Allāhumma bika aṣbaḥnā wa bika amsainā • wa bika naḥyā wa bika namūt • wa ilaika n-nushūr • (1 time)

O Allah, by You we have entered the morning and by You we have entered the evening · by You we live and by You we die · and to You is the resurrection.[12]

Sayyiduna **ABU HURAIRA'S** ؓ

EXPRESSION OF SUBMISSION (**EVENING**)

اَللّٰهُمَّ بِكَ اَمْسَيْنَا وَبِكَ اَصْبَحْنَا ❀ وَبِكَ
نَحْيٰي وَبِكَ نَمُوْتُ ❀ وَاِلَيْكَ الْمَصِيْرُ ❀ (١ مرة)

Allāhumma bika amsainā wa bika aṣbaḥnā • wa bika naḥyā wa bika namūt • wa ilaika l-maṣīr • (1 time)

O Allah, by You we have entered the evening and by You we have entered the morning · by You we live and by You we die · and to You is the return.

O Allah, by You
we have entered
the morning
and by You we
have entered the
evening
”

-١٣-

Sayyiduna ʿ**ABD ALLAH B. GHANNAM'S** ؓ
EXPRESSION OF GRATITUDE (**MORNING**)

اَللّٰهُمَّ مَا اَصْبَحَ بِيْ مِنْ نِعْمَةٍ اَوْ بِاَحَدٍ مِّنْ خَلْقِكَ فَمِنْكَ
وَحْدَكَ لَا شَرِيْكَ لَكَ ❀ فَلَكَ الْحَمْدُ وَلَكَ الشُّكْرُ ❀ (١ مرة)

Allāhumma mā aṣbaḥa bī min niʿmatin aw bi-aḥadin min khalqika fa minka waḥdaka lā sharīka lak(a) • fa laka l-ḥamdu wa laka sh-shukr(u) • (1 time)

O Allah, all the favours that I or any of Your creation have received this morning are from You alone; You have no partner. To You belong all praise and all thanks.[13]

Sayyiduna ʿ**ABD ALLAH B. GHANNAM'S** ؓ
EXPRESSION OF GRATITUDE (**EVENING**)

اَللّٰهُمَّ مَا اَمْسَى بِيْ مِنْ نِعْمَةٍ اَوْ بِاَحَدٍ مِّنْ خَلْقِكَ فَمِنْكَ
وَحْدَكَ لَا شَرِيْكَ لَكَ ❀ فَلَكَ الْحَمْدُ وَلَكَ الشُّكْرُ ❀ (١ مرة)

Allāhumma mā amsa bī min niʿmatin aw bi-aḥadin min khalqika fa minka waḥdaka lā sharīka lak(a) • fa laka l-ḥamdu wa laka sh-shukr(u) • (1 time)

O Allah, all the favours that I or any of Your creation have received this <u>evening</u> are from You alone; You have no partner. To You belong all praise and all thanks.

Sayyidatuna **FATIMA AZ-ZAHRA'S**
DIVINE EXALTATION

اَللّٰهُمَّ يَا اَوَّلَ الْاَوَّلِينَ ❊ وَيَا اٰخِرَ الْاٰخِرِينَ ❊
وَيَا ذَا الْقُوَّةِ الْمَتِينَ ❊ وَيَا رَاحِمَ الْمَسَاكِينَ ❊
وَيَا اَرْحَمَ الرَّاحِمِينَ ❊ (٣ مرات)

Allāhumma yā awwala l-awwalīn • wa yā āk͟hira l-āk͟hirīn • wa yā d͟ha l-quwwati l-matīn • wa yā rāḥima l-masākīn • wa yā arḥama r-rāḥimīn • (3 times)

O Allah, O First of the first · O Last of the last · O Possessor of absolute power · O He who shows mercy to the impoverished · O Quintessence of mercy.[14A]

Sayyidatuna FATIMA AZ-ZAHRA'S
ARDENT ENTREATY

يَا حَيُّ يَا قَيُّومُ ۞ بِرَحْمَتِكَ اَسْتَغِيْثُ ۞ اَصْلِحْ لِيْ شَأْنِيْ كُلَّهُ ۞ وَلَا تَكِلْنِيْ اِلٰى نَفْسِيْ طَرْفَةَ عَيْنٍ ۞ (٣ مرات)

yā Ḥayyu yā Qayyūm(u) • bi raḥmati-ka astag͟hīt͟h • aṣliḥ lī sha'nī kullah(u) • wa lā takilnī ilā nafsī ṭarfata 'ain • (3 times)

O Ever-Living, O Self-Sustaining • In Your Mercy do I seek relief • so, rectify my affair entirely • and do not leave me to myself for the blink of an eye. [14B]

Sayyiduna AL-HAKIM AT-TIRMIDHI'S
PRESERVATION OF FAITH
(MORNING ONLY)

يَا حَيُّ يَا قَيُّومُ ۞ يَا بَدِيْعَ السَّمٰوٰتِ وَالْاَرْضِ ۞ يَا ذَا الْجَلَالِ وَالْاِكْرَامِ ۞ يَا اَللهُ ۞ لَا اِلٰهَ اِلَّا اَنْتَ ۞

(٣ مرات)

اَللّٰهُمَّ بِحُرْمَةِ الْحَسَنِ وَاَخِيْهِ وَجَدِّهِ وَاَبِيْهِ وَاُمِّهِ وَبَنِيْهِ ۞ نَجِّنِيْ مِنَ الْغَمِّ الَّذِيْ اَنَا فِيْهِ ۞

يَا حَيُّ يَا قَيُّومُ ❁ يَا ذَا الْجَلَالِ وَالْإِكْرَامِ ❁
اَسْأَلُكَ اَنْ تُحْيِيَ قَلْبِيْ بِنُوْرِ مَعْرِفَتِكَ ❁
يَا اَللّٰهُ يَا اَللّٰهُ يَا اَللّٰهُ ❁ يَا اَرْحَمَ الرَّاحِمِيْنَ ❁

(١ مرة)

yā Ḥayyu yā Qayyūm(u) • yā badī'a s-samāwāti wa l-arḍ • yā dha l-Jalāli wa l-Ikrām • yā Allāh • lā ilāha illā ant(a) • (3 times)

Allāhumma bi ḥurmati l-Ḥasani wa akhīhi wa jaddihi wa abīhi wa ummihi wa banīh(i) • najjinī mina l-ghammi lladhī anā fīh(i) • yā Ḥayyu yā Qayyūm(u) • yā dha l-jalāli wa l-ikrām • as'aluka an tuḥyiya qalbī bi-nūri ma'rifatika • yā Allāh yā Allāh yā Allāh • yā arḥama r-rāḥimīn • (1 time)

O Ever-Living, O Self-Sustaining · O Originator of the heavens and the earth · O You of Majesty and Munificence · O Allah · there is no god worthy of worship but You ·

O Allah, by the sanctity of (Imam) al-Hasan ؑ, his brother (Imam al-Husain ؑ), his grandfather (the Prophet ﷺ), his father (Imam 'Ali ؑ), his mother (Lady Fatima ؑ), and his progeny ؑ—deliver me from the sorrow that I am in. O Ever-Living, O Self-Subsisting! O Possessor of Majesty and Honour!

I beseech You to purify and revive my heart with the light of Gnosis—mystical intuitive knowledge of spiritual truth [ma'rifa] · O Allah, O Allah, O Allah · O Quintessence of Mercy.[15A]

-١٥-

Sayyiduna **'ABD ALLAH B. 'AMR B. AL-'AS'** ﵁

PRESERVATION OF SELF

(EVENING ONLY)

يَا مَنْ اَظْهَرَ الْجَمِيْلَ وَسَتَرَ الْقَبِيْحَ ۞ يَا مَنْ لَا يُؤَاخِذُ
بِالْجَرِيْرَةِ وَلَا يَهْتِكِ السِّتْرَ ۞ يَا عَظِيْمَ الْعَفْوِ ۞ يَا حَسَنَ
التَّجَاوُزِ ۞ يَا وَاسِعَ الْمَغْفِرَةِ ۞

يَا بَاسِطَ الْيَدَيْنِ بِالرَّحْمَةِ ۞ يَا صَاحِبَ كُلِّ نَجْوٰى ۞ وَيَا
مُنْتَهٰى كُلِّ شَكْوٰى ۞ يَا كَرِيْمَ الصَّفْحِ ۞
يَا عَظِيْمَ الْمَنِّ ۞ يَا مُبْتَدِئَ النِّعَمِ قَبْلَ اسْتِحْقَاقِهَا ۞ يَا رَبَّنَا
وَيَا سَيِّدَنَا وَيَا مَوْلَانَا وَيَا غَايَةَ رَغْبَتِنَا ۞

اَسْأَلُكَ يَا اَللّٰهُ اَنْ لَّا تُشَوِّيَ خَلْقِيْ بِالنَّارِ ۞ (١ مرة)

yā man aẓhara l-jamīla wa satara l-qabīḥ(a) • yā man lā yu'ākhidh bi l-jarīrati wa lā yahtiki s-sitr(a) • yā aẓīma l-'afw(i) • yā ḥasana t-tajāwuz(i) • yā wāsi'a l-maghfirah •

yā bāsiṭa l-yadaini bi r-raḥmah • yā ṣāḥība kulli najwā • wa yā muntahā kulli shakwā • yā karīma ṣ-ṣafḥ(i) • yā 'aẓīma l-man-n(i) • yā mubtadi'a n-ni'mi qabla stiḥqāqihā •

yā Rabbanā wa yā Sayyidanā wa yā mawlānā wa yā ghāyata raghbatinā • as'aluka yā Allāhu an lā tushawwiya khalqī bi n-nār • (1 time)

O He who manifest what is beautiful and conceal what is ugly · O He who does not take a wrongdoer to task nor tear away the veil (covering the faults) · O supreme in pardon · O splendid in forbearance · O magnanimous in forgiveness ·

O whose Hands are outstretched in mercy · O Listener to all whisperings · O You to whom all complaints are made · O bounteous in remission · O supreme in bestowal · O giver of blessings to those who do not deserve ·

O our Lord, O our Master, O our Patron, O the Goal of our desires · I beseech You, O Allah, to not disfigure my being with the Fire (of Hell)![15B]

Sayyiduna **ABU HURAIRA'S**
SHIELD OF PROTECTION

اَعُوذُ بِكَلِمَاتِ اللهِ التَّامَّاتِ كُلِّهَا مِنْ شَرِّ مَا خَلَقَ

(٣ مرات)

a'ūdhu bi-kalimāti Llāhi t-tāmmāti kullihā
min sharri • mā khalaq • (3 times)

I seek refuge in the perfect words of Allah in entirety from the evil He has created.[16]

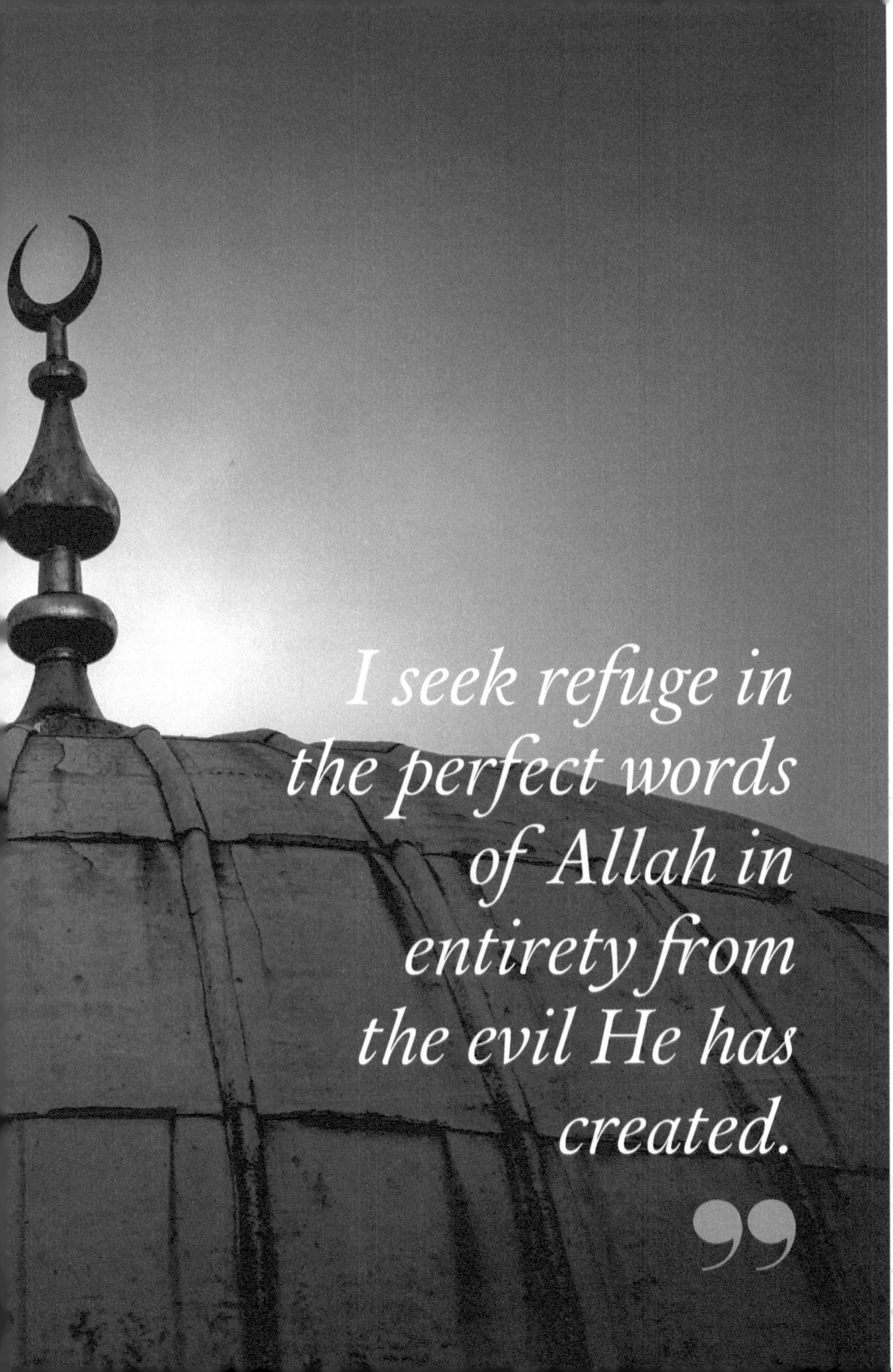

I seek refuge in the perfect words of Allah in entirety from the evil He has created.

”

-١٧-

Sayyiduna 'UTHMAN B. 'AFFAN'S ﷺ

SHIELD OF PROTECTION

بِسْمِ اللّٰهِ الَّذِي لَا يَضُرُّ مَعَ اسْمِهٖ شَيْءٌ فِي الْأَرْضِ وَلَا فِي السَّمَآءِ وَهُوَ السَّمِيْعُ الْعَلِيْمُ ۞

(٣ مرات)

bi-smi Llāhi lladhī lā yaḍurru ma'asmihi
shai'un fi l-arḍi wa lā fi s-samā'i wa
Huwa s-samī'u l-alīm • (3 times)

In the Name of Allah, against Whose Name nothing on the earth or in the heavens can do any harm; and He is the All-Hearing, the All-Knowing.[17]

-١٨-

Sayyiduna AL-KHIDR ﷺ & *Sayyiduna* ILYAS' ﷺ

GREETING OF DIVINE GLORIFICATION

بِسْمِ اللّٰهِ مَا شَآءَ اللّٰهُ لَا قُوَّةَ إِلَّا بِاللّٰه ۞

مَا شَآءَ اللّٰهُ كُلُّ نِعْمَةٍ مِّنَ اللّٰه ۞

مَا شَآءَ اللّٰهُ الْخَيْرُ كُلُّهُ بِيَدِ اللّٰه ۞

مَا شَآءَ اللّٰهُ لَا يَصْرِفُ السُّوٓءَ اِلَّا اللّٰه ۞

(٣ مرات)

bi-smi Llāhi
mā shā'a Llāhu lā quwwata illā bi Llāh •
mā shā'a Llāhu kullu ni'matin mina Llāh •
mā shā'a Llāhu l-khairu kulluhu bi yadi Llāh •
mā shā'a Llāhu lā yaṣrifu s-sū'a illa Llāh • (3 times)

In the Name of Allah,
what Allah has willed, there is no power save in Him ·
what Allah has willed, every grace is from Allah ·
what Allah has willed, All good is in Allah's Power ·
what Allah has willed, none dispels evil but Allah.[18]

-١٩-

Sayyiduna AS-SUYUTI'S ﷺ

PANACEA FOR EVERY AILMENT

بِسْمِ اللّٰه ۞ رَبِّيَ اللّٰه ۞ حَسْبِيَ اللّٰه ۞
تَوَكَّلْتُ عَلَى اللّٰه ۞ اِعْتَصَمْتُ بِاللّٰه ۞
فَوَّضْتُ اَمْرِيْ اِلَى اللّٰه ۞ مَا شَآءَ اللّٰه ۞
لَا قُوَّةَ اِلَّا بِاللّٰه ۞ (٣ مرات)

bi-smi Llāh • rabbiya Llāh • hasbiya Llāh •
tawakkaltu ʿala Lāh • iʿtaṣamtu bi Llāh •
fawwaḍtu amrī ila Llāh • mā shāʾa Llāh •
lā quwwata illā bi Llāh • (3 times)

*In the Name of Allah · my Lord is Allah ·
enough for me is Allah · my reliance is upon Allah ·
I seek protection with Allah · I entrust my affair to Allah · what Allah has willed · no power except with Allah.*[19]

-٢٠-

Sayyiduna **ʿABD ALLAH B. MAS'UD'S** ﷺ

FORTIFICATION OF BLESSINGS

بِسْمِ اللهِ عَلَى دِيْنِيْ وَنَفْسِيْ
وَوَلَدِيْ وَاَهْلِيْ وَمَالِيْ ۞ (١ مرة)

bi-smi Llāhi ʿalā dīnī wa nafsī wa
waladī wa ahlī wa mālī • (1 time)

*In the Name of Allah on my religion, my life,
my children, my family and my wealth.*[20]

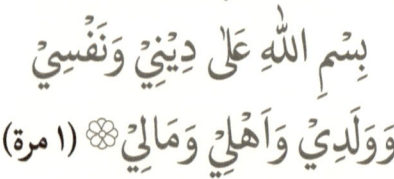

Sayyiduna **AL-GHAZALI'S**

EXPRESSION OF CONTENTMENT

رَضِيتُ بِاللهِ رَبًّا ۞ وَبِالْإِسْلَامِ دِينًا ۞ وَبِالْقُرْآنِ إِمَامًا ۞ وَبِمُحَمَّدٍ ﷺ نَبِيًّا رَسُولًا ۞ (١ مرة)

raḍītu bi Llāhi rabban • wa bi l-islāmi dīnan • wa bi l-qur'āni imāman • wa bi Muḥammadin ṣalla Llāhu 'alaihi wa sallama nabiyyan rasūlan • (1 time)

I am pleased with Allah as Lord · with Islam as religion · with the Qur'an as guide · and with Muhammad ﷺ as Prophet & Messenger.[21]

Sayyiduna **'ABD ALLAH B. MAS'UD'S**

EXPRESSION OF RELIANCE (**MORNING**)

أَصْبَحْنَا وَأَصْبَحَ الْمُلْكُ لِلَّهِ وَالْحَمْدُ لِلَّهِ ۞ لَا إِلٰهَ إِلَّا اللهُ وَحْدَهُ لَا شَرِيكَ لَهُ ۞ لَهُ الْمُلْكُ وَلَهُ الْحَمْدُ وَهُوَ عَلَىٰ كُلِّ شَيْءٍ قَدِيرٌ ۞ اَللّٰهُمَّ إِنِّي أَسْأَلُكَ مِنْ خَيْرِ هٰذَا الْيَوْمِ

وَخَيْرِ مَا فِيهِ ۞ وَأَعُوذُ بِكَ مِنْ شَرِّهِ وَشَرِّ مَا فِيهِ ۞ اَللّٰهُمَّ
إِنِّيْ أَعُوذُ بِكَ مِنَ الْكَسَلِ وَالْهَرَمِ وَسُوْءِ الْكِبَرِ ۞ وَفِتْنَةِ
الدُّنْيَا وَعَذَابِ النَّارِ وَعَذَابِ الْقَبْرِ ۞ (١ مرة)

aṣbaḥnā wa aṣbaḥa l-mulku li-Llāhi wa l-ḥamdu li-Llāh • lā ilāha illa Llāhu waḥdahu lā sharīka lah(u) • lahu l-mulku wa lahu l-ḥamdu wa Huwa ʿalā kulli shai'in qadīr • Allāhumma innī as'aluka min khairi hādha l-yawmi wa khairi mā fīh(i) • wa aʿūdhu bika min sharrihi wa sharri mā fīh(i) • Allāhumma innī aʿūdhu bika mina l-kasali wa l-haram(i) • wa sū'i l-kibar(i) • wa fitnati d-dunyā • wa ʿadhābi n-nāri wa ʿadhābi l-qabr(i)

• (1 time)

We have entered a new day and so has the Kingdom of Allah entered a new day; and praise is due to Allah · there is no god [worthy of worship] but Allah the One, and there is no partner with Him · to Him is the Sovereignty, to Him is all praise and He is Potent over every thing · O Allah, I beseech You for the goodness of this day and the goodness of what is in it · I seek refuge in You from the evil of it and what is in it · O Allah, I seek refuge in You from sloth, from decrepitude · from the evil of vanity · from trials of the world · from the torment of the Inferno and the torment of the grave.[22]

Sayyiduna 'ABD ALLAH B. MAS'UD'S
EXPRESSION OF RELIANCE (EVENING)

اَمْسَيْنَا وَاَمْسَى الْمُلْكُ لِلّٰهِ وَالْحَمْدُ لِلّٰهِ ۞ لَا اِلٰهَ اِلَّا اللّٰهُ وَحْدَهُ لَا شَرِيْكَ لَهُ ۞ لَهُ الْمُلْكُ وَلَهُ الْحَمْدُ وَهُوَ عَلٰى كُلِّ شَىْءٍ قَدِيْرٌ ۞ اَللّٰهُمَّ اِنِّىْ اَسْأَلُكَ مِنْ خَيْرِ هٰذِهِ اللَّيْلَةِ وَخَيْرِ مَا فِيْهَا ۞ وَاَعُوْذُ بِكَ مِنْ شَرِّهَا وَشَرِّ مَا فِيْهَا ۞ اَللّٰهُمَّ اِنِّىْ اَعُوْذُ بِكَ مِنَ الْكَسَلِ وَالْهَرَمِ وَسُوْءِ الْكِبَرِ ۞ وَفِتْنَةِ الدُّنْيَا وَعَذَابِ النَّارِ وَعَذَابِ الْقَبْرِ ۞ (۱ مرة)

amsainā wa amsa l-mulku li-Llāhi wa l-ḥamdu li-Llāh • lā ilāha illa Llāhu waḥdahu lā sharīka lah(u) • lahu l-mulku wa lahu l-ḥamdu wa Huwa 'alā kulli shai'in Qadīr • Allāhumma innī as'aluka min khairi hādhihi l-yawmi wa khairi mā fīhā • wa a'ūdhu bika min sharrihā wa sharri mā fīhā • Allāhumma innī a'ūdhu bika mina l-kasali wa l-haram(i) • wa sū'i l-kibar(i) • wa fitnati d-dunyā • wa 'adhābi n-nāri wa 'adhābi l-qabr(i) • (1 time)

We have entered a new evening and so has the Kingdom of Allah entered a new evening; and praise is due to Allah · there is no god [worthy of worship] but Allah the One, and there is no partner with Him · to Him is the Sovereignty, to Him is all praise and He is Potent over every thing · O Allah, I beseech You for the goodness of this night and the goodness of what is in it · I seek refuge in You from the evil of it and what is in it · O Allah, I seek refuge in You from sloth, from decrepitude · from the evil of vanity · from trial of the world · from the torment of the Inferno and the torment of the grave.

-٢٣-

Sayyiduna **ABU BAKR AS-SIDDIQ'S** ﵁

PROTECTIVE SUPPLICATION

اَللّٰهُمَّ فَاطِرَ السَّمٰوَاتِ وَالْاَرْضِ ۞ عَالِمَ الْغَيْبِ وَالشَّهَادَةِ ۞ رَبَّ كُلِّ شَيْءٍ وَّمَلِيْكَهُ ۞ اَشْهَدُ اَنْ لَّآ اِلٰهَ اِلَّآ اَنْتَ ۞ اَعُوْذُ بِكَ مِنْ شَرِّ نَفْسِيْ وَمِنْ شَرِّ الشَّيْطَانِ وَشِرْكِهٖ ۞ وَاَنْ اَقْتَرِفَ عَلٰى نَفْسِيْ سُوْءًا اَوْ اَجُرَّهُ اِلٰى مُسْلِمٍ ۞ (١ مرة)

Allāhumma fāṭira s-samāwāti wa l-arḍi • ʻālima l-ghaibi wa sh-shahādati • Rabba kulli shai'in wa malīkahu • ashhadu an lā ilāha illā anta • a'ūdhu bika min sharri nafsī wa min sharri sh-shaiṭāni wa shirkihi • wa an aqtarifa ʻalā nafsī sū'an aw ajurrahu ilā muslimin • (1 time)

O Allah, Creator of the heavens and the earth; Knower of the hidden and the manifest; Lord of everything and everyone; I bear witness that none has the right to be worshipped but You. I seek Your Protection from the evil of my own self, from the evil of Satan and from the evil of polytheism to which he calls. And from committing wrong against my soul or bringing such upon another Muslim.[23]

-٢٤-

Sayyiduna **ABU UMAMA'S** ﷺ

REPELLING OF WORRIES & DISCHARGING OF DEBTS

اَللّٰهُمَّ اِنِّيٓ اَعُوْذُ بِكَ مِنَ الْهَمِّ وَالْحَزَنِ ۞

وَاَعُوْذُ بِكَ مِنَ الْعَجْزِ وَالْكَسَلِ ۞

وَاَعُوْذُ بِكَ مِنَ الْجُبْنِ وَالْبُخْلِ ۞

وَاَعُوْذُ بِكَ مِنْ غَلَبَةِ الدَّيْنِ وَقَهْرِ الرِّجَالِ ۞

(١/٣ مرات)

Allāhumma innī a'ūdhu bi-ka mina l-hammi wa l-ḥazan(i) • wa a'ūdhu bi-ka mina l-'ajzi wa l-kasal(i) • wa a'ūdhu bi-ka mina jubni wa l-bukhl(i) • wa a'ūdhu bi-ka min ghalabati d-daini wa qahri r-rijāl(i) • (1/3 times)

O Allah, I seek Your protection from worries and grief · I seek Your protection from feebleness and laziness · I seek Your protection from cowardice and avarice · and I seek Your protection from the oppression of debts and the tyranny of men.[24]

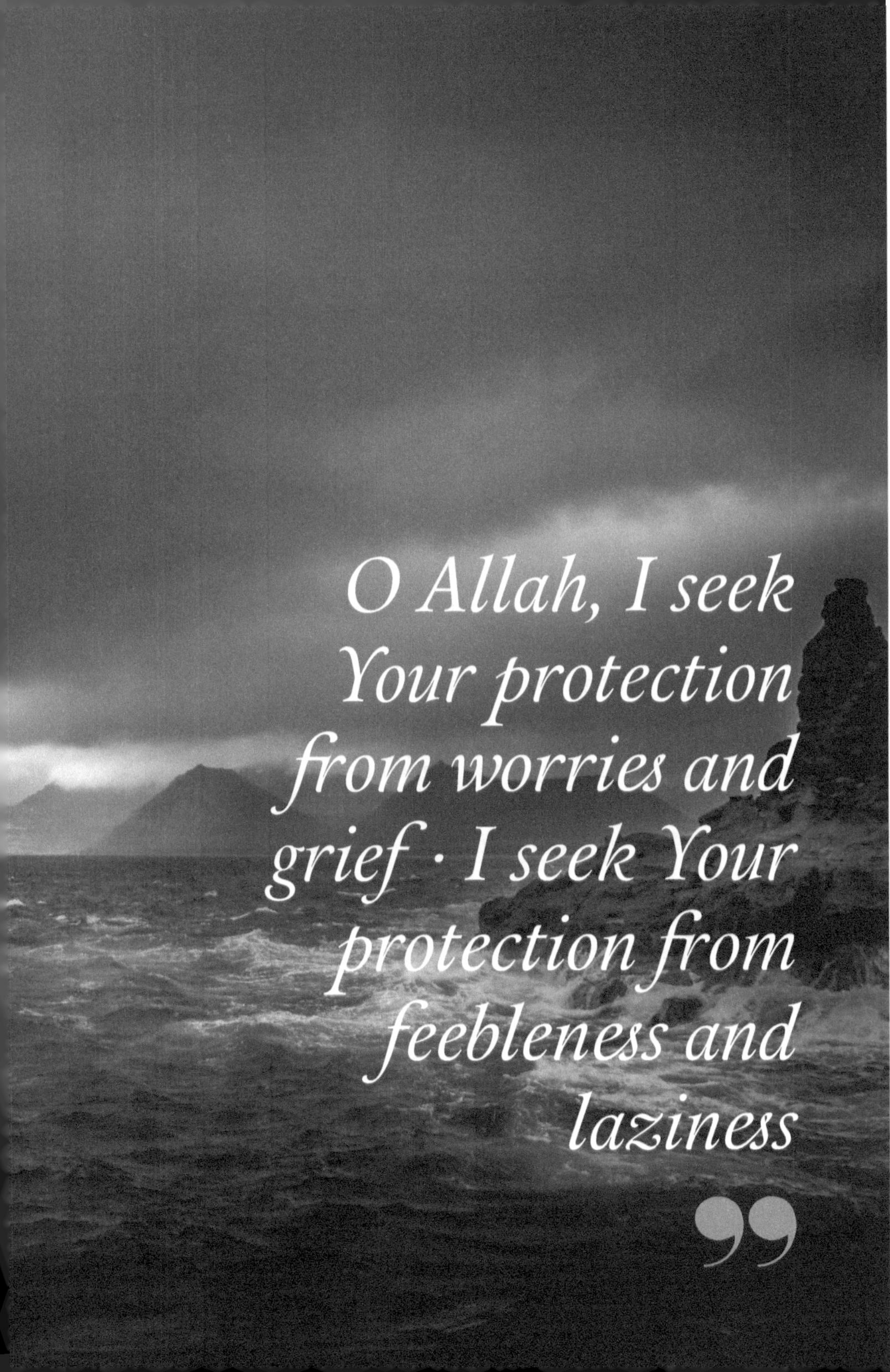

O Allah, I seek Your protection from worries and grief · I seek Your protection from feebleness and laziness

”

Sayyiduna **SHADDAD B. AWS'**
crème de la crème OF SEEKING FORGIVENESS

اَللّٰهُمَّ اَنْتَ رَبِّيْ ۞ لَاۤ اِلٰهَ اِلَّا اَنْتَ ۞ خَلَقْتَنِيْ وَاَنَا عَبْدُكَ ۞ وَاَنَا عَلٰى عَهْدِكَ وَوَعْدِكَ مَا اسْتَطَعْتُ ۞ اَعُوْذُ بِكَ مِنْ شَرِّ مَا صَنَعْتُ ۞ اَبُوْءُ لَكَ بِنِعْمَتِكَ عَلَيَّ وَاَبُوْءُ لَكَ بِذَنْبِيْ ۞ فَاغْفِرْ لِيْ ۞ فَاِنَّهٗ لَا يَغْفِرُ الذُّنُوْبَ اِلَّا اَنْتَ ۞ (١ مرة)

Allāhumma anta rabbī · lā ilāha illā anta · khalaqtanī wa anā 'abduk(a) · wa anā 'alā 'ahdika wa wa'dika ma-staṭa't(u) · a'ūdhu bi-ka min sharri mā ṣana't(u) · abū'u la-ka bi ni'mati-ka 'alayya wa abū'u la-ka bi dhanbī · fa-ghfirlī · fa-innahu lā yaghfiru dh-dhunūba illā anta · (1 time)

O Allah, You are my Lord · none has the right to be worshipped except You · You created me and I am Your slave · I abide by Your covenant and pledge [to fulfil it] as best I can ·

I seek refuge in You from the evil I have done · I acknowledge Your blessing on me and I admit my sin · so forgive me · for verily none forgives sins except You.[25]

-٢٦-

Sayyiduna **ABU AD-DARDA'S** ﵁

EXPRESSION OF COMPLETE RELIANCE

اَللّٰهُمَّ اَنْتَ رَبِّيْ ۞ لَآ اِلٰهَ اِلَّا اَنْتَ ۞ عَلَيْكَ تَوَكَّلْتُ ۞
وَاَنْتَ رَبُّ الْعَرْشِ الْعَظِيْمِ ۞ مَا شَآءَ اللّٰهُ كَانَ وَمَا لَمْ
يَشَأْ لَمْ يَكُنْ ۞ لَا حَوْلَ وَلَا قُوَّةَ اِلَّا بِاللّٰهِ الْعَلِيِّ الْعَظِيْمِ
۞ اَعْلَمُ اَنَّ اللّٰهَ عَلٰى كُلِّ شَيْءٍ قَدِيْرٌ ۞ وَاَنَّ اللّٰهَ قَدْ
اَحَاطَ بِكُلِّ شَيْءٍ عِلْمًا ۞ اَللّٰهُمَّ اِنِّيْٓ اَعُوْذُ بِكَ مِنْ
شَرِّ نَفْسِيْ وَمِنْ شَرِّ كُلِّ دَابَّةٍ اَنْتَ اٰخِذٌ بِنَاصِيَتِهَا
۞ اِنَّ رَبِّيْ عَلٰى صِرَاطٍ مُّسْتَقِيْمٍ ۞ (١ مرة)

Allāhumma anta rabbī • lā ilāha illā anta • ʿalaika tawakkaltu • wa anta rabbu l-ʿarshi l-ʿaẓīm • māshā'a Llāhu kāna wa mā lam yasha' lam yakun • lā ḥawla wa lā quwwata illā bi Llāhil ʿaliyyi l-ʿaẓīm •

aʿlamu anna Llāha ʿalā kulli shai'in qadīr • wa anna Llāha qad aḥāṭa bi kulli shai'in ʿilma(n) • Allāhumma innī aʿūdhu bi-ka min sharri nafsī wa min sharri kulli dābbatin anta ākhidhn bi nāṣiyatihā • inna rabbi ʿalā ṣirātin mustaqīm • (1 time)

O Allah, You are my Lord · none has the right to be worshipped except You · In You I place my trust · You are the Lord of the Mighty Throne · What Allah wills, shall be and what He does not will, shall not · There is no power or strength except by Allah, the Most High, the Mighty ·

I know that Allah has power over all things · and that He encompasses everything with His knowledge · O Allah, I seek protection with You from the evil of my soul and from the evil of every beast that You hold by the forelock · Verily, my Lord is on a straight path.²⁶

Sayyiduna **ANAS B. MALIK'S**
SUPPLICATION FOR GOOD SURPRISES

اَللّٰهُمَّ اِنِّيْ اَسْأَلُكَ مِنْ فُجَاءَةِ الْخَيْرِ
وَاَعُوْذُ بِكَ مِنْ فُجَاءَةِ الشَّرِّ (١ مرة)

Allāhumma innī as'aluka min fujā'ati l-khair ·
wa a'ūdhu bika min fujā'ati sh-sharr ·(1 time)

*O Allah I ask You for good surprises and I seek refuge in You from bad surprises.*²⁷

-٢٨-

Sayyiduna ‘ABD ALLAH B. ‘UMAR’S ﷺ ENCOMPASSING SUPPLICATION

اَللّٰهُمَّ اِنِّيْ اَسْأَلُكَ الْعَافِيَةَ فِي الدُّنْيَا وَالْاٰخِرَةِ ۞ اَللّٰهُمَّ اِنِّيْ
اَسْأَلُكَ الْعَفْوَ وَالْعَافِيَةَ فِيْ دِيْنِيْ وَدُنْيَايَ وَاَهْلِيْ وَمَالِيْ ۞
اَللّٰهُمَّ اسْتُرْ عَوْرَاتِيْ وَاٰمِنْ رَوْعَاتِيْ ۞ اَللّٰهُمَّ احْفَظْنِيْ مِنْ بَيْنِ
يَدَيَّ وَمِنْ خَلْفِيْ وَعَنْ يَمِيْنِيْ وَعَنْ شِمَالِيْ وَمِنْ فَوْقِيْ وَاَعُوْذُ
بِعَظَمَتِكَ اَنْ اُغْتَالَ مِنْ تَحْتِيْ ۞ (١ مرة)

Allāhumma innī as’aluka l-‘āfiyata fi d-dunyā wa l-ākhirati • Allāhumma innī as’aluka l-‘afwa wa l-‘āfiyata fī dīnī wa dunyāya wa ahlī wa mālī • Allāhumma stur ‘awrātī wa āmin raw‘ātī • Allāhumma ḥfaẓnī min baini yadayya wa min khalfī wa ‘an yamīnī wa ‘an shimālī wa min fawqī wa a‘ūdhu bi-‘aẓamatika an ughtāla min taḥtī • (1 time)

O Allah, I ask You for security in this world and in the Hereafter. O Allah, I ask You for forgiveness and security in my religion, my worldly affairs, my family and my wealth. O Allah, conceal my faults and keep me safe from the things which I fear. O Allah, guard me in my front, my back, my right, my left, above me, and I seek in You greatness from receiving unexpected harm from below me.[28]

-٢٩-

Sayyidatuna ‘AISHA AS-SIDDIQA’S ﷺ

COMPLETE SUPPLICATION

اَللّٰهُمَّ اِنِّيْٓ اَسْأَلُكَ مِنَ الْخَيْرِ كُلِّهٖ عَاجِلِهٖ وَاٰجِلِهٖ مَا عَلِمْتُ مِنْهُ وَمَا لَمْ اَعْلَمْ ۞ وَاَعُوْذُ بِكَ مِنَ الشَّرِّ كُلِّهٖ عَاجِلِهٖ وَاٰجِلِهٖ مَا عَلِمْتُ مِنْهُ وَمَا لَمْ اَعْلَمْ ۞ وَاَسْأَلُكَ الْجَنَّةَ وَمَا قَرَّبَ اِلَيْهَا مِنْ قَوْلٍ وَّعَمَلٍ ۞ وَ اَعُوْذُ بِكَ مِنَ النَّارِ وَمَا قَرَّبَ اِلَيْهَا مِنْ قَوْلٍ وَّعَمَلٍ ۞ وَاَسْأَلُكَ مِنَ الْخَيْرِ مَا سَئَلَكَ عَبْدُكَ وَرَسُوْلُكَ مُحَمَّدٌ ﷺ ۞ وَاَسْتَعِيْذُكَ مِمَّا اسْتَعَاذَكَ مِنْهُ عَبْدُكَ وَرَسُوْلُكَ مُحَمَّدٌ ﷺ ۞ وَاَسْأَلُكَ مَا قَضَيْتَ لِيْ مِنْ اَمْرٍ اَنْ تَجْعَلَ عَاقِبَتَهٗ رَشَدًا ۞

(١ مرة)

Allāhumma innī as’aluka mina l-khairi kullihi ‘ājilihi wa ājilihi mā ‘alimtu minhu wa mā lam a‘lam • wa a‘ūdhu bi-ka mina sh-sharri kullihi ‘ājilihi wa ājilihi mā ‘alimtu minhu wa mā lam a‘lam •

wa as’aluka l-jannata wa mā qarraba ilaihā min qawlin wa ‘amalin • wa a‘ūdhu bi-ka mina n-nāri wa mā qarraba ilaihā min qawlin wa ‘amalin •

wa as'aluka mina l-khairi mā sa'alaka 'abduka wa rasūluka Muḥammadun, ṣalla Llāhu 'alaihi wa sallam • wa asta'īdhuka mimma sta'ādhaka minhu 'abduka wa rasūluka Muḥammad-un, ṣalla Llāhu 'alaihi wa sallam •

wa as'aluka mā qaḍaita lī min amrin an taj'ala 'āqibatahu ra-shadan •(1 time)

O Allah, I beseech You for all the good in this world and the hereafter, what I know and what I do not know. And I seek refuge with You from all evil in this world and the hereafter, what I know and what I do not know.

I beseech You for the Garden, and for that which brings one closer to it, in word and deed. And I seek refuge with You from Hell and from that which brings one closer to it, in word and deed.

I beseech You for the good of what Your peerless-bondsman and Prophet ﷺ asked for. And I seek refuge with You from all evil which Your peerless-bondsman and Prophet ﷺ sought refuge in.

And I beseech You to make every decree You pronounce concerning me, good![29]

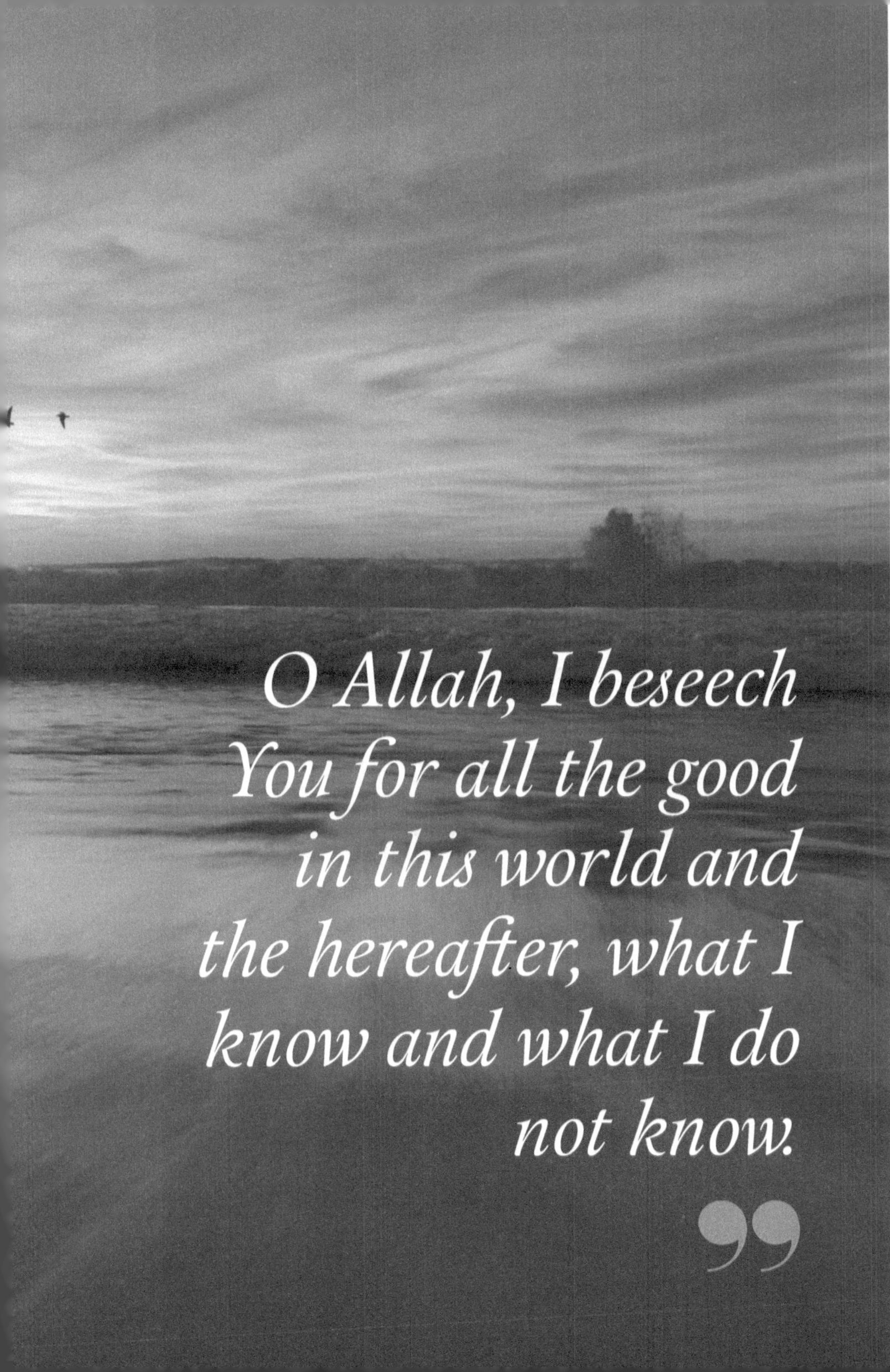
O Allah, I beseech
You for all the good
in this world and
the hereafter, what I
know and what I do
not know.
”

-٣٠-

Sayyiduna **MA'QIL B. YASAR'S** ﵁

VERSES TO ELICIT PRAYERS OF 70,000 ANGELS

اَعُوْذُ بِاللهِ السَّمِيْعِ الْعَلِيْمِ مِنَ الشَّيْطَانِ الرَّجِيْمِ

(٣مرات)

﴿لَوْ اَنْزَلْنَا هٰذَا الْقُرْاٰنَ عَلٰى جَبَلٍ لَّرَاَيْتَهٗ خَاشِعًا مُّتَصَدِّعًا مِّنْ خَشْيَةِ اللّٰهِؕ وَتِلْكَ الْاَمْثَالُ نَضْرِبُهَا لِلنَّاسِ لَعَلَّهُمْ يَتَفَكَّرُوْنَ ۞ هُوَ اللّٰهُ الَّذِيْ لَآ اِلٰهَ اِلَّا هُوَۚ عٰلِمُ الْغَيْبِ وَالشَّهَادَةِۚ هُوَ الرَّحْمٰنُ الرَّحِيْمُ ۞ هُوَ اللّٰهُ الَّذِيْ لَآ اِلٰهَ اِلَّا هُوَۚ اَلْمَلِكُ الْقُدُّوْسُ السَّلٰمُ الْمُؤْمِنُ الْمُهَيْمِنُ الْعَزِيْزُ الْجَبَّارُ الْمُتَكَبِّرُؕ سُبْحٰنَ اللّٰهِ عَمَّا يُشْرِكُوْنَ ۞ هُوَ اللّٰهُ الْخَالِقُ الْبَارِئُ الْمُصَوِّرُ لَهُ الْاَسْمَآءُ الْحُسْنٰىؕ يُسَبِّحُ لَهٗ مَا فِى السَّمٰوٰتِ وَالْاَرْضِۚ وَهُوَ الْعَزِيْزُ الْحَكِيْمُ﴾

(١ مرة)

a‘ūdhu bi Llāhi s-samī‘i l-‘alīmi
mina sh-shaiṭāni r-rajīm • (3 times)
law anzalnā hādha l-qur’āna ‘alā jabalin lara’aitahu khāshian mutaṣaddi‘an min khashyati Llāh(i) wa tilka l-amthālu naḍribuhā li n-nāsi la‘allahum yatafakkarūn •
huwa Llāhu lladhī la ilāha illā hu(wa) ‘ālimu l-ghaibi wa sh-shahāda(ti) huwa r-raḥmānu r-raḥīm •
huwa Llāhu lladhī la ilāha illā huwa l-maliku l-quddūsu s-salāmu l-mu’minu l-muhaiminu l-‘azīzu l-jabbāru l-mutakabbir(u) subḥāna Llāhi ‘ammā yushrikūn •
huwa Llāhu l-khāliqu l-bāri’u l-muṣawwiru lahu l-asmā’u l-ḥusnā yusabbiḥu lahū mā fi s-samāwāti wa l-arḍ(i) wa huwa l-‘azīzu l-ḥakīm • (1 time)

I seek refuge with Allah—the All-Hearing,
the All-Knowing—from the accursed devil

(**BENEFIT**: place hand on head and recite these verses)

59:21-24 ﴾*If We had sent this Quran down to a mountain, you [Prophet] would have seen it humbled and split apart in its awe of Allah: We offer people such illustrations so that they may reflect. He is Allah: there is no god other than Him. It is He who knows what is hidden as well as what is in the open, He is the Lord of Mercy, the Giver of Mercy. He is Allah: there is no god other than Him, the Controller, the Holy One, Source of Peace, Granter of Security, Guardian over all, the Almighty, the Compeller, the Truly Great; Allah is far above anything they consider to be His partner. He is Allah: the Creator, the Originator, the Shaper. The best names belong to Him. Everything in the heavens and earth glorifies Him: He is the Almighty, the Wise.*﴿[30]

Sayyiduna ABU DHARR AL-GHIFARI'S
VERSES TO ELICIT SUFFICIENCY

﴿وَمَنْ يَتَّقِ اللهَ يَجْعَلْ لَهُ مَخْرَجًا وَيَرْزُقْهُ مِنْ حَيْثُ لَا يَحْتَسِبُ وَمَنْ يَتَوَكَّلْ عَلَى اللهِ فَهُوَ حَسْبُهُ إِنَّ اللهَ بَالِغُ أَمْرِهِ قَدْ جَعَلَ اللهُ لِكُلِّ شَيْءٍ قَدْرًا﴾

(١ مرة)

wa ma(n) yattaqi Llāha yaj'al lahu makhraja(n) • wa yarzuq-hu min ḥaithu la yaḥtasibu wa ma(n) yatawakkal 'ala Llāhi fa huwa hasbuh(u) inna Llāha bālighu amrih(i) qad ja'ala Llāhu li kulli shai'in qadra(n) • (1 time)

65:2-3 ❴*Allah will find a way out for those who are mindful of Him, and will provide for them from an unexpected source; Allah will be enough for those who put their trust in Him. Allah achieves His purpose; Allah has set a due measure for everything.*❵[31]

-٣٢-

Sayyiduna **AL-HASAN AL-BASRI'S** ﷺ

VERSES TO REPEL EVIL EYE

﴿وَإِن يَكَادُ الَّذِينَ كَفَرُوا
لَيُزْلِقُونَكَ بِأَبْصَارِهِمْ لَمَّا سَمِعُوا
الذِّكْرَ وَيَقُولُونَ إِنَّهُ لَمَجْنُونٌ ۝
وَمَا هُوَ إِلَّا ذِكْرٌ لِّلْعَالَمِينَ﴾

(١ مرة)

wa in yakādu lladhīna kafarū la-yuzliqūnaka bi-abṣārihim lammā sami'u dh-dhikra wa yaqūlūna innahu la majnūn • wa ma huwa illa dhikrun li l-'ālamīn • (1 time)

68:51-52 ﴿*And indeed, those who disbelieve would almost make you slip with their eyes [of hatred & envy] when they hear the Qur'an and they say, "Indeed, he is mad," but truly it is nothing other than a Reminder to the entire cosmos.*﴾[32]

-٣٣-

Sayyiduna **MUSA'S** ﷺ

VERSE TO REPEL WITCHCRAFT & SORCERY

﴿قَالَ مُوسَىٰ مَا جِئْتُم بِهِ السِّحْرُ
إِنَّ اللَّهَ سَيُبْطِلُهُ إِنَّ اللَّهَ لَا يُصْلِحُ عَمَلَ الْمُفْسِدِينَ ۝ وَيُحِقُّ
اللَّهُ الْحَقَّ بِكَلِمَاتِهِ وَلَوْ كَرِهَ الْمُجْرِمُونَ﴾

(١ مرة)

qāla mūsā ma ji'tum bihi s-siḥr(u) inna Llāha sa-yubṭiluh(u) inna Llāha la yuṣliḥu 'amala l-mufsidīn • wa yuḥiqqu Llāhu l-ḥaqqa bi-kalimātihi wa law kariha l-mujrimūn • (1 time)

10:81 ﴾*Moses said, 'Everything you have brought is sorcery and Allah will show it to be false. Allah does not make the work of mischief-makers right; He will uphold the Truth with His words, even if the evildoers hate it.'*﴿ 33

-٣٤-

Sayyiduna KA'B B. AHBAR'S ﷺ

SEVEN VERSES OF PROTECTIVE ADEQUACY

١

﴿قُلْ لَّنْ يُّصِيْبَنَآ اِلَّا مَا كَتَبَ اللّٰهُ لَنَاۚ هُوَ
مَوْلٰنَاۚ وَعَلَى اللّٰهِ فَلْيَتَوَكَّلِ الْمُؤْمِنُوْنَ﴾

٢

﴿وَاِنْ يَّمْسَسْكَ اللّٰهُ بِضُرٍّ فَلَا كَاشِفَ لَهٗٓ اِلَّا هُوَۚ وَاِنْ يُّرِدْكَ
بِخَيْرٍ فَلَا رَآدَّ لِفَضْلِهٖ يُصِيْبُ بِهٖ مَنْ يَّشَآءُ مِنْ عِبَادِهٖ وَهُوَ
الْغَفُوْرُ الرَّحِيْمُ﴾

٣

﴿وَمَا مِنْ دَآبَّةٍ فِي الْاَرْضِ اِلَّا عَلَى اللّٰهِ رِزْقُهَا وَيَعْلَمُ مُسْتَقَرَّهَا
وَمُسْتَوْدَعَهَاؕ كُلٌّ فِيْ كِتٰبٍ مُّبِيْنٍ﴾

٤

﴿اِنِّيْ تَوَكَّلْتُ عَلَى اللّٰهِ رَبِّيْ وَرَبِّكُمْؕ مَا مِنْ دَآبَّةٍ اِلَّا هُوَ اٰخِذٌۢ
بِنَاصِيَتِهَاؕ اِنَّ رَبِّيْ عَلٰى صِرَاطٍ مُّسْتَقِيْمٍ﴾

٥

﴿وَكَاَيِّنْ مِّنْ دَآبَّةٍ لَّا تَحْمِلُ رِزْقَهَا ۖ اَللّٰهُ
يَرْزُقُهَا وَاِيَّاكُمْ ۖ وَهُوَ السَّمِيْعُ الْعَلِيْمُ﴾

٦

﴿مَا يَفْتَحِ اللّٰهُ لِلنَّاسِ مِنْ رَّحْمَةٍ فَلَا مُمْسِكَ لَهَا ۚ
وَمَا يُمْسِكْ ۙ فَلَا مُرْسِلَ لَهٗ مِنْۢ بَعْدِهٖ ؕ
وَهُوَ الْعَزِيْزُ الْحَكِيْمُ﴾

٧

﴿وَلَئِنْ سَاَلْتَهُمْ مَّنْ خَلَقَ السَّمٰوٰتِ وَالْاَرْضَ لَيَقُوْلُنَّ
اللّٰهُ ؕ قُلْ اَفَرَءَيْتُمْ مَّا تَدْعُوْنَ مِنْ دُوْنِ اللّٰهِ اِنْ اَرَادَنِيَ اللّٰهُ بِضُرٍّ
هَلْ هُنَّ كٰشِفٰتُ ضُرِّهٖٓ اَوْ اَرَادَنِيْ بِرَحْمَةٍ هَلْ هُنَّ مُمْسِكٰتُ
رَحْمَتِهٖ ؕ قُلْ حَسْبِيَ اللّٰهُ ؕ عَلَيْهِ يَتَوَكَّلُ الْمُتَوَكِّلُوْنَ﴾

(١ مرة)

1. qul lan yusībanā illā mā kataba Llāhu lanā huwa mawlānā wa ʻala Llāhi fa l-yatawakkali l-mu'minūn •
2. wa in yamsaska Llāhu bi ḍurrin falā kāshifa lahū illā huwa wa in yuridka bi khairin falā rādda li faḍlihi yuṣību bihi

man yas͟hā'u min 'ibādihi wa huwa l-g͟hafūru r-rahīm •

3. wa mā min dābbatin fi l-arḍi illā 'ala Llāhi rizquha wa ya'l-amu mustaqarrahā wa mustawda'ahā kullun fī kitābin mubīn •

4. innī tawakkaltu 'ala Llāhi rabbī wa rabbikum mā min dābbatin illā huwa āk͟hidun bi nāṣiyatiha inna rabbī 'alā ṣīraṭin mustaqīm •

5. wa ka'ayyin min dābbatin la taḥmilu rizqahā Allāhu yar-zuquhā wa iyyākum wa huwa s-samī'u l-'alīm •

6. mā yaftaḥi Llāhu li n-nāsi min raḥmatin falā mumsika lahā wa mā yumsik falā mursila lahu min ba'dihi wa huwa l-'azīzu l-hakīm •

7. wa la'in sa'altahum man k͟halaqa s-samāwati wa l-arḍa la-yaqūlunna Llāh(u) qul afara'aitum mā tad'ūna min dūni Llāhi in arādaniya Llāhu bi ḍurrin hal hunna kās͟hifātu ḍurrihi aw arādanī bi raḥmatin hal hunna mumsikātu raḥmatihi qul ḥasbiya Llāhu 'alaihi yatawakkalu l-mut-awakkilūn • (1 time)

9:51

1. ﴾*Say, "Only what Allah has decreed will happen to us. He is our Master: let the believers put their trust in Allah."*﴿

10:107

2. ﴾*If Allah inflicts harm on you, no one can remove it but Him, and if He intends good for you, no one can turn His bounty away; He grants His bounty to any of His servants He will. He is the Most*

Forgiving, the Most Merciful.❵

11:6

3. ❴*There is not a creature that moves on earth whose provision is not His concern. He knows where it lives and its [final] abode: it is all in a clear record.*❵

11:56

4. ❴*I put my trust in Allah, my Lord and your Lord. There is no moving creature which He does not control. My Lord's way is straight.*❵

29:60

5. ❴*How many are the creatures who do not store their sustenance! Allah sustains them and you: He alone is the All Hearing, the All Knowing.*❵

35:2

6. ❴*No one can withhold the blessing Allah opens up for people, nor can anyone but Him release whatever He withholds: He is the Almighty, the All Wise.*❵

39:38

7. ❴*If you [Prophet] ask them, "Who created the heavens and earth?" they are sure to answer, "Allah," so say, "Consider those you invoke beside Him: if Allah wished to harm me, could they undo that harm? If Allah wished to show me mercy, could they withhold that mercy?" Say, "Allah is enough for me: all those who trust should put their trust in Him."*❵[34]

-٣٥-

Sayyiduna **AL-QUSHAIRI'S** ﵁

SIX VERSES OF HEALING CURE

١

﴿وَيَشْفِ صُدُوْرَ قَوْمٍ مُّؤْمِنِيْنَ﴾

٢

﴿يَآ اَيُّهَا النَّاسُ قَدْ جَآءَتْكُمْ مَّوْعِظَةٌ مِّنْ رَّبِّكُمْ وَشِفَآءٌ لِّمَا فِي الصُّدُوْرِلا وَهُدًى وَّرَحْمَةٌ لِّلْمُؤْمِنِيْنَ﴾

٣

﴿يَخْرُجُ مِنْۢ بُطُوْنِهَا شَرَابٌ مُّخْتَلِفٌ اَلْوَانُهٗ فِيْهِ شِفَآءٌ لِّلنَّاسِؕ اِنَّ فِيْ ذٰلِكَ لَاٰيَةً لِّقَوْمٍ يَّتَفَكَّرُوْنَ﴾

٤

﴿وَنُنَزِّلُ مِنَ الْقُرْاٰنِ مَا هُوَ شِفَآءٌ وَّرَحْمَةٌ لِّلْمُؤْمِنِيْنَۙ﴾

٥

﴿وَاِذَا مَرِضْتُ فَهُوَ يَشْفِيْنِ﴾

٦

﴿قُلْ هُوَ لِلَّذِيْنَ اٰمَنُوْا هُدًى وَّشِفَآءٌؕ﴾

(١ مرة)

1. wa yashfi sudūra qawmin mu'minīn •
2. yā ayyuha n-nāsu qad jā'atkum maw'iẓatun min rabbikum wa shifā'un li mā fi ṣ-ṣudūr, wa hudan wa raḥmatun li l-mu'minīn •
3. yakhruju min buṭūnihā sharābun mukhtalifun alwānuhu fīhi shifā'un li n-nās, inna fī dhālika la āyatan li qawmin yatafakkarūn •
4. wa nunazzilu mina l-qur'āni mā huwa shifā'un wa raḥmatun li l-mu'minīna •
5. wa idhā mariḍtu fa huwa yashfīn •
6. qul huwa li-lladhīna āmanū hudan wa shifā'un • (1 time)

9:14

1. ❮*He will heal the believers' feelings*❯

10:57

2. ❮*People, a teaching from your Lord has come to you, a healing for what is in [your] hearts, and guidance and mercy for the believers.*❯

16:69

3. ❮*From their bellies comes a drink of different colours in which there is healing for people. There truly is a sign in this for those who think..*❯

17:82

4. ❮*We send down the Qur'an as healing and mercy to those who believe*❯

26:80

5. ❮*And when I am ill, it is He Who cures me*❯

41:44

6. ❮*Say, 'It is guidance and healing for those who have faith'*❯[35]

-٣٦-

Sayyiduna **'ABD AL-QADIR AL-JILANI'S** ﷺ SUBLIME *wazifa*

اَللّٰهُمَّ صَحًّا صَحًّا وَحًّا بَحًّا ﴿حمٓ﴾ ﴿لَا يُنْصَرُوْنَ﴾

﴿وَجَعَلْنَا مِنْۢ بَيْنِ اَيْدِيْهِمْ سَدًّا وَّمِنْ خَلْفِهِمْ سَدًّا فَاَغْشَيْنَاهُمْ

فَهُمْ لَا يُبْصِرُوْنَ﴾ ﴿كٓهٰيٰعٓصٓ﴾

﴿حمٓ ۞ عٓسٓقٓ﴾ ﴿لَا يُصَدَّعُوْنَ عَنْهَا وَلَا يُنْزِفُوْنَ﴾ يَا رَبُّ

۞ يَا رَبُّ ۞ يَا رَبُّ ۞

وَلَا حَوْلَ وَلَا قُوَّةَ اِلَّا بِاللّٰهِ الْعَلِيِّ الْعَظِيْمِ ۞ (٣ مرات)

Allāhumma ṣaḥḥan ṣaḥḥan ṣaḥḥan waḥḥan baḥḥan • Hā-Mīīīn · lā yunṣarūn • wa ja'alnā min(m) baini aidīhim sadda(n) wa min khalfihim sadda(n) fa-aghshainā-hum fa-hum lā yubṣirūn • kāāāf-hā-yā-'aīīīn-ṣāāād • Hā-Mīīīm • 'aīīīn-sīīīn-qāāāf • lā yuṣadda'ūna 'anhā wa lā yunzifūn • yā Rabb, yā Rabb, yā Rabb • wa lā ḥawla wa lā quwwata illā bi Llāhi l-'aliyyi l-aẓīm • (3 times)

O Allah, truly, truly, truly, verily, surely! ﴾Ha-Mim﴿[41:1] *﴾They will not be helped.﴿*[41:16] *﴾And We have set a bar before them and a bar behind them, and have covered them so that they cannot see.﴿*[36:9] *﴾Kaf-Ha-Ya-'Ain-Sad﴿*[19:1] *﴾Ha-Min, 'Ain-Sin-Kaf﴿*[42:1-2] *﴾From it they get no aching of the head nor any madness.﴿*[56:19] *O Lord, O Lord! There is no power nor any strength except with Allah, the All-High, the Almighty.*[36]

We send down the Qur'an as healing and mercy to those who believe

"

-٣٧-

Sayyiduna **'ABD AL-QADIR AL-JILANI'S** ﷺ SUBTLE *daqa'iq*

(**MORNING** ONLY)

قَلْبِيْ قُطْبِيْ وَقَالَبِيْ لُبْنَانِيْ ۞
۞ سِرِّيْ خَضِرِيْ وَعَيْنُهُ عِرْفَانِيْ
هَارُوْنُ عَقْلِيْ وَكَلِيْمِيْ رُوْحِيْ ۞
۞ فِرْعَوْنِيْ نَفْسِيْ وَالْهَوٰى هَامَانِيْ

(٦/٧ مرات)

qalbī quṭbī wa qālabī lubnānī •
• sirrī khaḍirī wa 'ainuhu 'irfānī
hārūnu 'aqlī wa kalīmī rūḥī •
• firawnī nafsī wa l-hawā hāmānī

(6/7 times)

My heart [qalb] is my cardinal pole [qutb] and
my physical form [qalab] is my lubnan
my innermost being [sirr] is my Khidr and
its eye ['ain] is the source of my Gnosis ['irfan]
Harun is my intellect ['aql] and
Musa [kalimi] is my spirit [ruh]
Fir'awn is my lower self [nafs] and
Haman is my passion [hawa].[37A]

Sayyiduna 'ABD AL-QADIR AL-JILANI'S ﵁ SUBTLE *daqa'iq*

(EVENING ONLY)

كَفَاكَ رَبُّكَ كَمْ يَكْفِيكَ وَاكِفَةً ۞ كِفْ كَافُهَا كَكَمِينٍ كَانَ مُنْكَلِكَا

تَكُرُّ كَرًّا كَكَرِّ الْكَرِّ فِي كَبِدٍ ۞ تَحْكِي مُشَكْشَكَةً كَلَّتْ لِكَلْ كَلِكَا

كَفَاكَ مَا بِي كَفَاكَ الْكَافُ كُرْبَتَهُ ۞ يَا كَوْكَبًا كَانَ تَحْكِي كَوْكَبَ الْفَلَكَا

★ ★ ★

كَكُرَيْرَةٍ كَفُّكُمْ كَالْكَهْفِ فَوْكُمْ لَكُمْ

كَكَعْكَعٍ كَبِدٍ يَكْفِيكُمُ الْكَافُ

(١ مرة)

kafāka rabbuka kam yakfīka wākifatan •
• kif kāfuhā kakamīnin kāna munkalikan
takarru karran kakarri l-karri fī kabidin •
• taḥkī mushakshakatan kallat likal kalikan
kafāka mā bī kafāka l-kāfu kurbatahu •
• yā kawkaban kāna taḥkī kawkaba l-falakan

★ ★ ★

kakurairatin kaffukum ka l-kahfi fawkum lakum
kaka'ka'in kabidin yakfīkumu l-kāf • (6/7 times)

[O my heart,] your Lord is [and has always been]
sufficient for you in removing obstacles [from your path].
Now, too, He will suffice for you; [as Divine Help
is] a tremendous force [for impending battle].
Like an entangled rope that appears straight, these
snares are severe [to mislead you from the Straight Path].
They come fast and furious, like a raft [on a
dangerous downstream].
[O my heart,] come what may, be like the star on its
orbit—[firm and unwavering],
He ﷻ will suffice for you in every affliction—
[now and forever][37B]

★ ★ ★

-٣٨-

Sayyiduna ʿABD AL-QADIR AL-JILANI'S ﵁ SPECIAL *awrad*

(MORNING ONLY)

أَشْرَقَ نُورُ اللهِ ۞ وَظَهَرَ كَلَامُ اللهِ ۞ وَثَبَتَ أَمْرُ اللهِ ۞ وَنَفَذَ
حُكْمُ اللهِ ۞ وَتَوَكَّلْتُ عَلَى اللهِ ۞ مَا شَآءَ اللهُ ۞ وَلَا حَوْلَ وَلَا
قُوَّةَ إِلَّا بِاللهِ ۞ تَحَصَّنْتُ بِخَفِيِّ لُطْفِ اللهِ ۞ وَبِلُطْفِ صُنْعِ
اللهِ ۞ وَبِجَمِيلِ سِتْرِ اللهِ ۞ وَبِعَظِيمِ ذِكْرِ اللهِ ۞ وَبِقُوَّةِ
سُلْطَانِ اللهِ ۞ دَخَلْتُ فِي كَنَفِ اللهِ ۞ وَاسْتَجَرْتُ بِرَسُولِ
اللهِ ﷺ ۞ تَبَرَّأْتُ مِنْ حَوْلِي وَقُوَّتِي وَاسْتَعَنْتُ بِحَوْلِ اللهِ
وَقُوَّتِهِ ۞ اَللّٰهُمَّ اسْتُرْنِي وَاحْفَظْنِي فِي دِينِي وَدُنْيَايَ وَأَهْلِي
وَمَالِي وَوَلَدِي وَأَصْحَابِي وَأَحْبَابِي بِسِتْرِكَ الَّذِي سَتَرْتَ بِهِ
ذَاتَكَ فَلَا عَيْنٌ تَرَاكَ وَلَا يَدٌ تَصِلُ إِلَيْكَ ۞

يَا أَرْحَمَ الرَّاحِمِينَ احْجُبْنِي عَنِ الْقَوْمِ الظَّالِمِينَ ٣

۞ بِقُدْرَتِكَ يَا قَوِيُّ يَا مَتِينُ ۞ يَا أَرْحَمَ الرَّاحِمِينَ بِكَ نَسْتَعِينُ
۞ اَللّٰهُمَّ يَا سَابِقَ الْفَوْتِ ۞ يَا سَامِعَ الصَّوْتِ ۞ وَيَا كَاسِيَ
الْعِظَامِ لَحْمًا بَعْدَ الْمَوْتِ ۞ أَغِثْنِي وَأَجِرْنِي مِنْ خِزْيِ

الدُّنْيَا وَعَذَابِ الْآخِرَةِ ❁ وَلَا حَوْلَ وَلَا قُوَّةَ إِلَّا بِاللّٰهِ الْعَلِيِّ
الْعَظِيمِ ❁ (١ مرة)

ashraqu nūru Llāhi wa ẓahara kalāmu Llāhi wa thabata amru Llāhi wa nafadha ḥukmu Llāhi wa tawakkaltu ʿala Llāh • māshā'a Llāhu wa lā ḥawla wa lā quwwata illā bi Llāh • taḥaṣṣantu bi khafiyyi luṭfi Llāhi wa bi luṭfi ṣunʿi Llāhi wa bi jamīli sitri Llāhi wa bi ʿaẓīmi dhikri Llāhi wa bi quwwati sulṭāni Llāh • dakhaltu fī kanafi Llāhi wa-stajartu bi rasūli Llāhi ṣalla Llāhu ʿalaihi wa sallam • tabarra'tu min ḥawlī wa quwwatī wa-staʿantu bi ḥawli Llāhi wa quwwatih •

Allāhumma-sturnī wa-ḥfaẓnī fī dīnī wa dunyāya wa ahlī wa mālī wa waladī wa aṣḥābī wa aḥbābī bi sitrika-lladhī satarta bihi dhātika fa-lā ʿainun tarāka wa-lā yadun taṣilu ilaika • yā arḥama r-rāḥimīna- ḥjubnī ʿani l-qawmi ẓ-ẓālimīn (3 times) • yā qudratika yā qawiyyu yā matīn • yā arḥama r-rāḥimīna bika nastaʿīn • Allāhumma yā sābiqa l-fawt • yā sāmiʿa ṣ-ṣawt • wa yā kāsiya l-ʿiẓāmi laḥman baʿda l-mawt • aghithnī wa ajirnī min khizyi d-dunyā wa ʿadhābi l-ākhirah • (1 time)

The Light of Allah has shone forth, the Word of Allah has become manifest, the Commandment of Allah has been established, the Law of Allah has come into effect, and I have put all my trust in Allah. What Allah has willed [will come to pass] and there is no power or strength except with Allah · I have found shelter in Allah's hidden grace, and in the grace of Allah's work, and in the beauty of Allah's protection, and in the splendour of Allah's remembrance, and in the strength of Allah's kingship · I have entered Allah's domain and I have sought refuge with Allah's Messenger ﷺ · I have washed my hands of my personal power and strength and have turned for help to the power of Allah and His strength.

O Allah, shield me and protect me in my religion, my worldly affairs, my family, my property, my children, my companions and my friends with that shield of Yours with which You have shielded Your Essence such that no eye can see You and no hand can reach You · O quintessence of Mercy, protect me from the oppressors! (thrice)—by Your power, O Strong One, O Firm One · O quintessence of Mercy, through You we seek help · O Allah, O Existent in every direction, O Hearer of every voice, O Clother of the bones with flesh after death· Help me and protect me from the disgrace of this world and the torment of the Hereafter · There is no power or strength except with Allah, the All-High, the Almighty · [38A]

Sayyiduna 'ABD AL-QADIR AL-JILANI'S ﵁ SPECIAL *awrad*
(EVENING ONLY)

اَللّٰهُمَّ حُلَّ هٰذِهِ الْعُقْدَةَ ۞ وَاَزِلْ هٰذِهِ الْعُسْرَةَ ۞
وَلَقِّنِيْ حُسْنَ الْمَيْسُوْرِ ۞ وَقِنِيْ سُوْءَ الْمَقْدُوْرِ ۞
وَارْزُقْنِيْ حُسْنَ الطَّلَبِ ۞ وَاكْفِنِيْ سُوْءَ الْمُنْقَلَبِ ۞
اَللّٰهُمَّ حُجَّتِيْ حَاجَتِيْ ۞ وَعُدَّتِيْ فَاقَتِيْ ۞ وَوَسِيْلَتِيْ
اِنْقِطَاعُ حِيْلَتِيْ ۞ وَرَاْسُ مَا لِيْ عَدَمُ احْتِيَالِيْ ۞
وَشَفِيْعِيْ دُمُوْعِيْ ۞ وَكَنْزِيْ عَجْزِيْ ۞ اِلٰهِيْ قَطْرَةٌ مِنْ
بِحَارِ جُوْدِكَ تُغْنِيْنِيْ ۞ وَذَرَّةٌ مِنْ تَيَّارِ عَفْوِكَ تَكْفِيْنِيْ
۞ فَارْحَمْنِيْ ۞ وَارْزُقْنِيْ ۞ وَاهْدِنِيْ ۞ وَعَافِنِيْ ۞ وَاعْفُ
عَنِّيْ ۞ وَاغْفِرْ لِيْ ۞ وَاقْضِ حَاجَتِيْ ۞ وَنَفِّسْ كُرْبَتِيْ
۞ وَفَرِّجْ هَمِّيْ ۞ وَاكْشِفْ غَمِّيْ ۞ بِرَحْمَتِكَ يَا اَرْحَمَ
الرَّاحِمِيْنَ ۞ وَالْحَمْدُ لِلّٰهِ رَبِّ الْعَالَمِيْنَ ۞ (١ مرة)

Allāhumma ḥulla hādhihi l-'uqdata wa azil hādhihi l-'usrat(a) • wa laqqinī ḥusna l-maisūri wa qinī sū'a l-maqdūr(i) • wa-rzuqnī ḥusna ṭ-ṭalabi wa-kfinī sū'a l-munqalab(i) •

Allāhumma ḥujjatī ḥājatī • wa ʿuddatī fāqatī • wa wasīlatī inqiṭāʿu ḥīlatī • wa raʾsu mālī ʿadamu htiyālī • wa shafīʿī dumūʿī • wa kanzī ʿajzī • ilāhī qaṭratun min(m) biḥāru jūdika tughnīnī • wa dharratun min tayyāri ʿafwika takfīnī •

fa-rḥamnī • wa-rzuqnī • wa-hdinī • wa ʿāfinī • wa-ʿfu ʿannī • wa-ghfir lī • wa-qḍi ḥājatī • wa naffis kurbatī • wa farrij hammī • wa-kshif ghammī • bi raḥmatika yā arḥama r-rāḥimīn(a) • wa l-ḥamdu li Llāhi Rabbi l-ʿālamīn • (1 time)

O Allah, loosen this knot · cause this hardship to ease · let me encounter the best of good fortune · guard me against the worst of destiny · provide me with the best of what is sought · protect me from the worst of the final upheaval ·

O Allah is my needful plea · my equipment is my neediness · my means is the cessation of my deceitfulness · my capital is the non-existence of my cunning · my intercessor is my tears · my treasure is my incapacity · My Lord, a drop from the oceans of Your Generosity will enrich me · an atom from the current of Your Pardon will suffice me ·

So have mercy on me · grant me provision · guide me · give me well-being · pardon me · forgive me · fulfil my need · disperse my sorrow · cheer my concern · & remove my anxiety · by Your Universal Mercy, O Quintessence of mercy! Praise to Allah, Lord of the cosmos.[38B]

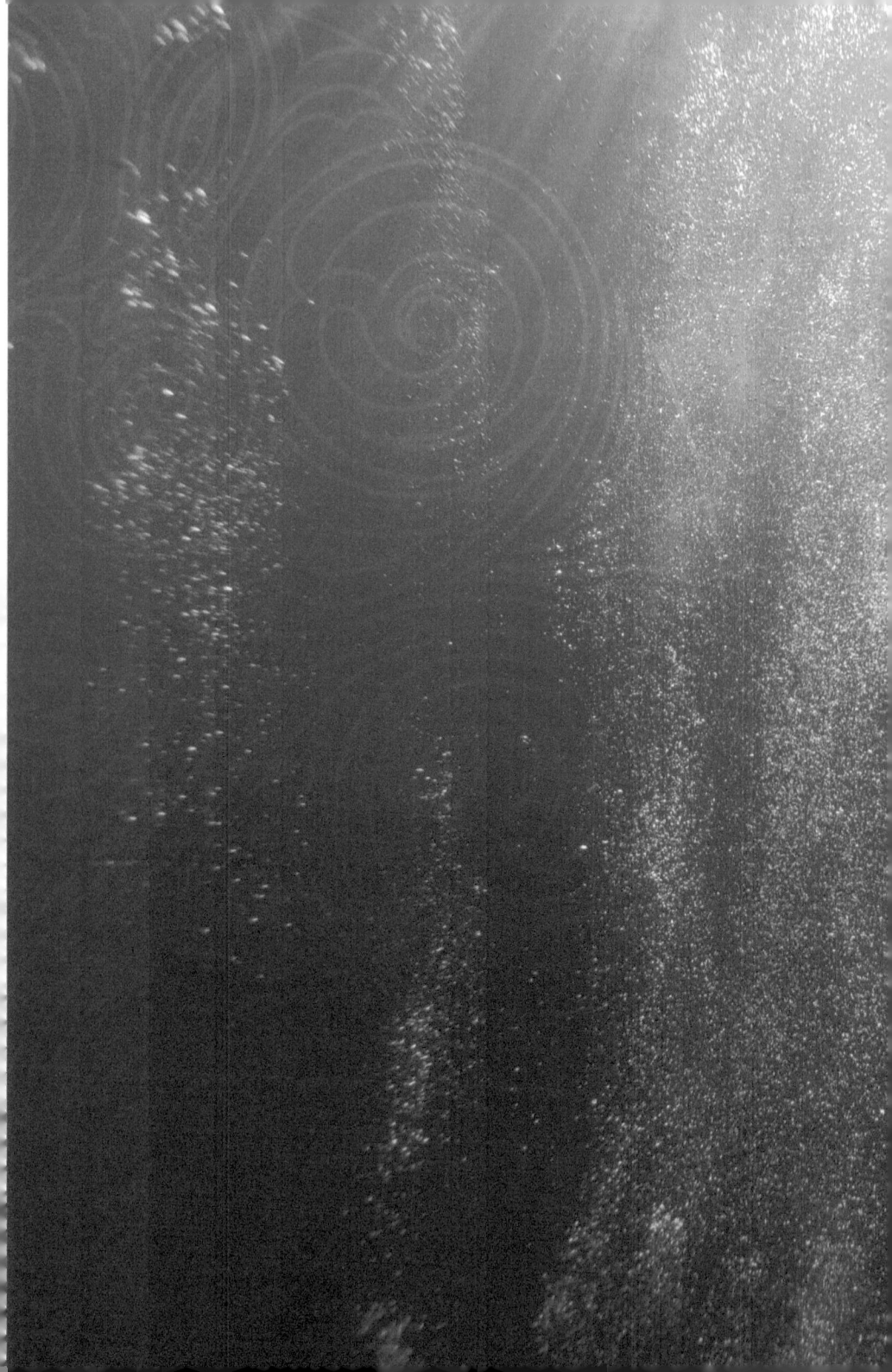

My Lord, a drop
from the oceans of
Your Generosity
will enrich me;
an atom from the
current of
Your Pardon will
suffice me.

”

-٣٩-

Sayyiduna **JABIR B. 'ABD ALLAH'S** ؓ STUPENDOUS *salawat* WITH *durud fathiyya* (**MORNING** ONLY)

﴿إِنَّ اللّٰهَ وَمَلٰٓئِكَتَهٗ يُصَلُّوْنَ عَلَى النَّبِيِّ
يٰٓاَيُّهَا الَّذِيْنَ اٰمَنُوْا صَلُّوْا عَلَيْهِ وَسَلِّمُوْا تَسْلِيْمًا﴾

اَلصَّلٰوةُ وَالسَّلَامُ عَلَيْكَ يَا رَسُوْلَ اللّٰهِ ۞

اَلصَّلٰوةُ وَالسَّلَامُ عَلَيْكَ يَا حَبِيْبَ اللّٰهِ ۞

اَلصَّلٰوةُ وَالسَّلَامُ عَلَيْكَ يَا خَلِيْلَ اللّٰهِ ۞

اَلصَّلٰوةُ وَالسَّلَامُ عَلَيْكَ يَا نَبِيَّ اللّٰهِ ۞

اَلصَّلٰوةُ وَالسَّلَامُ عَلَيْكَ يَا صَفِيَّ اللّٰهِ ۞

اَلصَّلٰوةُ وَالسَّلَامُ عَلَيْكَ يَا خَيْرَ خَلْقِ اللّٰهِ ۞

اَلصَّلٰوةُ وَالسَّلَامُ عَلَيْكَ يَا مَنِ اخْتَارَهُ اللّٰهُ ۞

اَلصَّلٰوةُ وَالسَّلَامُ عَلَيْكَ يَا مَنْ اَرْسَلَهُ اللّٰهُ ۞

اَلصَّلٰوةُ وَالسَّلَامُ عَلَيْكَ يَا مَنْ زَيَّنَهُ اللّٰهُ ۞

اَلصَّلٰوةُ وَالسَّلَامُ عَلَيْكَ يَا مَنْ شَرَّفَهُ اللّٰهُ ۞

اَلصَّلٰوةُ وَالسَّلَامُ عَلَيْكَ يَا مَنْ كَرَّمَهُ اللّٰه ۞

اَلصَّلٰوةُ وَالسَّلَامُ عَلَيْكَ يَا مَنْ عَظَّمَهُ اللّٰه ۞

اَلصَّلٰوةُ وَالسَّلَامُ عَلَيْكَ يَا سَيِّدَ الْمُرْسَلِيْنَ ۞

اَلصَّلٰوةُ وَالسَّلَامُ عَلَيْكَ يَا اِمَامَ الْمُتَّقِيْنَ ۞

اَلصَّلٰوةُ وَالسَّلَامُ عَلَيْكَ يَا خَاتَمَ النَّبِيِّيْنَ ۞

اَلصَّلٰوةُ وَالسَّلَامُ عَلَيْكَ يَا شَفِيْعَ الْمُذْنِبِيْنَ ۞

اَلصَّلٰوةُ وَالسَّلَامُ عَلَيْكَ يَا رَسُوْلَ رَبِّ الْعَالَمِيْنَ ۞

★ ★ ★

اَللّٰهُمَّ يَا رَبَّ مُحَمَّدٍ وَّاٰلِ مُحَمَّدٍ صَلِّ عَلٰى مُحَمَّدٍ وَّاٰلِ مُحَمَّدٍ وَّاَعْطِ مُحَمَّدًا
الدَّرَجَةَ وَالْوَسِيْلَةَ فِى الْجَنَّةِ ۞ اَللّٰهُمَّ يَا رَبَّ مُحَمَّدٍ وَّاٰلِ مُحَمَّدٍ
اِجْزِ مُحَمَّدًا ﷺ مَا هُوَ اَهْلُهٗ ۞ اَللّٰهُمَّ صَلِّ عَلٰى مُحَمَّدٍ وَّعَلٰٓى اٰلِ
مُحَمَّدٍ وَّعَلٰٓى اَهْلِ بَيْتِهٖ، وَسَلِّمْ تَسْلِيْمًا كَثِيْرًا ۞

(١ مرة)

inna Llāha wa malā'ikatahu yuṣallūna ‘ala n-nabiy, yā ayyuha lladhīna āmanū ṣallū ‘alaihi wa sallimū taslīma(n) • aṣ-ṣalātu wa s-salāmu ‘alaika yā rasūla Llāh • aṣ-ṣalātu wa s-salāmu 'alaika yā ḥabība Llāh • aṣ-ṣalātu wa s-salāmu 'alaika yā khalīla Llāh • aṣ-ṣalātu wa s-salāmu 'alaika yā nabiyya Llāh • aṣ-ṣalātu wa s-salāmu 'alaika yā ṣafiyya Llāh • aṣ-ṣalātu wa s-salāmu 'alaika yā khaira khalqi Llāh •

aṣ-ṣalātu wa s-salāmu 'alaika yā mani khtārahu Llāh • aṣ-ṣalātu wa s-salāmu 'alaika yā man arsalahu Llāh • aṣ-ṣalātu wa s-salāmu 'alaika yā man zayyanahu Llāh • aṣ-ṣalātu wa s-salāmu 'alaika yā man sharrafahu Llāh • aṣ-ṣalātu wa s-salāmu 'alaika yā man karramahu Llāh • aṣ-ṣalātu wa s-salāmu 'alaika yā man 'aẓẓamahu Llāh •

aṣ-ṣalātu wa s-salāmu 'alaika yā sayyida l-mursalīn • aṣ-ṣalātu wa s-salāmu 'alaika yā imāma l-muttaqīn • aṣ-ṣalātu wa s-salāmu 'alaika yā khātama n-nabiyyīn • aṣ-ṣalātu wa s-salāmu 'alaika yā shafī'a l-mudhnibīn • aṣ-ṣalātu wa s-salāmu 'alaika yā rasūla rabbi l-'ālamīn •

★ ★ ★

Allāhumma yā rabba Muḥammadin wa āli Muḥammadin ṣalli 'alā Muḥammadin wa āli Muḥammadin wa a'ṭi Muḥammadan ad-darajata wa l-wasīlata fi l-jannah •

Allāhumma yā rabba Muḥammadin wa āli Muḥammadin ijzi Muḥammadan ṣalla Llāhu 'alaihi wa sallam mā huwa ahluh(u) • Allāhumma ṣalli 'alā Muḥammadin wa 'alā āli Muḥammadin wa 'alā ahli baitih(i), wa sallama taslīman kathīra(n) • (1 time)

33:56 *﴾Allah and His angels whelm in blessings the Prophet. O you of faith! Ask blessings on him and salute him with a worthy salutation.﴿*

Salat and Salam upon you, O Messenger of Allah. Salat and Salam upon you, O Beloved of Allah. Salat and Salam upon you, O Friend of Allah. Salat and Salam upon you, O Prophet of Allah. Salat and Salam upon you, O Intimate of Allah. Salat and Salam upon you, O best of the creation of Allah.

Salat and Salam upon you, O whom Allah chose. Salat and Salam upon you, O whom Allah sent. Salat and Salam upon you, O whom Allah adorned. Salat and Salam upon you, O whom Allah honoured. Salat and Salam upon you, O whom Allah blessed. Salat and Salam upon you, O whom Allah exalted.

Salat and Salam upon you, O Master of Messengers. Salat and Salam upon you, O Leader of the devout. Salat and Salam upon you, O Seal of the Prophets. Salat and Salam upon you, O Intercessor of the sinners. Salat and Salam upon you, O Messenger of the Lord of the Cosmos.

★ ★ ★

O Allah, Lord of the praiseworthy one ﷺ and family of the praiseworthy one ﷺ, whelm the praiseworthy one ﷺ and family of the praiseworthy one ﷺ in divine exaltations, and grant the praiseworthy one ﷺ the highest rank and intercession in the Garden.

O Allah, Lord of the praiseworthy one ﷺ and family of the praiseworthy one ﷺ, reward the praiseworthy one such a reward that befits him. O Allah, whelm the praiseworthy one ﷺ and family of the praiseworthy one ﷺ in divine exaltations, and the scions of his house, and grant abundant peace immaculate.[39A]

Sayyiduna **JABIR B. 'ABD ALLAH'S** ﵁ STUPENDOUS *salawat* WITH *durud ruhiyya* (**EVENING** ONLY)

﴿إِنَّ ٱللَّهَ وَمَلَٰٓئِكَتَهُۥ يُصَلُّونَ عَلَى ٱلنَّبِيِّۚ
يَٰٓأَيُّهَا ٱلَّذِينَ ءَامَنُوا۟ صَلُّوا۟ عَلَيْهِ وَسَلِّمُوا۟ تَسْلِيمًا﴾

اَللّٰهُمَّ صَلِّ عَلٰى مُحَمَّدٍ مَّادَامَتِ الصَّلٰوةُ ۞

وَصَلِّ عَلٰى مُحَمَّدٍ مَّادَامَتِ الرَّحْمَةُ ۞

وَصَلِّ عَلٰى مُحَمَّدٍ مَّادَامَتِ الْبَرَكَاتُ ۞

وَصَلِّ عَلٰى رُوْحِ مُحَمَّدٍ فِى الْاَرْوَاحِ ۞

وَصَلِّ عَلٰى صُوْرَةِ مُحَمَّدٍ فِى الصُّوَرِ ۞

وَصَلِّ عَلٰى اِسْمِ مُحَمَّدٍ فِى الْاَسْمَاءِ ۞

وَصَلِّ عَلٰى نَفْسِ مُحَمَّدٍ فِى النُّفُوْسِ ۞

وَصَلِّ عَلٰى قَلْبِ مُحَمَّدٍ فِى الْقُلُوْبِ ۞

وَصَلِّ عَلٰى قَبْرِ مُحَمَّدٍ فِى الْقُبُوْرِ ۞

وَصَلِّ عَلٰى رَوْضَةِ مُحَمَّدٍ فِى الرِّيَاضِ ۞

وَصَلِّ عَلٰى جَسَدِ مُحَمَّدٍ فِى الْاَجْسَادِ ۞

وَصَلِّ عَلٰى تُرْبَةِ مُحَمَّدٍ فِى التُّرَابِ ۞
وَصَلَّى اللّٰهُ وَسَلَّمَ وَبَارَكَ عَلٰى خَيْرِ خَلْقِهِ
سَيِّدِنَا مُحَمَّدٍ وَّاٰلِهِ وَاَصْحَابِهِ وَاَزْوَاجِهِ
وَذُرِّيَاتِهِ وَاَهْلِ بَيْتِهِ وَاَحْبَابِهِ اَجْمَعِيْنَ ۞

★ ★ ★

اَللّٰهُمَّ يَا رَبَّ مُحَمَّدٍ وَّاٰلِ مُحَمَّدٍ صَلِّ عَلٰى مُحَمَّدٍ وَّاٰلِ مُحَمَّدٍ وَّاَعْطِ مُحَمَّدًا
الدَّرَجَةَ وَالْوَسِيْلَةَ فِى الْجَنَّةِ ۞ اَللّٰهُمَّ يَا رَبَّ مُحَمَّدٍ وَّاٰلِ مُحَمَّدٍ
اجْزِ مُحَمَّدًا ﷺ مَا هُوَ اَهْلُهُ ۞ اَللّٰهُمَّ صَلِّ عَلٰى مُحَمَّدٍ وَّعَلٰٓى اٰلِ
مُحَمَّدٍ وَّعَلٰٓى اَهْلِ بَيْتِهِ، وَسَلِّمْ تَسْلِيْمًا كَثِيْرًا ۞
(١ مرة)

inna Llāha wa malā'ikatahu yuṣallūna 'ala n-nabiy, yā ayyuha lladhīna āmanū ṣallū 'alaihi wa sallimū taslīma(n) • Allāhumma ṣalli 'alā Muḥammadin mādāmati ṣ-ṣalāt • wa ṣalli 'alā Muḥammadin mādāmatir-raḥmah • wa ṣalli 'alā Muḥammadin • mādāmati l-barakāt

wa ṣalli 'alā rūhi Muḥammadin fi l-arwāh • wa ṣalli 'alā ṣūrati Muḥammadin fi ṣ-ṣuwar • wa ṣalli 'alā ismi Muḥammadin fi l-asmā' • wa ṣalli 'alā nafsi Muḥammadin fi n-nufūs • wa ṣalli ʿalā qalbi Muḥammadin fi l-qulūb • wa ṣalli ʿalā qabri Muḥammadin fi l-qubūr • wa ṣalli ʿalā rawḍati Muḥammadin fi r-riyāḍ • wa ṣalli ʿalā jasadi Muḥammadin fi l-ajsād • wa ṣalli ʿalā turbati Muḥammadin fi t-turāb •

wa ṣalla Llāhu (wa sallama wa bāraka) ʿalā khairi khalqihi sayyidinā Muḥammadin wa ālihi wa aṣḥābihi wa azwājihi wa dhurriyātihi wa ahli baitihi wa aḥbābihi ajmaʿīn •

★ ★ ★

Allāhumma yā rabba Muḥammadin wa āli Muḥammadin ṣalli ʿalā Muḥammadin wa āli Muḥammadin wa aʿṭi Muḥammadan ad-darajata wa l-wasīlata fi l-jannah •

Allāhumma yā rabba Muḥammadin wa āli Muḥammadin ijzi Muḥammadan ṣalla Llāhu ʿalaihi wa sallam mā huwa ahluh(u) • Allāhumma ṣalli ʿalā Muḥammadin wa ʿalā āli Muḥammadin wa ʿalā ahli baitih(i), wa sallama taslīman kathīra(n) • (1 time)

33:56 *﴾Allah and His angels whelm in blessings the Prophet. O you of faith! Ask blessings on him and salute him with a worthy salutation.﴿*

O Allah, whelm the praiseworthy one ﷺ in divine exaltations till Your divine exaltations are completed · whelm the praiseworthy one ﷺ in divine exaltations till Your mercy is exhausted · whelm the praiseworthy one ﷺ in divine exaltations till Your blessings are fulfilled ·

[O Allah,] whelm the soul of the praiseworthy one ﷺ from amongst all souls, in Your divine exaltations · whelm the form of the praiseworthy one ﷺ from amongst all forms, in Your divine exaltations · whelm

the name of the praiseworthy one ﷺ from amongst all names, in Your divine exaltations · whelm the quintessence of the praiseworthy one ﷺ from amongst all essence, in Your divine exaltations · whelm the heart of the praiseworthy one ﷺ from amongst all hearts, in Your divine exaltations · whelm the grave of the praiseworthy one ﷺ from amongst all graves, in Your divine exaltations · whelm the garden of the praiseworthy one ﷺ from amongst all gardens, in Your divine exaltations · whelm the body of the praiseworthy one ﷺ from amongst all bodies, in Your divine exaltations · whelm the dust of the praiseworthy one ﷺ from amongst all dust, in Your divine exaltations ·

[O Allah,] whelm divine exaltations [salat], (salutations immaculate [salam] and blessings par excellence [baraka]) upon the best of creation, our liege Muhammad ﷺ and [upon] his family, companions, wives, progeny, the folks of his house and his lovers—one and all.

★ ★ ★

O Allah, Lord of the praiseworthy one ﷺ and family of the praiseworthy one ﷺ, whelm the praiseworthy one ﷺ and family of the praiseworthy one ﷺ in divine exaltations, and grant the praiseworthy one ﷺ the highest rank and intercession in the Garden.

O Allah, Lord of the praiseworthy one ﷺ and family of the praiseworthy one ﷺ, reward the praiseworthy one such a reward that befits him. O Allah, whelm the praiseworthy one ﷺ and family of the praiseworthy one ﷺ in divine exaltations, and the scions of his house, and grant abundant peace immaculate.[39B]

O Allah, Lord of the praiseworthy one and family of the praiseworthy one, reward the praiseworthy one such a reward that befits him.
”

-٤٠-

Sayyiduna **'ALI B. ABI TALIB'S** ﷺ VERSES OF *ikhtitam*

﴿دَعْوَىٰهُمْ فِيهَا سُبْحَٰنَكَ ٱللَّهُمَّ وَتَحِيَّتُهُمْ فِيهَا سَلَٰمٌ ۚ وَءَاخِرُ دَعْوَىٰهُمْ أَنِ ٱلْحَمْدُ لِلَّهِ رَبِّ ٱلْعَٰلَمِينَ﴾

(١ مرة)

daʿwāhum fīhā subḥānaka Llāhumma wa taḥiyyatu-hum fīhā salām(un) wa ākhiru daʿwāhum ani l-ḥamdu li Llāhi rabbi l-ʿālamīn • (1 time)

10:10 ﴿*Their prayer therein will be, "Glory to You, O Allah!" their greeting therein, "Peace," and the end of their prayer, "Praise to Allah, Lord of the Cosmos."*﴾[40]

﴿سُبْحَٰنَ رَبِّكَ رَبِّ ٱلْعِزَّةِ عَمَّا يَصِفُونَ ۞ وَسَلَٰمٌ عَلَى ٱلْمُرْسَلِينَ ۞ وَٱلْحَمْدُ لِلَّهِ رَبِّ ٱلْعَٰلَمِينَ﴾

(٣ مرات)

subḥāna rabbika rabbi l-ʿizzati ʿammā yaṣifūn • wa salāmun ʿala l-mursalīn • wa l-ḥamdu li Llāhi rabbi l-ʿālamīn • (3 times)

37:180-182 ﴿*Exalted is your Lord, the Lord of Might, far beyond their descriptions. Peace upon the Messengers. Praise to Allah, Lord of the Cosmos.*﴾

انتهى اذكار الصباح والمساء

THE TEN SEVENS BEFORE SUNRISE & BEFORE SUNSET

[al-musabba'at al-'ashr qabla tulu' ash-shams wa qabla al-ghurub]

THE WIDELY KNOWN *AL-MUSABBA'AT AL-'ASHR* OR "THE Ten Sevens" is a litany gifted by the Prophet ﷺ to Abu l-'Abbas Balyan b. Malkan al-Khidr ﷺ. The latter taught the *musabba'at* to the Kufan ascetic, Ibrahim at-Taimi ﷺ, in the vicinity of the honoured *ka'ba.* The story of how this litany came to be can be found in the works and commentaries of *Imam* Abu Talib al-Makki ﷺ (*qut al-qulub*), *Imam* Abu Hamid al-Ghazali ﷺ (*ihya' 'ulum ad-din*), *Sayyiduna sh-Shaikh* 'Abd al-Qadir al-Jilani[6] ﷺ (*al-ghunya*), *Imam* Ahmad as-Sawi al-Maliki al-Khalwati ﷺ (*hashiya 'ala tafsir jalalain*), and others. *Imam* 'Abd Allah al-Haddad ﷺ concludes his *wird al-kabir* with it while *Imam* Ahmad at-Tijani ﷺ considers it a mainstay.

Imam al-'Arus Syed Muhammad ﷺ says that the *musabba'at* is a cleanser to wash away one's sins and an aid to attain innumerable benefits. It offers the combined rewards of (a) recitation of the Qur'an *[tilawat al-Qur'an]*, (b) invocation *[dhikr]*, (c) contemplation *[fikr]*, and (d) supplication *[du'a]*. Recite it at least once a day. For those of high resolve and lofty spiritual aspirations, it should be read twice a day—before sunrise and before sunset. Once memorised, this is certainly feasible whilst going about one's daily affairs.

Sayyiduna ash-Shaikh 'Abd al-Qadir al-Jilani ﷺ relates an extraordinary traditional report in his *ghunya* where the *musabba'at*, its virtues and a particular means to seeing the Prophet ﷺ in a dream are mentioned. As the origin of the *musabba'at* is not widely known, the complete Arabic text from the *ghunya* is presented here together with a partial English translation.

---

6 A *musabba'at* attributed to *Sayyidina sh-Shaikh* ﷺ also exists. See *al-fuyudat*.

فصل آخر في ذكر ما ورد فعله بين العشاءين
ورؤية فاعله للنبي ﷺ ببركة فعله ذلك في المنام وغير ذلك من الثواب

More concerning worshipful acts between the two evening prayers by the blessing of which behold the Holy Prophet ﷺ in sleep & other rewards

عن عبد الرحمن بن حبيب الحارثي البصري، عن سعيد بن سعد بن أبي طيبة كرز ابن وبرة الحارثي رحمه الله، وكان من الأبدال، قال: أتاني أخ لي من أهل الشام فأهدى لي هدية وقال لي: أقبل مني هذه الهدية يا كرز فإنها نعم الهدية، قال: فقلت: يا أخي ومن أهدى إليك هذه الهدية؟ قال: أعطانيها إبراهيم التيمي رحمه الله، قال: فقلت: فهل سألت إبراهيم من أعطاه هذه العطية، قال: بلى. قال لي: كنت جالسٌ في قبالة الكعبة وأنا في التهليل والتسبيح والتحميد، فجاءني رجل فسلم علي وجلس عن يميني، فلم أر في زماني أحسن منه وجهاً ولا أحسن منه ثياباً ولا أطيب منه ريحاً ولا أشد منه بياضاً، فقلت: يا عبد الله من أنت ومن أين جئت وما أنت؟ فقال: أنا الخضر جئت للسلام عليك وحباً لك في الله، وعندي هدية أريد أن أهديها إليك، فقلت له: فأعلمني هديتك هذه ما هي؟ فقال الخضر عليه السلام: تقرأ قبل أن تطلع الشمس وتبسط على الأرض وقبل أن تغرب سورة ﴿الحمد ...﴾ سبع مرات، و ﴿قل أعوذ برب الناس ...﴾ سبع مرات، و ﴿قل أعوذ برب الفلق ...﴾ سبع مرات، و ﴿قل هو الله أحد ...﴾ سبع مرات، و ﴿قل يا أيها الكافرون ...﴾ سبع مرات، وآية الكرسي سبع مرات، وتقول {سبحان الله، والحمد لله، ولا إله إلا الله، والله أكبر} سبع مرات، وتصلي على النبي ﷺ سبع مرات، وتستغفر لنفسك ولوالديك وللمؤمنين والمؤمنات سبع مرات، وعقيب الاستغفار: {اللهم رب افعل بي وبهم عاجلاً وآجلاً في الدين والدنيا والآخرة ما أنت له أهل، ولا تفعل بنا يا مولانا ما نحن له أهل، إنك غفور حليم جواد كريم بر رؤوف رحيم} سبع مرات، وانظر ألا تدع ذلك غدوة وعشياً، فإن الذي أعطانيها قال لي: قلها مرة واحدة في دهرك؛ فقلت: أحب أن تعرفني من أعطاك هذه الهدية؟ قال أعطانيها محمد ﷺ ، قال: فقلت للخضر عليه السلام: علمني شيئاً إن قلته رأيت النبي ﷺ في منامي فأسأله أهو أعطاك هذه العطية؟ فقال لي: أمتهم أنت لي؟ قلت: لا، ولكني أحب أن أسمع ذلك من رسول الله ﷺ.

فقال لي: إن كنت تريد أن ترى النبي ﷺ في منامك، فاعلم أنك إذا صليت المغرب تقوم تصلي إلى العشاء الآخرة من غير أن تكلم أحداً من الآدميين، وأقبل على صلاتك التي أنت فيها، وتسلم في كل ركعتين، واقرأ في كل سورة ﴿الحمد ...﴾ مرة، و ﴿قل هو الله أحد ...﴾ سبع مرات، ثم تصلي صلاة العتمة في جماعة، ولا تكلمن أحداً، حتى تأتي منزلك، وتصلي الوتر، وتصلي عند نومك ركعتين، تقرأ في كل ركعة سورة {الحمد ...} و {قل هو الله أحد ...} سبع مرات، ثم اسجد بعد الصلاة، واستغفر الله تعالى في سجودك سبع مرات، وقل: سبحان الله، والحمد لله، ولا إله إلا الله، والله أكبر، ولا حول ولا قوة إلا بالله العلي العظيم سبع مرات، ثم ارفع

رأسك من السجود واستو جالساً، وارفع يديك وقل: يا حي يا قيوم، يا ذا الجلال والإكرام، يا إله الأولين والآخرين، ويا رحمن الدنيا والآخرة ورحيمهما، يا رب يا رب يا رب، يا الله يا الله يا الله، ثم قم فادع بمثل ما دعوت في قيامك، ثم اسجد وادع في سجودك مثل ما دعوت، ثم ارفع رأسك ونم حيث شئت مستقبل القبلة وأنت تصلي على النبي ﷺ وآدم حتى يغلبك النوم. فقلت له: أحب أن تعلمني ممن سمعت هذا الدعاء، فقال: أمهتم أنت لي؟ فقلت: والذي بعث محمداً ﷺ بالحق نبياً ما أنا بمتهم لك. فقال عليه السلام: إني حضرت محمداً ﷺ حيث علم هذا الدعاء، وأوحي إليه به وكنت عنده، فتعلمته ممن علمه إياه. قال إبراهيم: فقلت له: أخبرني بثواب هذا الدعاء. فقال لي الخضر عليه السلام: إذا لقيت محمداً ﷺ فاسأله عن ثوابه. قال إبراهيم، ففعلت ما قال لي الخضر عليه السلام، ولم أزل أصلي على النبي ﷺ وأنا في فراشي، فذهب عني النوم من شدة الفرح بما علمني الخضر عليه السلام وبما رجوته من لقاء النبي ﷺ، وأصبحت على تلك الحال إلى أن صليت الفجر، وجلست في محرابي إلى أن ارتفع النهار، فصليت الضحى وأنا أحدث نفسي: إن عشت الليلة فعلت كما فعلت في الليلة الماضية، فغلبني النوم، فجاءتني الملائكة فحملوني فأدخلوني الجنة، فرأيت قصوراً من الياقوت الأحمر، وقصوراً من زمرد أخضر، وقصوراً من لؤلؤ أبيض، ورأيت أنهاراً من عسل ولبن وخمر، ورأيت في قصر منها جارية أشرفت علي فرأيت صورة وجهها أشد من نور الشمس الصاحية، وإذا لها ذوائب قد سقطت على الأرض من أعلى القصر، فسألت الملائكة الذين أدخلوني: لمن هذا القصر ولمن هذه الجارية؟ فقالوا: للذي يعمل مثل عملك، فلم يخرجوني من تلك الجنان حتى أطعموني من ثمرها وسقوني من ذلك الشراب، ثم أخرجوني وردوني إلى الموضع الذي كنت فيه، فأتاني رسول الله ﷺ ومعه سبعون نبياً وسبعون صفاً من الملائكة، كل صف ما بين المشرق والمغرب، فسلم علي وأخذ بيدي، فقلت: يا رسول الله ﷺ، إن الخضر أخبرني أنه سمع منك هذا الحديث، فقال النبي ﷺ صدق الخضر وكل ما يحكيه فهو حق، وهو عالم أهل الأرض، وهو رئيس الأبدال، وهو من جنود الله في الأرض، فقلت: يا رسول الله ما لمن يعمل هذا العمل من الثواب سوى ما رأيت؟ فقال ﷺ لي: وأي ثواب يكون أفضل من هذا الذي رأيت وأعطيت، لقد رأيت موضعك من الجنة وأكلت من ثمارها وشربت من شرابها، ورأيت الملائكة والأنبياء معي، ورأيت الحور العين، فقلت: يا رسول الله فمن يعمل مثل ما عملت ولم ير مثل الذي رأيت في منامي، هل يعطي شيئاً مما أعطيته فقال النبي ﷺ: والذي بعثني بالحق نبياً، إنه ليغفر له جميع الكبائر التي عملها، ويرفع الله عنه غضبه ومقته، والذي بعثني بالحق نبياً ليعطي العامل لهذا، وإن لم ير الجنة في منامه مثل ما أعطيت، وإن منادياً ينادي من السماء: إن الله قد غفر لعامله ولجميع أمته ﷺ من المؤمنين والمؤمنات من المشرق والمغرب ويؤمر صاحب الشمال ألا يكتب على أحد منهم شيئاً من السيئات إلى السنة المقبلة، قال: فقلت له: بأبي أنت وأمي يا رسول الله، بالذي أراني جمالك وأراني الجنة، أله هذا الثواب والفضل، قال ﷺ: نعم يعطي ذلك جميعاً، قلت: يا رسول الله إنه ينبغي لجميع المؤمنين والمؤمنات أن يتعلموا هذا الدعاء ويعلموه، لما فيه من الثواب والفضل، فقال النبي ﷺ: والذي بعثني بالحق نبياً ما يعمل بهذا إلا من خلقه الله سعيداً، ولا يتركه إلا من خلقه الله

شقياً، فقلت: يا رسول الله فهل يعطي عامل هذا شيئاً غير هذا؟ فقال النبي ﷺ: والذي بعثني بالحق نبياً إن من عمل هذا العمل ليلة واحدة كتبت له بكل قطرة نزلت من السماء منذ خلق الله الدنيا إلى يوم ينفخ في الصور حسنات، ويمحى عنه بعدد كل حبة تنبت من الأرض سيئات له ولمن عمل به من المؤمنين والمؤمنات من الأولين والآخرين».

On the authority of 'Abd ar-Rahman b. Habib al-Harithi al-Basri, on the authority of Sa'id b. Sa'd b. Abu Tiba Karaz b. Wabra al-Harithi ﵁—one of the *'abdal*—who reported:

A brother from the people of Levant came to me and gave me a gift. He said: *"O Karaz, accept from me this gift, for it is truly a boon!"* So I asked: *"O my brother, who gave you this gift?"* He replied: *"Ibrahim at-Taimi (Allah have mercy on him) gave it to me"* So I said: *"Did you ask Ibrahim who gave him this gift?"* He replied: *"Yes, of course,'* then he said:

I was sitting in front of the *ka'ba* engaged in *tahlil*, *tasbih* and *tahmid*. A man came up to me, gave me *salam*, and sat on my right. Never in all my days had I seen anyone more stunning in countenance, more stunning in attire, more fragrant in perfume, or more radiating in complexion.

I said: *"O servant of Allah, who are you, where do you come from, and what are you?"* He replied: *"I am al-Khidr; I have come to give salam, for I love you for the sake of Allah; I also come with a gift for you."* I said: *"Please tell me about this gift of yours—what is it?"* al-Khidr ﵇ replied: *"You must recite the following, before the sun rises and spreads its light over the earth, and before it sets—*

[al-Khidr ﵇ then lists the musabba'at & says:]

—do not neglect, both in the morning and in the evening, for he who gave it to me said: 'You must recite it at least <u>once in your lifetime</u>.'"

I said: *"I would like to know who gave you this gift."* He said: *'It was Muhammad ﷺ who gave it to me."* I then said to al-Khidr ؏: *"Tell me something. If I see the Prophet ﷺ in my dreams, should I ask him if he gave you this boon?"* He asked: *"Are you doubting me?"* I said: *"No! I would love to hear it directly from the Messenger of Allah ﷺ."*

[al-Khidr ؏ then prescribes a prayer & some recitals to at-Taimi ؓ to see the Prophet ﷺ in his dream. at-Taimi follows the instructions, & eventually falls asleep. He sees some of the splendours of the Garden & meets the Prophet ﷺ who establishes the veracity & rank of al-Khidr ؏. Full translation is found in **THE TEN SEVENS.** *]*

-١-

سورة الفاتحة

surat al-fatiha – **THE OPENING** CHAPTER

بِسۡمِ اللّٰهِ الرَّحۡمٰنِ الرَّحِيۡمِ ﴿١﴾
اَلۡحَمۡدُ لِلّٰهِ رَبِّ الۡعٰلَمِيۡنَ ﴿٢﴾ الرَّحۡمٰنِ الرَّحِيۡمِ ﴿٣﴾ مٰلِكِ يَوۡمِ
الدِّيۡنِ ﴿٤﴾ اِيَّاكَ نَعۡبُدُ وَاِيَّاكَ نَسۡتَعِيۡنُ ﴿٥﴾ اِهۡدِنَا الصِّرَاطَ
الۡمُسۡتَقِيۡمَ ﴿٦﴾ صِرَاطَ الَّذِيۡنَ اَنۡعَمۡتَ عَلَيۡهِمۡ غَيۡرِ الۡمَغۡضُوۡبِ
عَلَيۡهِمۡ وَلَا الضَّآلِّيۡنَ ﴿٧﴾ اٰمِيۡنَ (٧ مرات)

bismi Llāhi r-raḥmani r-raḥīm • al-ḥamdu li Llāhi rabbi l-ʿālamīn • ar-raḥmāni r-raḥīm • māliki yawmi d-dīn • iyyāka naʿbudu wa iyyāka nastaʿīn • ihdina ṣ-ṣirāṭa l-mustaqīm • ṣirāṭa lladhīna anʿamta ʿalaihim ghairi l-maghḍūbi ʿalaihim wa la ḍ-ḍāllīn • āmīn • (7 times)

In the name of Allah,
the Universally Merciful, the Singularly Compassionate.
Praise belongs to Allah, Lord of the Worlds. The Universally Merciful, the Singularly Compassionate. Master of the Day of Reckoning. It is You we worship and it is You we seek succour. Guide us to the straight path: the path of those You have blessed, those who incur no anger and who have not gone astray.[41]

-٢-

سورة الناس

surat an-nass – **HUMANKIND** CHAPTER

بِسۡمِ ٱللَّهِ ٱلرَّحۡمَٰنِ ٱلرَّحِيمِ ۝

قُلۡ أَعُوذُ بِرَبِّ ٱلنَّاسِ ۝١ مَلِكِ ٱلنَّاسِ ۝٢ إِلَٰهِ ٱلنَّاسِ ۝٣ مِن شَرِّ ٱلۡوَسۡوَاسِ ٱلۡخَنَّاسِ ۝٤ ٱلَّذِي يُوَسۡوِسُ فِي صُدُورِ ٱلنَّاسِ ۝٥ مِنَ ٱلۡجِنَّةِ وَٱلنَّاسِ ۝٦

(٧ مرات)

bismi Llāhi r-raḥmani r-raḥīm • qul a'ūdhu bi rabbi n-nās • maliki n-nās • ilāhi n-nās • min sharri l-waswāsi l-khannās • al-ladhī yuwaswisu fī ṣudūri n-nās • mina l-jinnati wa n-nās • (7 times)

In the name of Allah,
the Universally Merciful, the Singularly Compassionate.
Say, "I seek refuge with the Lord of mankind, the Sovereign of mankind, and the God of mankind against the harm of the slinking whisperer—who whispers into the hearts of mankind—whether they be jinn or mankind."[42]

سورة الفلق

surat al-falaq – **DAYBREAK** CHAPTER

بِسْمِ اللهِ الرَّحْمٰنِ الرَّحِيْمِ ۝ قُلْ اَعُوْذُ بِرَبِّ الْفَلَقِ ۝ مِنْ شَرِّ مَا خَلَقَ ۝ وَمِنْ شَرِّ غَاسِقٍ اِذَا وَقَبَ ۝ وَمِنْ شَرِّ النَّفّٰثٰتِ فِي الْعُقَدِ ۝ وَمِنْ شَرِّ حَاسِدٍ اِذَا حَسَدَ ۝

(٧ مرات)

bismi Llāhi r-raḥmani r-raḥīm •
qul aʿūdhu bi rabbi l-falaq • min sharri mā khalaq • wa min sharri ghāsiqin idhā waqab • wa min sharri n-naffāthāti fi l-ʿuqad • wa min sharri ḥāsidin idhā ḥasad • (7 times)

*In the name of Allah,
the Universally Merciful, the Singularly Compassionate.*

Say, "I seek refuge with the Lord of daybreak against the harm of what He has created, the harm of the night when darkness gathers, the harm of witches when they blow on knots, and the harm of the envier when he envies."[43]

-٤-

سورة الاخلاص

surat al-ikhlas – **SINCERITY** CHAPTER

بِسۡمِ ٱللَّهِ ٱلرَّحۡمَٰنِ ٱلرَّحِيمِ ۝
قُلۡ هُوَ ٱللَّهُ أَحَدٌ ۝١ ٱللَّهُ ٱلصَّمَدُ ۝٢ لَمۡ يَلِدۡ
وَلَمۡ يُولَدۡ ۝٣ وَلَمۡ يَكُن لَّهُۥ كُفُوًا أَحَدُۢ ۝٤ (٧ مرات)

bismi Llāhi r-raḥmani r-raḥīm •
qul huwa Llāhu aḥad • Allāhu ṣ-ṣamad • lam yalid wa lam
yūlad • wa lam ya kun lahu kufuwan aḥad • (7 times)

In the name of Allah,
the Universally Merciful, the Singularly Compassionate.
Say, "He is Allah, the One; Allah, the eternal.
He begot none and He was not begotten.
None is comparable to Him."[44]

-٥-

سورة الكافرون

surat al-kafirun – **DISBELIEVERS** CHAPTER

بِسْمِ اللّٰهِ الرَّحْمٰنِ الرَّحِيْمِ ۝
قُلْ يٰٓاَيُّهَا الْكٰفِرُوْنَ ۝١ لَآ اَعْبُدُ مَا تَعْبُدُوْنَ ۝٢
وَلَآ اَنْتُمْ عٰبِدُوْنَ مَآ اَعْبُدُ ۝٣ وَلَآ اَنَا عَابِدٌ مَّا عَبَدْتُّمْ ۝٤
وَلَآ اَنْتُمْ عٰبِدُوْنَ مَآ اَعْبُدُ ۝٥ لَكُمْ دِيْنُكُمْ وَلِيَ دِيْنِ ۝٦

(٧ مرات)

bismi Llāhi r-raḥmani r-raḥīm •
qul yā ayyuha l-kāfirūn(a) • lā aʿbudu mā taʿbudūn(a) • wa lā antum ʿābidūna mā aʿbud(u) • wa lā anā ʿābidun mā ʿabad tum • wa lā antum ʿābidūna mā aʿbud(u) • lakum dīnukum wa liya dīn(i) • (7 times)

In the name of Allah,
the Universally Merciful, the Singularly Compassionate.
Say, "O disbelievers, I do not worship what you worship and you do not worship what I worship. I will never worship what you worship and you will never worship what I worship. You have your religion and I have mine."[45]

-٦-

اية الكرسي

ayat al-kursi – THE THRONE VERSE

اَللّٰهُ لَآ اِلٰهَ اِلَّا هُوَۚ اَلْحَيُّ الْقَيُّوْمُۚ لَا تَاْخُذُهٗ سِنَةٌ وَّلَا نَوْمٌۗ لَهٗ مَا فِى
السَّمٰوٰتِ وَمَا فِى الْاَرْضِۗ مَنْ ذَا الَّذِيْ يَشْفَعُ عِنْدَهٗٓ اِلَّا بِاِذْنِهٖۗ
يَعْلَمُ مَا بَيْنَ اَيْدِيْهِمْ وَمَا خَلْفَهُمْۚ وَلَا يُحِيْطُوْنَ بِشَيْءٍ مِّنْ عِلْمِهٖٓ اِلَّا
بِمَا شَآءَۚ وَسِعَ كُرْسِيُّهُ السَّمٰوٰتِ وَالْاَرْضَۚ وَلَا يَـُٔوْدُهٗ
حِفْظُهُمَاۚ وَهُوَ الْعَلِيُّ الْعَظِيْمُ ﴿٢٥٥﴾ (٧ مرات)

Allāhu lā ilāha illā Huwa[1] al-ḥayyu l-qayyūm[2] lā ta'khudhuhu sinatun wa lā nawmun[3] lahū mā fi s-samāwāti wa mā fi l-arḍi[4] man dha l-ladhī yashfa'u *** 'indahu illā bi idhnihi[5] ya'lamu mā baina aidīhim wa mā khalfahum[6] wa lā yuḥīṭū-na bi shai'in min 'ilmihi illā bimā shā'a[7] wasi'a kursiyyuhu s-samāwāti wa l-arḍa[8] wa lā ya'ūduhu hifẓuhumā[9] wa huwa l-'aliyyu l-aẓīm[10] • (7 times)

Allah: there is no god but Him, the Ever-Living, the Ever-Watchful. Neither slumber nor sleep overtakes him. All that is in the heavens and in the earth belongs to Him. Who is there that can intercede with Him except by His leave. He knows what is before them and what is behind them, but they do not comprehend any of His knowledge except what He wills. His throne extends over the heavens and the earth; it does not weary Him to preserve them both. He is the Most-High, the Tremendous.[46]

-٧-

تسبيح وتحميد وتهليل وتكبير وحوقلة

tasbih, tahmid, tahlil, takbir & hawqala – DIVINE INVOCATIONS

سُبْحَانَ اللهِ ۞ وَالْحَمْدُ لِلّٰهِ ۞ وَلَا اِلٰهَ اِلَّا اللهُ ۞ وَاللهُ اَكْبَرُ ۞
وَلَا حَوْلَ وَلَا قُوَّةَ اِلَّا بِاللهِ الْعَلِيِّ الْعَظِيمِ ۞
(٧ مرات)

subḥāna Llāh(i) • wa l-ḥamdu li Llāh(i) • wa lā ilāha illa Llāh(u) • wa Llāhu akbar(u) • wa lā ḥawla wa lā quwwata illā bi Llāhi l-ʿaliyyi l-ʿaẓīm • (7 times)

Glory be to Allah; praise is for Allah; there is no God but Allah; Allah is Great. There is no might or power except by & with Allah, the Most-High, the Incomparably Great.[47]

There is no might or power except by & with Allah, the Most-High, the Incomparably Great.”

-٨-

صلاة على النبي ﷺ

salat 'ala n-nabi ﷺ – **EXALTATION** UPON THE **PROPHET** ﷺ

اَللّٰهُمَّ صَلِّ عَلٰى سَيِّدِنَا مُحَمَّدٍ عَبْدِكَ وَرَسُوْلِكَ
النَّبِيِّ الْأُمِّيِّ ۞ وَعَلٰى اٰلِهِ وَصَحْبِهِ وَسَلِّمْ ۞ (٧ مرات)

Allāhumma ṣalli 'alā sayyidinā Muḥammadin 'abdika wa rasūlika n-nabiyyi l-ummiyy(i) • wa 'alā ālihi wa ṣaḥbihi wa sallim • (7 times)

O Allah, whelm in salawat and salam our liege Muhammad ﷺ—Your most perfect slave & Your most beloved envoy, the prophet sent to a people without a scripture & not taught by any human—and upon his family and companions.[48]

-٩-

استغفار

istighfar – SEEKING **FORGIVENESS**

أَسْتَغْفِرُ اللّٰهَ الْعَظِيْمَ لِيْ وَلِوَالِدَيَّ ❀

وَلِلْمُؤْمِنِيْنَ وَالْمُؤْمِنَاتِ ❀ وَالْمُسْلِمِيْنَ وَالْمُسْلِمَاتِ ❀

اَلْأَحْيَاءِ مِنْهُمْ وَالْأَمْوَاتِ ❀

إِنَّكَ سَمِيْعٌ قَرِيْبٌ مُجِيْبُ الدَّعَوَاتِ ❀ (٧ مرات)

astaghfiru Llāha l-ʿaẓīma lī wa li wālidayya • wa li l-muʾminīna wa l-muʾmināt • wa l-muslimīna wa l-muslimāt • al-aḥyāʾi minhum wa l-amwāt • innaka samīʿun qarībun mujību d-daʿawāt • (7 times)

O Allah, forgive me and my parents, all believing men and women, and all Muslim men and women—those who are alive and those who have passed away. Truly You are the Hearer, the Near One, the Acceptor of supplications.[49]

-١٠-

دعاء

dua' – **EARNEST ENTREATY**

اَللّٰهُمَّ رَبِّ افْعَلْ بِيْ وَبِهِمْ عَاجِلًا وَاٰجِلًا فِى الدِّيْنِ
وَالدُّنْيَا وَالْاٰخِرَةِ مَا اَنْتَ لَهُ اَهْلٌ ۞ وَلَا تَفْعَلْ
بِنَا يَا مَوْلَانَا مَا نَحْنُ لَهُ اَهْلٌ ۞ اِنَّكَ غَفُوْرٌ حَلِيْمٌ
جَوَادٌ كَرِيْمٌ بَرٌّ رَّءُوْفٌ رَّحِيْمٌ ۞ (٧ مرات)

Allāhumma f'al bī wa bi him 'ājilan wa ājilan fi d-dīni wa d-dunyā wa l-ākhirati mā anta lahu ahl(un) • wa lā taf'al binā yā mawlānā mā naḥnu lahu ahl(un) • innaka ghafūrun ḥalīmun jawādun karīmun barrun ra'ūfun raḥīm(un) • (7 times)

O Allah, Lord, give me and them—now and in the future; in religion, in this world and in the Hereafter—that which befits You. Do not give us, O our Patron, that which befits us [wretched ones]. Verily, You are All-Forgiving, All-Forbearing, All-Generous, All-Bountiful, the Doer of All-Good, All-Kind and All-Merciful.[50]

انتهى المسبعات العشر

BENEFIT

[fa'ida]

هذا مثال خاتم النبوة الذى كان بين كتفيه صلى الله عليه وسلم
ومكتوب من الشعر بقلم القدرة

ومن خواصه ما نقله الترمذى أن من توضأ ونظر اليه وقت الصبح حفظه الله تعالى الى وقت المغرب. ومن نظر اليه وقت المغرب حفظه الله تعالى إلى وقت الصبح. ومن نظر اليه أول الشهر يحفظه الله إلى آخره. ومن نظر إليه فى أول السنة يحفظه الله إلى إلى آخرها من البلاء والآفات. ومن نظر اليه فى أول السفر يصير ذلك مباركاً عليه. وإن مات فى تلك السنة يختم له بالايمان.
وقال وأتم هذا وأرجو الله تعالى أن من نظر اليه بصدق المحبة والايمان فى عمره مرة واحدة يحفظه الله تعالى من جميع ما يكرهه الى أن يلقى الله تعالى. وصلى اللهم على سيدنا محمد كلما ذكرك الذاكرون وغفل عن ذكره الغافلون ورضى الله عن أصحاب رسول الله أجمعين والتابعين لهم بإحسان الى يوم الدين.
والحمد لله رب العالمين

SEAL OF PROPHETHOOD

"Between his blessed shoulders was the Seal of Prophethood, and he is the Seal of the Prophets."—Imam 'Ali b. Abi Talib

THIS IS AN ILLUSTRATION OF THE *KHATAM AN-NUBUWWA* or "Seal of Prophethood" that is between the Prophet's shoulders. It is made with hair by the Pen of Divinity. [Based on *ahadith* or "Prophetic narrations", scholars say that it is a piece of flesh on the Messenger of Allah's ﷺ blessed back. Scholars differ in opinion concerning its shape and what is written on it.] As for its merits and benefits, *Imam* at-Tirmidhi states:

> *Whosoever performs ablution [wudu'] and looks at it at the time of subh (i.e. morning), Allah Most High will protect him till the time of maghrib (i.e. evening); whosoever looks at it at the time of maghrib, Allah Most High will protect him till the time of subh.*
>
> *Whosoever looks at it at the beginning of the month, Allah Most High will protect him till the end of the month. Whosoever looks at it at the beginning of the year, Allah Most High will protect him till the end of the year from afflictions and calamities.*
>
> *Whosoever looks at it at the beginning of a journey, Allah Most High will make the travel blessed. If he were to die in that year, his life will be sealed with faith [iman].*

> *I hope to Allah Most High that whosoever looks at it with sincere love and true faith once in his lifetime, Allah Most High protects him from all that he dislikes until he meets Allah Most High.*

O Allah, bless our liege Muhammad ﷺ whenever You are remembered and whenever he is forgotten. Allah be pleased with the Messenger of Allah's companions and their successors in excellence till the Day of Judgment. Praise be to Allah, Lord of the cosmos.

POSTFACE

As we complete this work, I remind myself and all readers of two extraordinary *hadith qudsi* that give tremendous hope to broken hearts and stir yearning souls into an enrapturing whirlwind:

(١) عَنْ اَبِيْ هُرَيْرَةَ ﵁ قَالَ : قَالَ النَّبِيُّ ﷺ : يَقُولُ اللّٰهُ تَعَالٰى:
اَنَا عِنْدَ ظَنِّ عَبْدِيْ بِيْ ❁ وَاَنَا مَعَهُ اِذَا ذَكَرَنِيْ ❁ فَاِنْ ذَكَرَنِيْ فِيْ نَفْسِهِ ❁
ذَكَرْتُهُ فِيْ نَفْسِيْ ❁ وَاِنْ ذَكَرَنِيْ فِيْ مَلَاٍ ❁ ذَكَرْتُهُ فِيْ مَلَاٍ خَيْرٍ مِنْهُمْ ❁
وَاِنْ تَقَرَّبَ اِلَيَّ بِشِبْرٍ ❁ تَقَرَّبْتُ اِلَيْهِ ذِرَاعًا ❁ وَاِنْ تَقَرَّبَ اِلَيَّ ذِرَاعًا ❁
تَقَرَّبْتُ اِلَيْهِ بَاعًا ❁ وَاِنْ اَتَانِيْ يَمْشِيْ ❁ اَتَيْتُهُ هَرْوَلَةً ❁
رواه البخاري (وكذلك مسلم والترمذي وابن ماجه)

On the authority of Abu Huraira ﵁
who said: The Prophet ﷺ said: Allah the Almighty said:

I am as My servant thinks I am[7]*. I am with him when he makes mention of Me. If he makes mention of Me to himself, I make mention of him to Myself; if he makes mention of Me in an assembly, I make mention of him in an assembly better than it. If he draws near to Me an arm's length, I draw near to him a cubit; if he draws near to Me a cubit, I draw near to him a fathom; and if he comes to Me walking, I go to him at speed.*

Related by Buhkari (7405) and likewise by Muslim (2675), Tirmidhi and Ibn Maja

---

7 Another possible rendering of the Arabic is: *I am as My servant expects Me to be*. The meaning is that forgiveness and acceptance of repentance by the Almighty is subject to His servant truly believing that He is forgiving and merciful. However, not to accompany such belief with right action would be to mock the Almighty.

At the core of our every act of worship—*salat, zakat, sawm, hajj, dhikr, fikr, du'a, munajat, tasbih, tahmid, takbir, tahlil, hawqala, hasbala, salat 'ala n-Nabi* ﷺ—there must be a burning desire to gain proximity to Allah ﷻ. The invocations here are a means to attaining just that.

(٢) عَنْ اَبِيْ هُرَيْرَةَ رَضِيَ اللّٰهُ عَنْهُ قَالَ : قَالَ رَسُوْلُ اللهِ ﷺ:
اِنَّ اللّٰهَ قَالَ مَنْ عَادٰى لِيْ وَلِيًّا فَقَدْ اٰذَنْتُهُ بِالْحَرْبِ ❀ وَمَا تَقَرَّبَ اِلَيَّ عَبْدِيْ بِشَيْءٍ اَحَبَّ اِلَيَّ مِمَّا افْتَرَضْتُ عَلَيْهِ ❀ وَمَا يَزَالُ عَبْدِيْ يَتَقَرَّبُ اِلَيَّ بِالنَّوَافِلِ حَتّٰى اُحِبَّهُ ❀ فَاِذَا اَحْبَبْتُهُ كُنْتُ سَمْعَهُ الَّذِيْ يَسْمَعُ بِهِ ❀ وَبَصَرَهُ الَّذِيْ يُبْصِرُ بِهِ ❀ وَيَدَهُ الَّتِيْ يَبْطُشُ بِهَا وَرِجْلَهُ الَّتِيْ يَمْشِيْ بِهَا ❀ وَاِنْ سَاَلَنِيْ لَاُعْطِيَنَّهُ ❀ وَلَئِنِ اسْتَعَاذَنِيْ لَاُعِيْذَنَّهُ ❀ وَمَا تَرَدَّدْتُ عَنْ شَيْءٍ اَنَا فَاعِلُهُ تَرَدُّدِيْ عَنْ نَفْسِ الْمُؤْمِنِ ❀ يَكْرَهُ الْمَوْتَ وَاَنَا اَكْرَهُ مَسَاءَتَهُ ❀
رواه البخاري (وكذلك أحمد)

On the authority of Abu Huraira ﷺ who said:
The Prophet ﷺ said:

Allah said, "I will declare war against him who shows hostility to a pious worshipper of Mine. The most beloved things with which My slave comes nearer to Me, is what I have enjoined upon him. My slave keeps on coming closer to Me through performing Nawafil [supererogatory deeds besides what is obligatory] till I love him, so I become his sense of hearing with which he hears, and his sense of sight with which he sees, and his hand with which he grips, and his leg with which he walks; and if he asks Me, I will give him, and if he asks My protection [Refuge], I will protect him; [i.e. give him My Refuge] and I do not hesitate to do anything as I hesitate to take the soul of the believer, for he hates death, and I hate to disappoint him."

Related by Buhkari (6502) and likewise by Ahmad (6.256)

Allah Most High reinforces here the importance of obligatory acts of worship and emphatically states the benefit of supererogatory acts of worship. This is enough of an encouragement and incentive to embrace the invocations here as part of one's daily liturgical schedule.

★ ★ ★

THE BELOVED LOVING SEEKERS LONGING FOR THE DIVINE COUNTEnance will also do well to remember these two unequivocal Prophetic statements on the reality of *dhikr Allah* or "the remembrance of Allah":

قَالَ سَمِعْتُ اَبَا هُرَيْرَةَ رَضِيَ اللهُ عَنْهُ: يَقُوْلُ سَمِعْتُ رَسُوْلَ اللهِ ﷺ:
اَلَا اِنَّ الدُّنْيَا مَلْعُوْنَةٌ مَلْعُوْنٌ مَا فِيْهَا اِلَّا ذِكْرَ اللهِ وَمَا وَالَاهُ وَعَالِمًا اَوْ مُتَعَلِّمًا A
رواه الترمذي: (٦٣) كتاب الزهد عن رسول الله ﷺ: ٩١ (وكذلك ابن ماجه)

Abu Huraira ﵁ said: The Messenger of Allah ﷺ said:

Verily the world is cursed—cursed is everything in it—except the remembrance of Allah, and what follows from it, and someone who knows [& teaches], and someone who learns.—Related by Tirmidhi: 2322 (and likewise by Ibn Maja)

قَالَ معاذ بن جبل رَضِيَ اللهُ عَنْهُ: قَالَ رَسُوْلَ اللهِ ﷺ:
ألا أخبركم بخير أعمالكم وأزكاها عند مليككم وأرفعها في درجاتكم وخير لكم من تعاطي الذهب والفضة ومن أن تلقوا عدوكم غدا فتضربوا أعناقهم ويضربوا أعناقكم A قالوا بلى يا رسول الله ۞ قال ذكر الله عَزَّ وَجَلَّ ۞
مسند أحمد بن حنبل: مسند الأنصار: ٢١٠٦٥

Mu'adh b. Jabal ﵁ said: The Messenger of Allah ﷺ said:

"Shall I not inform you about the best of your actions, the purest of them with your Master, the loftiest of them in ranks, better for you than spending gold and silver, and [better than] meeting your enemies in the future as you smite their necks and they yours?" They said, "Certainly, O Messenger of Allah." He said, "The remembrance of Allah, Mighty & Majestic."—Related by Ahmad: 21065

★ ★ ★

WE BEGAN THIS WORK WITH VERSES 41-44 OF *SURAT AL-AHZAB.* We shall end with the subsequent comforting verses between 45-48*:*

﴿ يَا أَيُّهَا النَّبِيُّ إِنَّا أَرْسَلْنَاكَ شَاهِدًا وَمُبَشِّرًا وَنَذِيرًا ۝ وَدَاعِيًا إِلَى اللَّهِ بِإِذْنِهِ
وَسِرَاجًا مُنِيرًا ۝ وَبَشِّرِ الْمُؤْمِنِينَ بِأَنَّ لَهُمْ مِنَ اللَّهِ فَضْلًا كَبِيرًا ۝ وَلَا تُطِعِ
الْكَافِرِينَ وَالْمُنَافِقِينَ وَدَعْ أَذَاهُمْ وَتَوَكَّلْ عَلَى اللَّهِ ۚ وَكَفَىٰ بِاللَّهِ وَكِيلًا ﴾

ALLAH MOST HIGH SAYS IN **AL-AHZAB,** 33:45-48

O [beloved] Prophet, We have sent you as a witness, as a bearer of glad tidings, as a warner, as one who calls people to Allah by His leave, as a light-giving lamp. So announce to the believers the glad tidings that a great bounty awaits them from Allah. And incline not to the disbelievers and the hypocrites. Disregard their noxious talk, and place your trust in Allah. Allah is sufficient as Trustee.

O Allah, make us amongst Your pious friends, among Your prosperous company, and among Your upright servants. Use us in accordance with Your good pleasure with us. Give us success in achieving the things which You love to see from us. Govern us in accordance with Your good choice for us.

اَللّٰهُمَّ اجْعَلْنَا مِنْ اَوْلِيَائِكَ الْمُتَّقِيْنَ وَحِزْبِكَ الْمُفْلِحِيْنَ وَعِبَادِكَ الصَّالِحِيْنَ ۞ وَاسْتَعْمِلْنَا
لِمَرْضَاتِكَ عَنَّا ۞ وَوَفِّقْنَا لِمُحَابِّكَ مِنَّا ۞ وَصَرِّفْنَا بِحُسْنِ اخْتِيَارِكَ لَنَا ۞ وَصَلَّى اللّٰهُ
عَلٰى سَيِّدِنَا مُحَمَّدٍ وَاٰلِهِ وَصَحْبِهِ وَسَلَّمْ ۞ سُبْحَانَ رَبِّكَ رَبِّ الْعِزَّةِ عَمَّا يَصِفُوْنَ ۞ وَسَلَامٌ عَلَى
الْمُرْسَلِيْنَ ۞ وَالْحَمْدُ لِلّٰهِ رَبِّ الْعٰلَمِيْنَ ۞ وَالسَّلَامُ عَلَيْكُمْ وَرَحْمَةُ اللّٰهِ وَبَرَكَاتُهُ وَمَغْفِرَتُهُ
وَرِضْوَانُهُ وَجَنَّتُهُ ۞

THAIKA SHU'AIB
10 *Muharram* 1442
Kanhangad, INDIA

PUBLISHERS' AFTERWORD

IT IS WITH MIXED FEELINGS THAT THIS IS WRITTEN. ON THE ONE hand, we are deeply honoured and extremely privileged that *Shaikh* Dr Thaika Shuaib ﵀ tasked members of our team with the publication of this work. On the other, we are pained that we could only bring this to the public domain after his entering the isthmus. We take solace in his regular utterance, *"Things happen at their appointed time."*

The noble Shaikh regularly quoted a *hadith* which delights the people of remembrance *[ahl adh-dhikr]*: *"Intensify in the remembrance of Allah until they say you are crazy." [akthiru dhikru Llahi hatta yaqulu majnun]*. He used to lamentingly comment that modern men and women do not engage in enough *dhikr Allah* to keep sane, let alone to be labelled crazy!

We hope and pray that the Shaikh's lament is partly addressed by this work. We beseech Allah ﷻ to accept this from us and to make it a lasting legacy for the noble Shaikh. May Allah ﷻ continue benefiting us by him in both abodes and raise us all together—under the banner of the Holy Prophet ﷺ—on the day when all will scramble to him ﷺ for Him ﷻ.

MUHAMMAD IDRIS *JALALI*

ON BEHALF OF THE PUBLISHERS

Ramadan 13th, 1443 / April 14th, 2022

BIOGRAPHICAL NOTES

BIOGRAPHICAL NOTES OF THE PROPHETS, COMPANIONS AND Saints whose invocations adorn this work are presented below. Most are brief while some are lengthy. As this edition is released as an e-book, we have left the longer ones as they are without redaction.

'ABD ALLAH B. 'ABBAS B. 'ABD AL-MUTTALIB, ABU L-'ABBAS AL-HASHIMI ﷺ (INVOCATION 6)

Ibn 'Abbas was a beloved paternal cousin of the Prophet ﷺ for whom the Prophet ﷺ performed *tahnik*. He was born in Mecca three years before the *hijra* in excruciating circumstances for the Muslims. He grew up in the blessed company of the Prophet ﷺ. He would, amongst other tasks, bring the Prophet ﷺ water for ablution and stand up with him for prayer even as a child. He was only 13 years old when the Prophet ﷺ left this world for the isthmus. Once, the Prophet ﷺ entered a lavatory and found water for his ablution. He asked, *Who placed it?* He was informed accordingly and so made the prayer, *O Allah, make him (Ibn 'Abbas) a learned scholar in religion.* True to the prayer, he became one of the greatest *mufassir* (exegete) of the Qur'an.

Sayyiduna 'Umar ﷺ would keep him close in his council and resort to his abundant knowledge and formidable intellect.

Likewise, other senior companions would engage him for his opinions although he was a young man. He said: *The Messenger of Allah embraced me and said: "O Allah, teach him wisdom and the interpretation of the Book."* A narration attributed to him states: *...I went to him (another companion) during the time of the afternoon siesta and spread my cloak in front of his door. The wind blew dust on me (as I sat waiting for him). If I wished I could have sought his permission to enter and he would certainly have given me permission. But I preferred to wait on him so that he could be completely refreshed. Coming out of his house and seeing me in that condition he said, "O cousin of the Prophet, what's the matter with you? If you had sent for me I would have come to you." I said: "I am the one who should come to you, for knowledge is sought, it does not just come." Then I asked him about the hadith and learnt from him.*

His house was the equivalent of a university with specialized teaching. He taught every day and held classes on a variety of subjects including *tafsir, fiqh, halal & haram,* poetry, Arab history, inheritance laws, Arabic language and etymology. He entered the isthmus in Ta'if in the year 71 AH.

'ABD ALLAH B. 'AMR B. AL-'AS, AS-SUHAMI AL-QURASHI (INVOCATION 15)

A noble *sahabi* who embraced Islam before his father. He is regarded as one of the scholars and devout worshippers. He possessed the ability to write and so sought (and received) the permission of the Prophet ﷺ to write down whatever he heard from the Prophet ﷺ. He is known for fighting in battles with two swords. He carried his father's banner on the day of Yarmuk and witnessed Siffin with Mu'awiyya who also placed him in charge of Kufa for a short period of time. He entered the isthmus in the year 65 AH. He has narrated 700 *ahadith.*

'ABD ALLAH B. GHANNAM B. AWS B. MALIK AL-ANSARI AL-BAYADI - ﵁ (INVOCATION 13)

A noble *sahabi* counted amongst the people of the Hejaz.

'ABD ALLAH B. MAS'UD B. GHAFIL, ABU 'ABD AR-RAHMAN AL-HUDHALI ﵁ **(INVOCATION 20 AND 22)**

Ibn Mas'ud was one of the earliest converts—the sixth—to Islam and was the first person to publicly recite the Qur'an in Mecca. His mother was Umm 'Abd who was also from the tribe of Hudhail. He was a short and thin man with dark skin and of humble origin. The Prophet ﷺ once commanded him to climb a tree. When the other companions looked at his legs, they laughed at his lean stature. The Prophet ﷺ said, *Why are you laughing? 'Abd Allah's foot is heavier in the balance than the mountain of 'Uhud.*

When the companions were concerned that people of Quraish have not heard the Qur'an being recited to them loudly, he declared that he will do it. The companions warned him that the Quraish will beat him up because he was thin and short and had no one to protect him. He said, *Allah will protect me!* He then recited a portion from *Surat ar-Rahman* loudly in front of the Quraish; they beat him up. He responded, *The sweetness of faith that I experienced, I would not mind returning tomorrow and doing it again!* Thus, after the Prophet ﷺ, he became the first person to recite the Qur'an publicly in Mecca.

He migrated to Abyssinia and then to Medina. He was with

the Prophet ﷺ at Badr, at the *bai'at ar-ridwan* and at every subsequent battle. He was also at Yarmuk. As a *khadim*, he was on close terms with the Prophet ﷺ who loved him, honoured him and trusted him with his ﷺ secrets. He walked with the Prophet ﷺ, carried his blessed *siwak*, his ennobled sandals and water for his washing.

He was a *hafiz* of the Qur'an and an eminent scholar who was an authority on *qira'at, tafsir, shari'a* and *hadith*. 848 *ahadith* are recorded from him. The Prophet ﷺ once addressed him by saying: *"You are a schooled boy." Sayyiduna* 'Umar ؓ looked at him one day and said: *"A vessel filled with knowledge."*

The Prophet ﷺ enjoyed listening to his recitation of the Qur'an. He said, *The Prophet ﷺ said to me: "Recite for me." I said: "O Messenger of Allah, shall I recite for you while it is to you whom it was revealed?" He ﷺ said: "I love to hear it from other than me." So I recited Surat an-Nisa until I reached: "...and We bring you (Muhammad) as a witness against these people* (4:41)*" and I saw the eyes of the Prophet ﷺ overflowing with tears."*

After the passing of the Prophet ﷺ he was put in charge of the treasury of Kufa. He moved back to Medina during the caliphate of *Sayyiduna* 'Uthman ؓ. He entered the isthmus in Medina sometime between 30 and 33 AH (652/3 or 653/4) at the age of sixty.

'ABD ALLAH B. 'UMAR B. AL-KHATTAB, ABU 'ABD AR-RAHMAN ؓ (INVOCATION 28)

A noble *sahabi* who was born after the mission of the Prophet ﷺ had begun. He embraced Islam while still a child and migrated with his parents. He presented himself to the Prophet

ﷺ on the day of Badr. As he was only 13 years, the Prophet ﷺ deemed him too young and sent him back. The same thing happened a year later on the day of ‘Uhud. The following year—when he was 15—the Prophet ﷺ permitted him to partake at Khandaq (the Battle of the Trench). After that, he participated in all the battles of the Prophet ﷺ.

He is from amongst the young companions who benefitted tremendously from the companionship of the Prophet ﷺ. He possessed vast knowledge, was a *hafiz* of the Qur’an and related 1,630 *ahadith*. He adhered to the Prophetic *Sunna* strictly and is considered the most stringent of the companions in imitating the Prophet ﷺ. It has been reported that the Prophet ﷺ said about him: *“‘Abd Allah is a righteous man.”* He entered the isthmus in Mecca in the year 73 AH (652/3 or 653/4) at the age of eighty-four.

‘ABD AL-QADIR AL-JILANI (INVOCATIONS 36, 37 AND 38)

(Imam) Abu Muhammad *Muhyi d-Din* ‘Abd al-Qadir b. Abu Salih Musa b. Abu ‘Abd Allah b. Yahya az-Zahid b. Muhammad b. Dawud b. Musa b. ‘Abd Allah b. Musa al-Jawn b. ‘Abd Allah al-Mahd b. al-Hasan al-Muthanna b. Abu Muhammad al-Hasan b. ‘Ali b. Abi Talib ؓ is the eponym of *at-Tariqa al-Qadiriyya*. He was born in the town Nip/Nif/Na’if in Jilan[8] in 470 AH to pious parents who descended from the Messenger of Allah ﷺ: his father from al-Hasan ؓ and his mother from al-Husain ؓ.

He received his early religious education at home before mi-

8 Recent studies have also suggested that he was in fact born in a village called “al-Jil” near the city of Mada’in, 40 km south of Baghdad.

grating to Baghdad at the age of eighteen to continue his learning and embark on what turned out to be a unique and amazing spiritual journey. Baghdad was then the capital of the Abbasid caliphate and, more importantly, it was a centre of knowledge and education that was vibrant with spiritual and intellectual activities. But this was also a period of political upheaval, with the crusaders in action in Palestine, Syria, and Antakya in Turkey, and Baghdad at the mercy of the neighbouring Turkish and Seljuq Sultans.

In Baghdad, he first accompanied the Sufi Sheikh Hammad ad-Dabbas (d. 525/1131), and later *Sheikh* Abu Sa'id al-Mukharrami (al-Makhzumi). It has also been reported that he was a student of *Imam* Abu Hamid al-Ghazali (d. 505/1111), and that his book *al-Ghunya* reflects influences from al-Ghazali's *ihya' 'ulum ad-din*.

When Sheikh Abu Sa'id saw how his student was developing, he asked him in 521/1127 to teach in his school. He used to lecture three days a week. His audience grew quickly until a lecture would attract tens of thousands. Many students used to write down his lectures, preserving his words. Nobilities and rulers attended his lectures, while he did not spare them any criticism he had of how they governed.

He continued to preach in his school until his death in 561/1165. The fame that this school developed as a result of the respect and following that he had, and it being his burial place, guaranteed its status as one of the most revered and visited Islamic sites in the world.

He went for pilgrimage to Mecca twice, the first in 505/1112, when he was still little known. In this trip he met Sheikh Udayy

b. Musafir (d. 557/1162). In his second in 555/1160 he met the famous Moroccan Sheikh Abu Madyan al-Ghawth (d. 594/1197). By then, he had become one of the most, if not the most, famous Sufi Sheikh, with countless followers everywhere.

There is no personality in the history of Sufism who has been linked to as many miracles as him. His influence on Muslims and his role in the spread of Islam are impossible to exaggerate. There are far more Sufi *Tariqas* whose chains of masters trace themselves back to him than any other Sheikh. Accordingly, the followers of *Tariqa Qadiriyya* far outnumber the followers of any other Sufi path. Sufis in general and Qadiris in particular played a major role in spreading Islam in Asia and Africa. He left a large corpus of sermons and writings, some of which he authored while others were compiled by his students.

'AISHA AS-SIDDIQA, UMM 'ABD ALLAH (INVOCATION 29)

Beloved wife of the Prophet ﷺ and daughter of *Sayyiduna* Abu Bakr as-Siddiq ؓ, she is honoured as *umm al-mu'minin* (mother of the believers). The Prophet ﷺ cemented his relationship with his bosom friend *Sayyiduna* Abu Bakr as-Siddiq ؓ by marrying her. She was christened with the agnomen *Umm 'Abd Allah* by the Prophet ﷺ due to her nephew 'Abd Allah b. Zubair ؓ, who was the son of her sister 'Asma.

After *Sayyidatuna* Khadija al-Kubra ؓ and *Sayyidatuna* Fatima az-Zahra' ؓ, she is regarded as the best woman in Islam. Due to the strength of her personality, she was a leader in every field: knowledge, society, politics and war. She often regretted her involvement in war but lived long enough to regain her position as the most respected woman of her time.

She is proof that a woman can be far more learned than men and that she can be the teacher of scholars and experts. Her life is also proof that a woman can exert influence over men and women and provide them with inspiration and leadership. Her life is also proof that the same woman can be totally feminine and be a source of pleasure, joy and comfort to her husband. She did not graduate from any institutions. Yet, her utterances are studied in faculties of universities and her legal pronouncements are researched by students and teachers all over the world.

The bulk of her vast treasure of knowledge was obtained while she was still young. In her early childhood she was brought up by her father who was greatly liked and respected, for he was a man of wide knowledge, gentle manners, and an agreeable presence. Moreover, he was the closest friend of the Prophet ﷺ who was a frequent visitor to their home since the very early days of his mission. In her youth, already known for her striking beauty and her formidable memory, she came under the loving care and attention of the Prophet ﷺ himself. As his wife and close companion, she acquired from him knowledge and insight such as no woman has ever acquired. She became the wife of the Prophet ﷺ in Mecca and had the wedding in Medina after the *hijra*. Before and after her wedding, she maintained a natural jollity and innocence and did not seem at all overawed by the thought of being wedded to him who was the Messenger of Allah ﷺ whom all his companions—including her own mother and father—treated with such love and reverence as they gave to no one else.

Her early life in Medina also had its more serious and anxious times. Once her father and two companions who were staying with him fell ill with a dangerous fever that was common in Medina at certain seasons. One morning she went to visit him and was dismayed to find the three men lying completely weak and exhausted. She asked her father how he was and he answered her in verse but she did not understand what he was saying. The two others also answered her with lines of poetry, which seemed to her to be nothing but unintelligible babbling. She was deeply troubled and went home to the Prophet ﷺ saying: *They are raving, out of their minds, through the heat of the fever.*" The Prophet ﷺ asked what they had said and was somewhat reassured when she repeated almost word for word the line they had uttered and which made sense although she did not fully understand them then. This was a demonstration of the great retentive power of her memory which, as the years went by, preserved so many of the priceless sayings of the Prophet ﷺ.

Of the Prophet's wives in Medina, it was clear that she was loved by the Prophet ﷺ most. From time to time, one or the other of his companions would ask: *O Messenger of Allah ﷺ, whom do you love most in the world?* He ﷺ did not always give the same answer to this question for he felt great love for many—for his daughters and their children, for Abu Bakr, for 'Ali, for Zaid and his son Usama. But of his wives, the only one he named in this connection was her. She too loved him greatly in return and often would seek reassurance from him that he loved her. Once she asked the Prophet ﷺ: *How is your love for me?* He ﷺ replied: *Like the rope's knot.* (meaning it was strong and secure). And time after time thereafter, she would ask the Prophet ﷺ:

How is the knot?" and he ﷺ would reply: *In the same condition.*

As she loved the Prophet ﷺ so was her love a jealous love and she could not bear the thought that the Prophet's attentions should be given to others more than seemed enough for her. Of her jealousy, she would say in her later years: *I was not jealous of any other wife of the Prophet ﷺ as I was jealous of Khadija, because of his constant mentioning of her and because Allah Most High had commanded him to give her glad tidings of a mansion in Paradise of precious stones. And whenever he sacrificed a sheep he would send a fair portion of it to those who had been her intimate friends. Many a time I said to him: "It is as if there had never been any other woman in the world except Khadija."*

Despite her feelings of jealousy which nonetheless were not of a destructive kind, she was really a generous and patient soul. She bore with the rest of the Prophet's household poverty and hunger, which often lasted for long periods. For days on end no fire would be lit in the sparsely furnished house of the Prophet ﷺ for cooking or baking bread and they would live merely on dates and water. Poverty did not cause her distress or humiliation; self-sufficiency when it did come did not corrupt her.

Once the Prophet ﷺ stayed away from his wives for a month because they had distressed him by asking of him that which he did not have. This was after the Khaibar expedition when an increase of riches whetted the appetite for presents. Returning from his self-imposed retreat, he went first to her apartment. She was delighted to see him but he said that he had received Revelation, which required him to put two options before her. He then recited the verses: *O Prophet, say to your wives: "If you desire the life of this world and its adornments, then come and I will bestow its goods upon you, and I will release you with a fair release. But if you desire Allah and His Messenger and the abode of the Hereafter, then verily Allah has laid in store for you an immense reward for such as you who do good."* (*Surat al-Ahzab*, 33:28)

Her reply was: *Indeed, I desire Allah and His Messenger and the abode of the Hereafter,* and her response was followed by all the others. She stuck to her choice both during the lifetime of the Prophet ﷺ and afterwards. Later, when the Muslims were favoured with enormous riches, she was given a gift of one hundred thousand dirhams. She was fasting when she received the money and she distributed the entire amount to the poor and the needy even though she had no provisions in her house. Shortly after, a maidservant said to her: *Could you buy meat for a dirham with which to break your fast?* She replied: *If I had remembered, I would have done so.*

The Prophet's affection for her remained to the last. During his final illness, it was to her apartment that he went at the suggestion of his wives. For much of the time he lay there on a couch with his head resting on her breast or on her lap. She it was who took a tooth stick *[miswak]* from her brother, chewed upon it to soften it and gave it to the Prophet ﷺ. Despite his weakness, he rubbed his teeth with it vigorously. Not long afterwards, he lost consciousness and she thought it was the onset of death, but after an hour he opened his eyes. She it is who has preserved for us these last moments of the most honoured of Allah's creation. When the Prophet ﷺ opened his eyes again, she remembered his having said to her: *No Prophet is taken by death until he has been shown his place in Paradise and then offered the choice to live or to die.* She said to herself: *He will not now choose us.* Then she heard the Prophet ﷺ murmur: *With the supreme company in Paradise, with those upon whom Allah has showered His favour—the Prophets, the martyrs and the righteous...* Again she heard the Prophet ﷺ murmur: *O Lord, with the supreme company...* and these were the last words she heard the Prophet ﷺ speak. Gradually his head grew heavier upon her breast, until others in the room began to lament, and she laid his head on a pillow. In the floor of her room where the Prophet ﷺ was, a grave was dug in which was buried the Seal of the Prophets ﷺ amid much bewilderment and great sorrow.

She lived on almost fifty years after the passing away of the Prophet ﷺ. She had been his wife for a decade. Much of the time was spent in learning and acquiring knowledge of the two most important sources of Allah's guidance viz. the Qur'an and the *Sunna* of His Prophet. She was one of three wives (the other two being Hafsa and Umm Salama) who memorised the Revelation. Like Hafsa, she had her own *mushaf* (codex) of the Qur'an written after the Prophet ﷺ had entered the isthmus.

As for the *ahadith* or sayings of the Prophet ﷺ, she is one of four (the others being Abu Huraira, 'Abd Allah b. 'Umar, and Anas b. Malik) who transmitted more than two thousand sayings. Many of these pertain to some of the most intimate aspects of personal behaviour, which only someone in her position could have learnt. What is most important is that her knowledge of *ahadith* was passed on in written form by at least three persons including her nephew 'Urwa who became one of the greatest scholars among the generation after the companions.

Many of the learned companions of the Prophet ﷺ and their followers benefited from her knowledge. Abu Musa al-Ash'ari once said: *If we companions of the Messenger of Allah ﷺ had any difficulty on a matter, we asked 'Aisha about it.* Her nephew 'Urwa asserts that she was proficient not only in *fiqh* but also in medicine *[tibb]* and poetry. Many of the senior companions of the Prophet ﷺ came to her to ask for advice concerning questions of inheritance—a subject which required a highly skilled mathematical mind. Scholars regard her as one of the earliest *fuqaha'* of Islam along with persons like 'Umar b. al-Khattab, 'Ali and 'Abd Allah b. 'Abbas. The Prophet ﷺ referring to her extensive knowledge of Islam is reported to have said: *Learn a portion of your religion [din] from this red-hued [humaira] lady.* "Humaira" meaning "red-hued" was an epithet given to her by the Prophet ﷺ.

She not only possessed great knowledge, but took an active part in education and social reform. As a teacher she had a clear and persuasive manner of speech and her power of oratory has been described in superlative terms by al-Ahnaf, who said: *I have heard speeches of Abu Bakr and 'Umar, 'Uthman and 'Ali and the Khulafa' up to this day, but I have not heard speech more persuasive and more beautiful from the mouth of any person than from the mouth of 'Aisha.* Men and women came from far and wide to benefit from her knowledge. The number of women is said to have been greater than that of men. Besides answering questions, she took boys and girls, some of them orphans, into her custody and trained them under her care and guidance. This was in addition to her relatives who received instruction from her. Her house thus became a school and an academy. Two of her outstanding students were her nephew 'Urwa and 'Umra bint 'Abd ar-Rahman were two distinguished reporters of *ahadith.* The latter is regarded by scholars as one of the trustworthy narrators of *ahadith* and is said to have acted as Lady 'Aisha's secretary, receiving and replying to letters addressed to her.

She entered the isthmus in 57 or 58 AH (676/7 or 677/8) in the month of Ramadan. *Sayyiduna* Abu Huraira, the governor of Medina under Marwan b. al-Hakam, prayed over her. As she had instructed, she was buried in the Baqi' Graveyard.

'ALI B. ABI TALIB B. 'ABD AL-MUTTALIB, ABU TURAB AL-MURTADA ﷺ (INVOCATION 40)

He was born in Mecca in 598 CE, with some sources indicating the he was born in the sacred sanctuary of the Ka'ba. He was the fourth caliph and cousin of the Prophet ﷺ, later becoming the Prophet's ﷺ son-in-law though marriage to the Prophet's ﷺ daughter, Fatima az-Zahra ﷺ. He has the distinction of being the first child to accept Islam. The personal qualities for which he is renowned are innumerable and include being an exemplary warrior, statesman, husband, father and scholar of immense eloquence. He was respected for his courage, knowledge, belief, honesty, piety, nobility, unbending devotion to Islam, deep loyalty to the Holy Prophet ﷺ, consistent treatment of all Muslims and generosity in forgiving his defeated foe. He is seen as an exemplar of *futuwwa* (spiritual chivalry). Almost all *silsila* (initiatic chain) of the *turuq* (Sufi orders) trace their lineage through him. On the 19th of Ramadan 40 AH, he was attacked with a poison-coated dagger while prostrating during the *fajr* prayer. Rather than seek out revenge, he stipulated that if he survived his attacker would be pardoned and if he passed away his attacker should receive only one equal hit. He entered the isthmus a few days after the attack in Iraq in 40 AH /661 CE.

ABU BAKRA, NUFAI' B. MASRUH AL-HABASHI ؓ (INVOCATION 10)
A noble *sahabi*, he belonged to Harith b. Kaldah ath-Thaqafi. His mother, Sumayya, was the slave girl of Harith. Nufay' was commonly attributed to Harith, as per the pagan custom, but he disapproved of this and insisted that he be attributed to his father, Masruh the Abyssinian.

His journey to Islam began down the wall of the fort of Ta'if. The year was 8 AH and the Prophet ﷺ had just conquered Mecca and defeated the Hawazin at Hunain, and then turned his attention to Ta'if, where he besieged the fort of the Thaqif. The siege was strenuous, but the Thaqif persevered.

The Prophet's ﷺ announcer called out, *Whichever slave comes down from the fort to us is free.* Hearing this, a group of them exited among whom was Nufai'. He descended using the aid of a *bakra* (winch), hence he was called Abu Bakra. Moreover, the Prophet ﷺ freed him, in accordance to the announcement, thus he is listed among the freed slaves of the Prophet ﷺ. He would boast over this saying, *I am from your brothers in religion and I am the freed slave of the Prophet ﷺ. If people insist on attributing me, then I am Nufai' b. Masruh."* His previous master requested the Prophet ﷺ to return him, the Prophet ﷺ refused saying that he was the emancipated individual of Allah and His Messenger.

After embracing Islam, he lived in the close company of the Prophet ﷺ. He derived maximum benefit from his piety and knowledge and passed a great amount of knowledge to this *umma*. Although his stay with the Prophet ﷺ was brief, he is reckoned among the eminent and devout companions. He has transmitted over 130 valuable *ahadith*. His sons, 'Abd Allah and

Muslim, as well as famous *tabi'un,* viz. Rib'i b. Harash, al-Hasan al-Basri, and Ahnaf narrate from him.

Imam Bukhari and *Imam* Muslim collectively transmit 8 of his reports. A significant *hadith* found in both their collections is the following: The Messenger of Allah ﷺ said, *Shall I not inform you of one of the gravest of the cardinal sins?* We said, *Yes, O Messenger of Allah!* He ﷺ said, *To join others as partners with Allah in worship and to be undutiful to one's parents.* The Messenger of Allah ﷺ sat up from his reclining position (in order to stress the importance of what he was going to say) and added, *I warn you making a false statement and giving a false testimony. I warn you against making a false statement and giving a false testimony.* The Messenger of Allah ﷺ kept repeating this (warning) till we wished he should stop.

He is responsible for transmitting the legendary *hadith* about *Sayyiduna* al-Hasan ؓ. He begins by relating the affection the Prophet ﷺ showed to his grandson. He would look at the companions and speak to them and then turn and look at *Sayyiduna* al-Hasan ؓ with fondness. Thereafter the Prophet ﷺ said, *This son of mine is a leader. If he lives, he will reconcile between two Muslim groups.* In another narration, he describes how *Sayyiduna* al-Hasan ؓ would jump on the back of the Prophet ﷺ while the latter was performing ritual prayer.

His knowledge proved beneficial. When the *fitna* erupted between the Muslims, he practiced diligently upon those reports that he transmitted regarding bloodshed and kept away from the strife. He never wished to soil his hands with the blood of any Muslim.

He simply kept to himself, just as the Prophet ﷺ commanded, *There will soon be turmoil. Behold! There will be turmoil in which the one who is seated will be better than one who stands and the one who stands will be better than one who runs. Behold! When the affliction appears, the one who has camel should stick to his camel and he who has sheep or goats should stick to his sheep and goats and he who has land should stick to the land.*

He became famous for his knowledge and excellence to the extent that Hasan al-Basri would say that Abu Bakra and 'Imran b. Husain were the two most prominent companions who settled in Basra. He strenuously exerted himself in worship until he entered the isthmus in Basra circa. 51 AH. Abu Barza al-Aslami performed his funeral prayer as per his bequest, as a bond of brotherhood had been contracted between them by the Prophet ﷺ.

ABU AD-DARDA' AL-KHAZRAJI AL-ANSARI ﷺ (INVOCATIONS 4 AND 26)

A noble *sahabi* who was an authority on the Qur'an. He was renowned for his piety, abstinence and strict adherence to the religion. Faith in Allah and His Messenger ﷺ permeated his entire being. He was one of the few who collected the Qur'an as it was being revealed.

From the time he became a Muslim, he devoted himself completely to Islam. He deeply regretted every moment he had spent as a *mushrik* and the opportunities he had lost to do well. He realized how much his friends had learned about Islam in the preceding two or three years, how much of the Qur'an they had memorized and the opportunities they had to devote themselves to Allah and His Messenger ﷺ. He made up his mind to expend every effort to try to make up for what he had missed. *'ibada* occupied his days and nights. His search for knowledge was restless. He memorised the Qur'an and sought to understand the profundity of its message.

When he saw that business and trade disturbed the sweetness of his *'ibada* and kept him away from the mosque, he reduced his involvement without hesitation or regret. Someone asked him why he did this and he replied: *I was a merchant before my pledge to the Messenger of Allah ﷺ. When I became a Muslim, I wanted to combine tijara (trade) and 'ibada (worship), but I did not achieve what I desired. So I abandoned tijara and inclined towards 'ibada.* He added, *By Him in Whose Hand is the soul of Abu ad-Darda', what I want to have is a shop near the door of the mosque so that I do not miss any salat with the congregation. Then I shall sell and buy and make a modest profit every day. I am not saying that Allah—Great and Majestic is He—has prohibited trade, but I want to be among those whom neither trade nor selling distracts from the remembrance of Allah.* He also abandoned his hitherto soft and luxurious lifestyle. He ate only what was sufficient to keep him upright and wore clothes that were simple and sufficient to cover his body.

During his Caliphate, *amir al-mu'minin* 'Umar b. al-Khattab ﷺ wanted to appoint him as a governor in Syria. The latter refused. 'Umar persisted, and so he replied: *If you are content that I should go to them to teach them the Book of their Lord and the Sunna of their Prophet ﷺ and pray with them, I shall go.* 'Umar agreed and he left for Damascus. There he found the people immersed in luxury and soft living. This appalled him. He called the people to the Masjid and rebuked them, moving them to sobs and tears. From then on, he began to frequent the meeting places of the people of Damascus and market places where he taught and answered questions and exhorted anyone who had become heedless. He used every opportunity and every occasion to awaken people and to set them on the right path.

He left the Hejaz and sought seclusion *['uzla]* in Syria after he witnessed a sign of change in morals which the Prophet ﷺ had warned him to look for: Two men appeared before him quarrelling over ownership of a span *[shibr]* of earth. He said, *"I heard the Messenger of Allah ﷺ say, 'When you are in a certain land and hear two men quarrelling over ownership of a span of earth, depart thence.'"* Then he departed for the Levant.

Once, *Sayyiduna* 'Umar visited him at his home during a visit to Damascus. It was night and there was no light in the house. He welcomed 'Umar and sat him down. The two men conversed in darkness. As they did so, 'Umar felt his "pillow" and realized it was an animal's saddle. He touched the place where he lay and knew it was covered with small pebbles. He felt the sheet with which he covered himself and found it so flimsy that there was no way it could possibly protect him from the cold of Damascus. 'Umar asked him: *Shouldn't I make things more comfortable for you? Shouldn't I send something for you?* He replied: *Do you remember a hadith that the Prophet ﷺ told us?* 'Umar asked: *What is it?* He said: *Did he not say, "Let what is sufficient for anyone of you in this world be like the provisions of a rider?"* 'Umar replied: *Yes.* He said: *And what have we done after this, O 'Umar?* Both men were moved to tears, thinking about the vast riches that had come the way of Muslims with the expansion of Islam and their preoccupation with amassing wealth and worldly possessions. With deep sorrow and sadness, both men continued to reflect on this situation until the break of dawn. He entered the isthmus in 32 AH (652).

ABU DHARR AL-GHIFARI, JUNDUB B. JUNADA ﵁ (INVOCATION 31)

A noble *sahabi*, he was one of the earlier converts to Islam. The Prophet ﷺ said of him: *The earth does not carry nor the heavens cover a man more true and faithful than Abu Dharr.*

Before becoming Muslim, he was known for his courage, his calmness, his far-sightedness and also for the repugnance he felt against the idols that his people worshipped. He rejected the religious beliefs of the Arabs and the religious corruption in their midst.

While he was in the Waddan desert, news reached him that a Prophet had appeared in Mecca. He sent his brother to the city to gather information about the new Prophet and his teachings. He hoped that if this Prophet was true, it would change the hearts and minds of people and lead them away from the darkness of superstition.

Not satisfied with the findings of his brother, he set off for Mecca to find out more himself. After receiving the hospitality of *Imam* 'Ali b. Abi Talib for three days, he revealed his purpose for coming to Mecca. *Imam* 'Ali then led him to the Prophet ﷺ. When he saw the Prophet ﷺ, he greeted: *as-salamu 'alaika ya rasula Llah,* and the Prophet ﷺ replied *wa 'alaika salamu Llahi wa rahmatuhu wa barakatuhu.* He was thus the first person to greet Prophet ﷺ in this manner, and it has become a universal greeting since.

The Prophet ﷺ welcomed him, invited him to Islam and recited some of the Qur'an for him. Before long and without any hesitation, he pronounced the *shahada* (testification of faith). Despite the caution of the Prophet ﷺ to conceal his acceptance of Islam, he announced his conversion to the Quraish; they beat him mercilessly, until the uncle of the Prophet ﷺ, 'Abbas b. 'Abd al-Muttalib, came to his rescue.

At the behest of the Prophet ﷺ, he returned back to his tribe and invited them to Islam. First, his brother became Muslim. Then, their mother converted. From there, this family of believers went out tirelessly inviting the Ghifar to Allah and did not flinch from their purpose. Eventually, a large number became Muslims and the congregational prayer was instituted among them.

He remained in his desert abode until after the Prophet ﷺ had gone to Medina and the battles of Badr, 'Uhud and Khandaq had been fought. When he was finally in Medina, he requested to be in the personal service of the Prophet ﷺ. The Prophet ﷺ agreed and was pleased with his companionship. The Prophet ﷺ sometimes showed preference to him above others and whenever he met with him, he would pat him and smile and show his happiness.

After the passing of the Prophet ﷺ, he could not bear to stay in Medina because of grief and the knowledge that there was to be no more of his guiding company. He left for the Syrian desert and stayed there during the caliphates of *Sayyiduna* Abu Bakr and *Sayyiduna* 'Umar ؓ.

During the caliphate of *Sayyiduna* 'Uthman ؓ, he was increasingly perceived as summoning people to an overly strict religious regimen: he would stand at the Ka'ba and threaten fire and brimstone unless people gave up their gold and silver and official posts. *Sayyiduna* 'Uthman pressured him to give up public life altogether: *Why do you not retire?* He first went to the Levant and stayed in Damascus. Here he saw the growing laxity of the Muslims, their love for the world and their consuming desire for luxury. He was saddened and repelled by this. Mu'awiyya wrote to 'Uthman at this juncture complaining that he (i.e. Abu Dharr) was declaring asceticism obligatory. .

He was recalled him to Medina lest he be harmed. Here too he was critical of the people's pursuit of worldly pursuits and pleasures. The people were critical in turn of his reviling them. *Sayyiduna* 'Uthman therefore ordered that he should go to Rubdhah, a small village 100 km west of Medina. There he stayed far away from people, renouncing their preoccupation with the world, and holding on to the legacy of the Prophet ﷺ and his companions in seeking the everlasting abode of the Hereafter, in preference to this transitory world.

Once, a man visited him and began looking at the contents of his house but found it quite bare. He asked him: *Where are your possessions?* He replied: *We have a house yonder (i.e. the Hereafter) to which we send the best of our possessions.* The man understood and commented: *But you must have some possessions so long as you are in this abode?* To which he replied: *The owner of this abode will not leave us in it.*

He persisted in his simple and frugal life to the end. He was noted for his humility and asceticism. He had a zeal for knowledge and is said to have matched Ibn Mas'ud in religious learning. In complete isolation and poverty, he entered the isthmus in 31 or 32 AH (652 or 653).

ABU BAKR AS-SIDDIQ ﵁ (INVOCATION 23)

He was born in Mecca in 573 CE. He was the first caliph, the father-in-law of the Prophet Muhammad ﷺ, and one of the closest companions of the Prophet Muhammad ﷺ. Many Sufi poets refer to him as the "*Friend of the Cave*", referring to the incident when he accompanied the Prophet ﷺ on the dangerous journey from Mecca to Medina. The two left Mecca, followed by a group from the Quraish with ill intent, and sought refuge in a cave. Allah ﷻ caused a spider to spin a web across the mouth of the cave and birds to nest there, leading the pursuers to believe that no one could possibly have entered the cave without disturbing these creatures and destroying their homes. While the pursuers were at the mouth of the cave, he was repeatedly stung by a scorpion, causing him significant pain. Rather than cry out, he refrained from making a noise and even caught his tears to minimise the possibility that the pursuers be alerted to someone in the cave due to the sound of his tears hitting the ground. This image of the "*Friend of the Cave*" became a model of dedication and love of the Prophet ﷺ, a spiritual state lauded and prized by many. Once, he donated all his wealth for the sake of Allah. When the Prophet ﷺ heard this he asked him what he had left for his family, to which he was replied "Allah and His Prophet." As Caliph, he was instrumental in preserving the Koran, appointing a committee, headed by Zaid b. Thabit, to collect all verses of the book and then verify them. He entered the isthmus in 13 AH/634 CE in Medina and is interred next to the Prophet ﷺ.

ABU HANIFA AN-NU'MAN B. THABIT AT-TAIMI AL-KUFI ﵁ (INVOCATION 8)

Renowned as *al-imam al-a'zam* (the Great Imam), he met the companions of the Prophet ﷺ and is counted amongst the *tabi'un* (followers). He is renowned for his piercing intellect as *faqih* (jurist), his scrupulousness, integrity of character and his resoluteness in the face of oppression. His school is historically associated with the Ottomans and the Mughals of India; it is the most widely followed school of thought and is still followed by the majority of the Muslims in the world.

He is the first in Islam to organize the writing of *fiqh* under sub-headings embracing the whole of the Law, beginning with *tahara* (ritual purification) followed by *salat* (prayer), an order which was retained by all subsequent scholars such as Malik, Shafi'i, Abu Dawud, Bukhari, Muslim, Tirmidhi, and others. All these and their followers are indebted to him and give him a share of their reward because he was the first to open that road for them. Ash-Shafi'i summed it up with: *"People are all the children of Abu Hanifa in fiqh, of Ibn Ishaq in history, of Malik in hadith, and of Muqatil in tafsir."*

ABU HURAIRA AD-DAWSI AL-YAMANI ﵁ (INVOCATIONS 12 AND 16)

A noble *sahabi*. He is the most prolific narrator of *ahadith* in spite of the shortness of his contact with the Prophet ﷺ. He is revered by the folk of *tasawwuf* as one of the *ahl as-suffa*.

He became a Muslim at the hands of at-Tufail b. 'Amr ﵁, the chieftain of the Daws tribe to which he belonged. The Daws lived in the region of Tihama which stretches along the coast of the Red Sea in southern Arabia. When at-Tufail returned to his village after meeting with the Prophet ﷺ and becoming a Muslim in the early years of his mission, he was one of the first to respond to his call, unlike the majority of the Daws who remained stubborn in their old beliefs for a long time. When at-Tufail visited Mecca again, he accompanied him. There he had the honour and privilege of meeting the Noble Prophet ﷺ who asked him: *What is your name?* He replied: *'Abd ash-Shams (Servant of a Sun).* The Prophet ﷺ said: *Let it be 'Abd ar-Rahman (Servant of the Beneficent Lord)* He said: *Yes, 'Abd ar-Rahman (it shall be), O Messenger of Allah.* His *kunya* continued to be *Abu Huraira,* literally "father of a kitten", as he was fond of cats (just like the Prophet ﷺ) and often had a cat with him since his childhood.

He stayed in Tihama for several years and it was only at the beginning of the seventh year of the *hijra* that he arrived in Medina with others of his tribe. The Prophet ﷺ had gone on a campaign to Khaibar. Being destitute, he took up his place in the Masjid with others of the *ahl as-suffa.* He was single, without wife or child. With him however was his mother who was still a unbeliever. He longed and prayed for her to become a Muslim but she adamantly refused. One day, he invited her to have faith in Allah alone and follow His Prophet ﷺ but she uttered some words about the Prophet ﷺ which saddened him greatly. With tears in his eyes, he went to the Noble Prophet ﷺ who asked: *What makes you cry, O Abu Huraira?* He replied: *I have not let up in inviting my mother to Islam but she has always rebuffed me. Today, I invited her again and I heard words from her which I do not like. Do make supplication to Allah* ﷻ *to make the heart of Abu Huraira's mother incline to Islam.* The Prophet ﷺ

responded to his request and prayed for his mother. He then said: *I went home and found the door closed. I heard the splashing of water and when I tried to enter, my mother said: "Stay where you are, O Abu Huraira." And after putting on her clothes, she said, "Enter!" I entered and she said: "I testify that there is no god but Allah and I testify that Muhammad is His Servant and His Messenger." I returned to the Prophet ﷺ weeping with joy just as an hour before I had gone weeping from sadness and said: "I have good news, O Messenger of Allah ﷺ. Allah has responded to your prayer and guided the mother of Abu Huraira ﷺ to Islam."*

He loved the Prophet ﷺ immensely and found favour with him. He was never tired of looking at the Prophet ﷺ whose face appeared to him as having all the radiance of the sun and he was never tired of listening to him. Often he would praise Allah for his good fortune and say: *Praise be to Allah Who has guided Abu Huraira to Islam. Praise be to Allah Who has taught Abu Huraira the Qur'an. Praise be to Allah Who has bestowed on Abu Huraira the companionship of Muhammad ﷺ.*

On reaching Medina, he set his heart on attaining knowledge. Zaid b. Thabit ؓ the notable companion of the Prophet ﷺ reported: *While Abu Huraira and I and another friend of mine were in the mosque praying to Allah Almighty and performing dhikr to Him, the Messenger of Allah ﷺ appeared. He came towards us and sat among us. We became silent and he said: "Carry on with what you were doing." So my friend and I made a supplication to Allah before Abu Huraira ؓ did and the Prophet ﷺ began to say "Amin" to our du'a. Then Abu Huraira ؓ made a supplication saying: "O Lord, I ask You for what my two companions have asked and I ask You for knowledge which will not be forgotten." The Prophet*

ﷺ said: "Amin". We then said: "And we ask Allah ﷻ for knowledge which will not be forgotten", and the Prophet ﷺ replied: "The Dawsi youth has asked for this before you."

He had free time at his disposal. Unlike many of the *muhajirun* he did not busy himself in the market places, with buying and selling. Unlike many of the *ansar*, he had no land to cultivate nor crops to tend. He stayed with the Prophet ﷺ in Medina and went with him on journeys and expeditions. With his formidable memory, he set out to memorise in the four years that he spent with the Prophet ﷺ the gems of wisdom that emanated from his lips. He realized that he had a great gift and he set about to use it to the full in the service of Islam. Many companions were amazed at the number of *hadith* he had memorized and often questioned him on when he had heard a certain *hadith* and under what circumstances.

Once Marwan b. al-Hakam ﷺ wanted to test his power of memory. He sat with him in one room and behind a curtain he placed a scribe, unknown to Abu Huraira, and ordered him to write down whatever Abu Huraira said. A year later, Marwan called Abu Huraira again and asked him to recall the same *ahadith* which the scribe had recorded. It was found that he had not forgotten a single word.

He was concerned to teach and transmit the *hadith* he had memorized and knowledge of Islam in general. It is reported that one day he passed through the souk of Medina and naturally saw people engrossed in the business of buying and selling. *How feeble are you, O people of Medina!* he said. *What do you see that is feeble in us, Abu Huraira?* they asked. *The inheritance of the Messenger of Allah ﷺ is being distributed and you remain here!*

Won't you go and take your portion? he said. *Where is this, O Abu Huraira?* they asked. *In the mosque,"* he replied.

They left quickly. He waited until they returned. When they saw him, they said: *O Abu Huraira, we went to the mosque and entered and we did not see anything being distributed.* He asked: *Didn't you see anyone in the Masjid?* They replied: *O yes, we saw some people performing salat, some people reading Qur'an and some people discussing about what is halal and what is haram.* He replied: *Woe unto you, that is the inheritance of Muhammad ﷺ.*

He underwent much hardship and difficulties as a result of his dedicated search for knowledge. He was often hungry and destitute. He said about himself: *When I was afflicted with severe hunger, I would go to a companion of the Prophet ﷺ and ask him about an ayat of the Qur'an and (stay with him) learning it so that he would take me with him to his house and give me food. One day, my hunger became so severe that I placed a stone on my stomach. I then sat down in the path of the companions. Abu Bakr passed by and I asked him about and ayat of the Book of Allah. I only asked him so that he would invite me but he didn't. Then 'Umar b. al-Khattab passed by me and I asked him about an ayat but he also did not invite me. Then the Messenger of Allah ﷺ passed by and realized that I was hungry and said: "Abu Huraira!" I replied: "At your command," and followed him until we entered his house. He found a bowl of milk and asked his family: "From where did you get this?" They replied: "Someone sent it to you." He then said to me: "O Abu Huraira, go to the ahl as-suffa and invite them."* He did as he was told and they all drank from the milk.

The time came of course when the Muslims were blessed with great wealth and material goodness of every description.

He eventually got his share of wealth. He had a comfortable home, a wife and child. But this turn of fortune did not change his personality. Neither did he forget his days of destitution. He would say: *I grew up as an orphan and I emigrated as a poor and indigent person. I used to take food for my stomach from Busra bint Ghazwan ﵂. I served people when they returned from journeys and led their camels when they set out. Then Allah caused me to marry her (Busra). So praise to Allah who has strengthened His religion and made Abu Huraira an imam.* (This last statement is a reference to the time when he became governor of Medina)

Much of his time would be spent in spiritual exercises and devotion to Allah. *qiyam al-lail*—staying up the night in prayer and devotion—was a regular practice of his family, including his wife and his daughter. He would stay up for a third of the night, his wife for another third and his daughter for a third. In this way, in the house of Abu Huraira ﵁, no hour of the night would pass without *'ibada, dhikr* and *salat.*

During his caliphate, *Sayyiduna* 'Umar ﵁ appointed him as governor of Bahrain. 'Umar was very scrupulous about the type of persons whom he appointed as governors. He was always concerned that his governors should live simply and frugally and not acquire much wealth even though this was through lawful means.

In Bahrain, he became quite rich. 'Umar heard of this, recalled him to Medina and questioned him about where and how he had acquired such a fortune. He replied: *From breeding horses and gifts which I received.* 'Umar ordered: *Hand it over to the treasury of the Muslims.* He did as he was told and raised his hands to the heavens and prayed: *O Lord, forgive the amir al-mu'minin.*

Subsequently, 'Umar asked him to become governor once again but he declined. 'Umar asked him why he refused and he said: *So that my honour would not be besmirched, my wealth taken and my back beaten.* And he added: *And I fear to judge without knowledge and speak without wisdom.*

Throughout his life, he remained kind and courteous to his mother. Whenever he wanted to leave home, he would stand at the door of her room and say: *as-salamu 'alaikum, ya ummata, wa rahmatu Llahi wa barakatuhu (peace be on you, mother, and the mercy and blessings of Allah).* She would reply: *wa 'alaika s-salam, ya bunayya, wa rahmatu Llahi wa barakatuhu* (And on you be peace, my son, and the mercy and blessings of Allah).

Often he would also say: *May Allah have mercy on you as you cared for me when I was small.* She would reply: *May Allah have mercy on you as you delivered me from error when I was old.* He always encouraged other people to be kind and good to their parents. One day, he saw two men walking together, one older than the other. He asked the younger one: *What is this man to you?* The person replied: *My father.* He advised: *Don't call him by his name. Don't walk in front of him and don't sit before he does.*

Muslims owe an enormous debt of gratitude to him for helping to preserve and transmit the valuable legacy of the Prophet ﷺ. He entered the isthmus between 57 and 59 AH (676–679), when he was seventy-eight years old.

ABU SA'ID AL-KHUDRI, SA'D B. MALIK B. SINAN AL-KHAZRAJI AL-ANSARI ؓ (INVOCATION 1)

An eminent young *sahabi,* his lineage goes back to Khudra Batn of the Khazraj, one of the original inhabitants of Yathrib.

His mother was Anisa b. Abi Haritha of Bani 'Adl. He resided in Medina all his life.

He was prevented from fighting at 'Uhud as he was deemed too young by the Prophet ﷺ. His father was killed in that battle. Thereafter he took part in 12 battles with the Prophet ﷺ. He travelled to Syria once to visit the 'Umayyad caliph, Mu'awiyya. He also defended the city of Medina in the Battle of Harra in 64 AH. He is counted amongst the jurists and scholars amongst the companions and has narrated 1,170 *ahadith.* He entered the isthmus in Medina in 74 AH (693/4) or between 63 and 65 AH (682/3–684/5).

ABU UMAMA ؓ, **SUDAI B. 'AJLAN B. WAHB AL-BAHILI (INVOCATION 24)**

An esteemed companion about whom the Prophet ﷺ said: *"O Abu Umama, you are from me and I am with you."* He was with *Imam* 'Ali ؓ at the Battle of Siffin. He later settled in Homs where he breathed his last in a village named Danwah sometime either in 81 AH or 86 AH at the ripe old age of 91 or 106. He was the last of the companions in Syria to leave for the isthmus. He has narrated some 250 *ahadith* on significant matters such as giving *salam, talqin,* fasting, charity and backbiting.

The Prophet ﷺ sent him to his tribe to spread the message of Islam. When he arrived there, they were eating *Haram* food, and they offered him some also, but he said, *"I have come to forbid you from eating this food, and I am the emissary of the Prophet ﷺ, and I have come so that you embrace faith upon him."* Seeing this, the tribe belied him and scolded him. Thus, hungry and thirsty, he left that place reaching another place where he was overcome with tiredness and fell asleep. In his dream, he saw an angel placing a bowl full of milk in his hands, which he drank until he was quenched.

In the meantime, some members of his tribe censured the people, saying, *"A respected person from your own tribe came to the village, but you sent him back."* Hearing this, the people of the tribe felt great regret, so they took some food and water, and came to him. He said, *"I have no need for your food or drink; my Almighty creator, Allah, has fed me and given me to drink and satiated me,"* and then he relayed his dream. The people observed his state and began to realise that he had in fact eaten and drank to his fill. (They were amazed at this) and recited the *kalima* and entered the fold of Islam.

ANAS B. MALIK, ABU HAMZA AL-KHAZRAJI AL-ANSARI ﷺ (INVOCATIONS 11 AND 27)

A noble *sahabi* who was a devoted *khadim* to the Prophet ﷺ. He was born in Medina ten years before the *hijra*. His family belonged to the Najjar clan of the Khazraj tribe, which was one of the two leading tribes of Medina. The Prophet ﷺ christened him with the agnomen *Abu Hamza*.

When he was ten, his noble mother—Umm Sulaim ﷺ—placed him in the care of the Prophet ﷺ. He lived in close proximity to the Prophet ﷺ, thus observing and recording to memory minute details of the Prophet's daily life and way of living. Consequently, he was a prolific narrator of *ahadith*; he is one of the seven companions who are named "the Increasers" *[mukthirun]* for having transmitted an extraordinarily high number of reports from the Prophet ﷺ. With approximately

2,286 *ahadith* (including repetitions), he ranks third among the *mukthirun*. In addition to the *ahadith* that he heard directly from the Prophet ﷺ himself, he learned and transmitted *hadith* from the following companions: Abu Bakr ؓ, 'Umar ؓ, 'Uthman ؓ, Fatima ؓ, Mu'adh b. Jabal ؓ, 'Usaid b. Hudair ؓ, Abu Dharr al-Ghifari ؓ, his mother Umm Sulaim ؓ, his maternal aunt Umm Haram bint Milhan ؓ, his aunt's husband 'Ubada b. Samit ؓ, and his stepfather Abu Talha ؓ. He also taught *hadith* to such famous personalities as Hasan al-Basri, Ibn Sirin, Sha'bi, Abu Kilaba al-Jarmi, Makhul b. Abi Muslim, 'Umar b. 'Abd al-'Aziz, Zuhri, Qat'ada b. Diama, and Abu Amr b. Ala.

He narrates the excitement and joy of the Medinans upon the arrival of the Prophet ﷺ with the following account: *The children of Medina were screaming: "Muhammad is coming! Muhammad is coming!" I started to run and cry out with them. Finally, the Messenger of Allah ﷺ appeared with Abu Bakr ؓ. When we saw them approaching, a man sent us back to the city, asking us to tell everybody that the Messenger of Allah had arrived. We ran back right away and informed everyone. Around five hundred Medinan Ansar came out to greet them.* After the Prophet ﷺ came to Medina, the Ansar competed with each other to be of service to him. In this, Anas b. Malik's mother was at a serious disadvantage, since she had nothing to offer. So she held Anas by the hand and went to the Prophet ﷺ, saying: *"O Messenger of Allah, I am a poor woman. I have nothing to offer that could be of help to you. This is my son; I am leaving him to you so that he can help and serve you. Please accept him."* The Prophet ﷺ did not decline her request.

From this moment on for ten years until the Prophet ﷺ left for the isthmus, he was the Prophet's ﷺ personal attendant. He had a great love for the Prophet ﷺ and took great joy and pride in attending to his needs. He would wake up before everyone else in the mornings and go to the Prophet's ﷺ mosque to take care of his needs and wishes. If the Prophet ﷺ intended to fast that day, he would prepare his pre-dawn meal and perform the morning prayer with him after the meal ended. After Anas entered the service of the Prophet ﷺ, he performed his morning prayers with him every day. Due to his young age, Anas did not participate in the battles of Badr, 'Uhud and Khandaq. However, he was present on the battlefield during Badr, attending to the Prophet ﷺ and assisting the fighters where possible. He also took his place in the Prophet's ﷺ closest personal party during such milestone events as the Treaty of Hudaibiya, the Expedition of Khaibar, the pilgrimage of the year 629 AD *['umra al-qada']*, the Conquest of Mecca, the Battle of Hunain, the Siege of Taif, and the Farewell Pilgrimage.

After the passing of the Prophet ﷺ, the newly-elected Caliph *Sayyiduna* Abu Bakr ؓ assigned him to the post of alms collector and sent him to Bahrain. During the rule of *Sayyiduna* 'Umar ؓ, he was preoccupied with the education of the Muslims in Basra. He was also a member of a council of leading Companions, which was assembled by *Sayyiduna* 'Umar ؓ to advice and counsel him. After a brief stint in Damascus, he returned to Basra and continued his work. He participated in the military campaigns that took place during the rule of *Sayyiduna* 'Umar ؓ, including the conquest of Tustar. After the conquest, he was charged with the duty of transporting the war booty back to Medina. He managed to stay away from the political disturbances and polarization that started during the rule of the *Sayyiduna* 'Uthman ﷺ and which steadily kept intensifying. In this period, the only official post he held was the governorship of Basra, which coincided with the caliphate of 'Abd Allah b. Zubair and lasted only forty days. After this brief official engagement, he returned to his life of education and teaching.

He was always courageous and adamant in his struggle against oppression and injustice, and he never shrunk from telling the truth. When the severed head of the Prophet's ﷺ grandson, Husain ﷺ, was brought to the governor of 'Iraq, 'Ubaid Allah b. Ziyad, the latter started defaming Husain ﷺ. He was present during this incident, and he rebuked the governor by interrupting him and saying: "*This head looks like the head of the Prophet* ﷺ". Because he opposed the practices of the 'Umayyad regime, he was censured and persecuted, along with other Companions like Jabir b. 'Abd Allah ﷺ and Sahl b. Sa'd ﷺ. One of their oppressors was the governor of 'Iraq, Hajjaj, who branded their necks and hands in order to humiliate them in front of the public and went so far as to seize all of his property, claiming that he aided the rebels opposing the government. He wrote a letter of complaint to the 'Umayyad caliph 'Abd al-Malik b. Marwan and informed him of the injustice he endured, and the caliph sent orders from the capital to Hajjaj, commanding him to return his property and apologize to him.

The most important quality distinguishing him among the companions was his years-long service to the Prophet ﷺ and the fact that he was raised under his tutelage. He also learned about many religious issues from the Prophet ﷺ himself, and he later spent his life trying to teach and spread this knowledge. A great many reports about the Prophet's ﷺ conduct towards others, especially children; his way of teaching and education; and many other ethical practices come down to us from him. He narrates, for example, that he stayed with the Prophet ﷺ for a very long time and that he never heard a single word of reproach from him even though he could not always behave the way the Prophet ﷺ wanted him to. He goes on to say that when the wives of the Prophet ﷺ were once about to scold him for a mistake he made, the Prophet ﷺ told them: *"Leave the child alone. He has done nothing but what God has willed."* Such reports provide priceless prophetic guidance and information about the education of children and youth. He was a companion who tried to shape all aspects of his life according to the example of the Prophet ﷺ, and he succeeded in this endeavour in large measure. *Sayyiduna* Abu Huraira ؓ testifies that the way he performed his prayer was extremely similar to the way the Prophet ﷺ prayed.

He has related 2,286 *ahadith*. The Prophet ﷺ had supplicated for him: *"O Allah, increase his wealth and his children, grant him a long life, bless him and enter him into paradise."* He was from the wealthiest of people and had some 120 children. Having spent the great majority of his life in Basra, he entered the isthmus between 91 and 93 AH (709/10–711/12) in Basra at a very advanced age (97–107). He was the last companion who passed away in Basra. (AFTERNOTE: On February 25, 2006, his tomb west of Basra was attacked and vandalized.)

FATIMA ؓ BINT RASUL ALLAH ﷺ (INVOCATION 14)

She is the esteemed daughter of the Prophet ﷺ and Lady Khadija al-Kubra, beloved wife of *amir al-mu'minin Imam* 'Ali b.

Abi Talib and honourable mother of the princes of Paradise, al-Hasan and al-Husain. She was born at a time when her holy father had begun to spend long periods in the solitude of mountains around Mecca, meditating and reflecting on the great mysteries of creation. She is regarded as one of the four exemplary women in the history of humanity (along with Asiya, wife of Pharaoh; Mary, mother of Jesus; and Khadija) and is universally known as Fatima az-Zahra (Fatima the resplendent). Numerous marvels are attributed to her and she is seen by many as an important model for female piety and sanctity. She entered the isthmus in 11 AH (632-3 CE) at the young age of eighteen. She was buried in the graveyard of Baqi' in Medina in an unmarked grave, which was according to her will.

When she was young, she saw her three elder sisters—Zainab, Ruqayya and Umm Kulthum—leave home one after the other to live with their husbands. She was too young to understand the meaning of marriage and the reasons why her sisters had to leave home. She loved them dearly and was sad and lonely when they left. It is said that a certain silence and painful sadness came over her then. She still had for company (1) her noble mother, (2) Baraka, the maid-servant of Lady Amina, (3) Zaid b. Haritha, and (4) 'Ali b. Abi Talib. However, in none of them did she find the carefree joy and happiness that she enjoyed with her sisters.

When she was five, she heard that her father had become the Messenger of Allah. His first task was to convey the good news of Islam to his family and close relations. They were to worship Allah Almighty alone. Her mother, who was a tower of strength and support, explained to her what her father had to do. From this time on, she became more closely attached to him ﷺ and felt a deep and abiding love for him ﷺ. Often she would be at his side walking through the narrow streets and alleys of Mecca, visiting the *ka'ba* or attending secret gatherings of the early Muslims who had accepted Islam.

One day, when she was not yet ten, she accompanied her father to *masjid al-haram.* He stood in the place known as *al-hijr* facing the *ka'ba* and began to pray. She stood by his side. A group of Quraish, by no means well-disposed to the Prophet ﷺ, gathered around him. They included Abu Jahl b. Hisham, 'Uqba b. Abi Mu'ait, 'Umayya b. Khalaf, and Shaiba and 'Utba, both sons of ar-Rabi'a. Menacingly, the group went up to the Prophet ﷺ and Abu Jahl, the ringleader, asked: *"Which of you can bring the entrails of a slaughtered animal and throw it on Muhammad ﷺ?"* 'Uqba, one of the vilest of the lot, volunteered and hurried off. He returned with the obnoxious filth and threw it on the shoulders of the Prophet ﷺ while he was still prostrating. *Sayyiduna* 'Abd Allah b. Mas'ud ﵁ was present but he was powerless to do or say anything.

But the devastated yet determined ten-year old young Fatima went up to her father, removed the offensive matter, stood firmly and angrily before the group of Quraish thugs and lashed out against them. They didn't say a single word to her. The Prophet ﷺ raised his head on completion of the prostration and went on to complete the prayer. He then said: *"O Lord, may you punish the Quraish!"* and repeated this imprecation three times. Then he continued: *"May You punish 'Utba, 'Uqba, Abu Jahl and Shaiba."* (All four perished many years later at the Battle of Badr.)

On another occasion, she was with the Prophet ﷺ as he made *tawaf* (circumambulation) around the *ka'ba.* A Quraish mob gathered around him. They seized him and tried to strangle him with his own clothes. She screamed and shouted for help. *Sayyiduna* Abu Bakr ؓ rushed to the scene and managed to free the Prophet ﷺ. While he was doing so, he pleaded: *"Would you kill a man who says, 'My Lord is God?'"* Far from giving up, the mob turned on *Sayyiduna* Abu Bakr ؓ and began hitting him until blood flowed from his head and face.

Such scenes of vicious opposition and harassment against her father and the early Muslims were witnessed by the young Fatima. She did not meekly stand aside but joined in the struggle in defence of her father and his noble mission. She was still a young girl and instead of the cheerful romping, the gaiety and liveliness which children of her age are and should be accustomed to, she had to witness and participate in such ordeals.

Of course, she was not alone in this. The whole of the Prophet's ﷺ family suffered from the mindless violence of the disbelieving Quraish. Her sisters, Ruqayya and Umm Kulthum ؓ, also suffered. They were living at this time in the very nest of hatred and intrigue against the Prophet ﷺ. Their husbands were 'Utba and 'Utaiba, sons of Abu Lahab and Umm Jamil. Umm Jamil was known to be a hard and harsh woman who had a sharp and evil tongue. It was mainly because of her that Khadija ؓ was not pleased with the marriages of her daughters to Umm Jamil's sons in the first place. It must have been painful for Ruqayya and Umm Kulthum ؓ to be living in the household of such inveterate enemies who not only joined but led the campaign against their father.

As a mark of disgrace to the Prophet ﷺ and his family, 'Utba and 'Utaiba were prevailed upon by their parents to divorce their wives. This was part of the process of ostracizing the Prophet ﷺ totally. The Prophet ﷺ in fact welcomed his daughters back to his home with joy, happiness and relief. Fatima, no doubt, must have been happy to be with her sisters once again. They all wished that their eldest sister, Zainab, would also be divorced by her husband. In fact, the Quraish brought pressure on Abu-l 'As to do so but he refused. When the Quraish leaders came up to him and promised him the richest and most beautiful woman as a wife should he divorce Zainab ؓ, he replied: *"I love my wife deeply and passionately and I have a great and high esteem for her father even though I have not entered the religion of Islam."*

Both Ruqayya and Umm Kulthum were happy to be back with their loving parents and to be rid of the unbearable mental torture to which they had been subjected in the house of Umm Jamil. Shortly afterwards, Ruqayya married again, to the young and shy 'Uthman b. 'Affan ؓ who was among the first to have accepted Islam. They both left for Abyssinia among the first *muhajirun* (emigrants) who sought refuge in that land and stayed there for several years. Fatima was not to see Ruqayya again until after their mother had left for the isthmus.

The persecution of the Prophet ﷺ, his family and his followers continued and even became worse after the migration of the first Muslims to Abyssinia. In about the seventh year of his mission, the Prophet ﷺ and his family were forced to leave their homes and seek refuge in a rugged little valley enclosed by hill on all sides and which could only be entered from Mecca by a narrow defile. To this arid valley, the Prophet ﷺ and the clans of Banu Hashim and al-Muttalib were forced to retire with limited supplies of food. Fatima was one of the youngest members of the clans—just about twelve years old—and had to undergo months of hardship and suffering. The wailing of hungry children and women in the valley could be heard from Mecca. The Quraish allowed no food and contact with the Muslims whose hardship was only relieved somewhat during the season of pilgrimage.

The boycott lasted for three years. When it was lifted, the Prophet ﷺ had to face even more trials and difficulties. Lady Khadija ؓ, the faithful and loving, left for the isthmus shortly afterwards. With her passing, the Prophet ﷺ and his family lost one of the greatest sources of comfort and strength, which had sustained them through the difficult period. The year in which the noble Khadija ؓ, and later Abu Talib, passed away is known as the Year of Sadness. Fatima, now a young lady, was greatly distressed by her mother's death. She wept bitterly and for some time was so grief-stricken that her health deteriorated. It was even feared she might die of grief.

Although her older sister, Umm Kulthum, stayed in the same household, Fatima realized that she now had a greater responsibility with the passing away of her mother. She felt that she had to give even greater support to her father ﷺ. With loving tenderness, she devoted herself to looking after his needs. So concerned was she for his welfare that she came to be called *Umm Abiha* (the mother of her father). She also provided him with solace and comfort during times of trial, difficulty and crisis. Often the trials were too much for her. Once, about this time, an insolent mob heaped dust and earth upon his gracious head. As he entered his home, she wept profusely as she wiped the dust from her father's head. *"Do not cry, my daughter,"* he ﷺ said, *"for Allah shall protect your father."*

The Prophet ﷺ had a special love for her. He ﷺ once said: *"Whoever has pleased Fatima has indeed pleased Allah and whoever has caused her to be angry has indeed angered Allah. Fatima is a part of me. Whatever pleases her pleases me and whatever angers her angers me."* He ﷺ also said: *"The best women in all the world are four: the Virgin Mary; Asiya, the wife of Pharaoh; Khadija, Mother of the Believers, and Fatima, daughter of Muhammad."* She thus acquired a place of love and esteem in the Prophet's heart that was only occupied by his wife Khadija.

She was given the title of *az-Zahra* which means "the Resplendent One". That was because of her beaming face that seemed to radiate light. It is said that when she stood for prayer, the *mihrab* (prayer niche) would reflect the light of her countenance. She was also called *al-Batul* because of her purity and asceticism. Instead of spending her time in the company of women, much of her time would be spent in *salat*, in reading the Qur'an and in other acts of *'ibada*. She had a strong resemblance to her father, the Messenger of Allah ﷺ. Lady 'Aisha, the wife of the Prophet ﷺ, said of her: *"I have not seen any one of Allah's creation resemble the Messenger of Allah ﷺ more in speech, conversation and manner of sitting than Fatima. When the Prophet ﷺ saw her approaching, he would welcome her, stand up and kiss her, take her by the hand and sit her down in the place where he was sitting."* She would do the same when the Prophet ﷺ came to her.

Her fine manners and gentle speech were part of her lovely and endearing personality. She was especially kind to poor and indigent folk and would often give all the food she had to those in need even if she herself remained hungry. She had no craving for the ornaments of this world nor the luxury and comforts of life. She lived simply, although on occasion as we shall see, circumstances seemed to be too much and too difficult for her. She inherited from her father a persuasive eloquence that was rooted in wisdom. When she spoke, people would often be moved to tears. She had the ability and the sincerity to stir their emotions, move people to tears and fill their hearts with praise and gratitude to Allah for His grace and His inestimable bounties.

She migrated to Medina a few weeks after the Prophet ﷺ did. She went with Zaid b. Haritha رضي الله عنه who was sent by the Prophet ﷺ back to Mecca to bring the rest of his family. The party included Fatima and Umm Kulthum, Sawda' (the Prophet's wife), Zaid's wife Baraka and her son Usama. Traveling with the group also were 'Abd Allah the son of Abu Bakr who accompanied his mother and his sisters, 'Aisha and Asma'—رضي الله عنهم. In Medina, she lived with her father in the simple dwelling he had built adjoining the mosque.

In the second year after the *hijra,* she received proposals of marriage through her father, two of which were turned down. Then 'Ali the son of Abu Talib رضي الله عنه, plucked up courage and went to the Prophet ﷺ to ask for her hand in marriage. In the presence of the Prophet, however, 'Ali رضي الله عنه became over-awed and tongue-tied. He stared at the ground and could not say anything. The Prophet ﷺ then asked: *"Why have you come? Do you need something?"* 'Ali ؓ still could not speak and then the Prophet ﷺ suggested: *"Perhaps you have come to propose marriage to Fatima."*

"Yes," replied 'Ali. At this, according to one report, the Prophet ﷺ said simply: "*marhaban wa ahlan* - Welcome to the family," and this was taken by 'Ali ؓ and a group of Ansar who were waiting outside for him as indicating the Prophet ﷺ approved and went on to ask 'Ali if he had anything to give as *mahr*. 'Ali ؓ replied that he didn't. The Prophet ﷺ reminded him that he had a shield that could be sold. 'Ali sold the shield to 'Uthman ؓ for four hundred dirhams and as he was hurrying back to the Prophet ﷺ to hand over the sum as *mahr*, 'Uthman ؓ stopped him and said: *"I am returning your shield to you as a present from me on your marriage to Fatima."*

She and 'Ali ؓ were thus married most probably at the beginning of the second year after the *hijra*. She was about nineteen years old at the time and 'Ali was about twenty-one. The Prophet ﷺ himself performed the marriage ceremony. At the *walima*, the guests were served with dates, figs and *hais* (a mixture of dates and butter fat). A leading member of the Ansar donated a ram and others made offerings of grain. All Medina rejoiced. On her marriage, the Prophet ﷺ is said to have presented her and 'Ali ؓ with a wooden bed intertwined with palm leaves, a velvet coverlet, a leather cushion filled with the leaves of the *idhkhir* plant, a sheepskin, a pot, a water-skin and a quern for grinding grain.

She left the home of beloved father for the first time to begin life with her husband. The Prophet ﷺ was clearly anxious on her account and sent Baraka ؓ with her should she be in need of any help. And no doubt Baraka was a source of comfort and solace to her. The Prophet ﷺ prayed for them: *"O Lord, bless them both, bless their house and bless their offspring."* In 'Ali's humble dwelling, there was only a sheepskin for a bed. In the morning after the wedding night, the Prophet ﷺ went to 'Ali's house and knocked on the door. Baraka ؓ came out and the Prophet said to her: *"O Umm Aiman, call my brother for me."*

"Your bother? That's the one who married your daughter?" asked Baraka ؓ somewhat incredulously as if to say: *Why should the Prophet (saw) call 'Ali his "brother"?* (He referred to 'Ali ؓ as his brother because just as pairs of Muslims were joined in brotherhood after the *hijra*, so the Prophet ﷺ and 'Ali ؓ were linked as "brothers".) The Prophet ﷺ repeated what he had said in a louder voice. 'Ali ؓ came and the Prophet ﷺ made a *du'a*, invoking the blessings of Allah on him. Then he asked for Fatima ؓ. She came almost cringing with a mixture of awe and shyness and the Prophet ﷺ said to her: *"I have married you to the dearest of my family to me."* In this way, he sought to reassure her. She was not starting life with a complete stranger but with one who had grown up in the same household, who was among the first to become a Muslim at a tender age, who was known for his courage, bravery and virtue, and whom the Prophet ﷺ described as his *"brother in this world and the hereafter".*

Her life with 'Ali was as simple and frugal as it was in her father's household. In fact, so far as material comforts were concerned, it was a life of hardship and deprivation. Throughout their life together, 'Ali remained poor because he did not set great store by material wealth. Fatima ؓ was the only one of her sisters who was not married to a wealthy man. In fact, it could be said that her life with 'Ali was even more rigorous than life in her father's home. At least before marriage, there were always a number of ready helping hands in the Prophet's household. But now she had to cope virtually on her own. To relieve their extreme poverty, 'Ali worked as a drawer and carrier of water and she as a grinder of corn. One day she said to 'Ali: *"I have ground until my hands are blistered."*

"I have drawn water until I have pains in my chest," said 'Ali and went on to suggest to her: *"Allah has given your father some captives of war, so go and ask him to give you a servant."* Reluctantly, she went to the Prophet ﷺ who said: *"What has brought you here, my little daughter?"*

"I came to give you greetings of peace," she said, for in awe of him she could not bring herself to ask what she had intended. *"What did you do?"* asked 'Ali when she returned alone. *"I was ashamed to ask him,"* she said. So the two of them went together, but the Prophet ﷺ felt they were less in need than others. *"I will not give to you,"* he ﷺ said, *"and let the ahl as-suffa (poor Muslims who stayed in the mosque) be tormented with hunger. I have not enough for their keep..."* She and 'Ali returned home feeling somewhat dejected but that night, after they had gone to bed, they heard the voice of the Prophet ﷺ asking permission to enter. Welcoming him, they both rose to their feet, but he told them: *"Stay where you are,"* and sat down beside them. *"Shall I not tell you of something better than that which you asked of me?"* he asked and when they said yes he said: *"Words which Jibril ﵇ taught me, that you should say 'subhana Llah (Glory be to Allah)' ten times after every prayer, and ten times 'al-hamdu li-Llah (All Praise is for Allah)' and ten times 'Allahu Akbar (Allah is Great)'.*

And that when you go to bed you should say them thirty-three times each." 'Ali used to say in later years: *"I have never once failed to say them since the Messenger of Allah ﷺ taught them to us."*

There are many reports of the hard and difficult times that she had to face. Often there was no food in her house. Once the Prophet ﷺ was hungry. He went to one after another of his wives' apartments but there was no food. He then went to his daughter's house and she had no food either. When he eventually got some food, he sent two loaves and a piece of meat to her. At another time, he went to the house of Abu Ayyub al-Ansari and from the food he was given, he saved some for her. She also knew that the Prophet ﷺ was without food for long periods and she in turn would take food to him when she could. Once she took a piece of barley bread and he said to her: *"This is the first food you father has eaten in three days."* Through these acts of kindness she showed how much she loved her father; and he loved her, really loved her in return.

Once he returned from a journey outside Medina. He went to the mosque first of all and prayed two *rak'ats* as was his custom. Then, as he often did, he went to Fatima's house before going to his wives. She welcomed him and kissed his face, his mouth and his eyes and cried. *"Why do you cry?"* the Prophet ﷺ asked. *"I see you, O Rasul Allah,"* she said, *"your colour is pale and sallow and your clothes have become worn and shabby."*

"O Fatima," the Prophet ﷺ replied tenderly, *"don't cry, for Allah has sent your father with a mission which He would cause to affect every house on the face of the earth whether it be in towns, villages or tents (in the desert) bringing either glory or humiliation until this mission is fulfilled, just as night (inevitably) comes."* With

such comments she was often taken from the harsh realities of daily life to get a glimpse of the vast and far-reaching vistas opened up by the mission entrusted to her noble father.

She eventually returned to live in a house close to that of the Prophet ﷺ. The place was donated by an Ansari who knew that the Prophet ﷺ would rejoice in having his daughter as his neighbour. Together they shared in the joys and triumphs, the sorrows and the hardships of the crowded and momentous Medina days and years.

In the middle of the second year after the *hijra,* her sister Ruqayya ؓ fell ill with fever and measles. This was shortly before the great campaign of Badr. *Sayyiduna* 'Uthman ؓ, her husband, stayed by her bedside and missed the campaign. Ruqayya entered the isthmus just before her father returned. On his return to Medina, one of the first acts of the Prophet ﷺ was to visit her grave. Fatima went with him ﷺ. This was the first bereavement they had suffered within their closest family since the death of Lady Khadija ؓ. She was greatly distressed by the loss of her sister. The tears poured from her eyes as she sat beside her father at the edge of the grave. And he comforted her and sought to dry her tears with the corner of his cloak.

The Prophet ﷺ had previously spoken against lamentations for the dead, but this had led to a misunderstanding, and when they had returned from the cemetery the voice of *Sayyiduna* 'Umar ؓ was heard raised in anger against the women who were weeping for the martyrs of Badr and for Ruqayya ؓ. *"'Umar, let them weep,"* he ﷺ said and then added, *"What comes from the heart and from the eye, that is from Allah and His mercy, but what comes from the hand and from the tongue, that is from Sa-*

tan." By the hand he meant the beating of breasts and the smiting of cheeks, and by the tongue he meant the loud clamour in which women often joined as a mark of public sympathy.

Sayyiduna 'Uthman later married the other daughter of the Prophet, Umm Kulthum, and on this account came to be known as *dhu n-nurain* (Possessor of the Two Lights). The bereavement in which the family suffered by the death of Ruqayya was followed by happiness when, to the great joy of all the believers, Fatima gave birth to a boy in Ramadan of the third year after the *hijra.* The Prophet spoke the words of the *adhan* in to the ear of the newborn babe and christened him al-Hasan, which means the Beautiful One. One year later, she gave birth to another son who was christened al-Husain, which means "little Hasan" or the little beautiful one. She would often bring her two sons to see their grandfather who was exceedingly fond of them. Later he would take them to the Mosque and they would climb onto his back when he prostrated. He did the same with his little granddaughter *Umama,* the daughter of Zainab.

In the eighth year after the *hijra,* she gave birth to a third child, a girl whom she named after her eldest sister Zainab who had passed away shortly before her birth. This Zainab (bint 'Ali) was to grow up and become famous as the "Heroine of Karbala". Fatima's fourth child was born two years later. This child was also a girl and the Prophet chose for her the name Umm Kulthum after Fatima's sister who had passed away the year before after an illness.

It was only through Fatima that the progeny of the Prophet was perpetuated. All the Prophet's male children had passed away in their infancy and the two children of Zainab, named 'Ali and Umama, passed away young. Ruqayya's child, 'Abd Allah, also passed away when he was yet two years old. This is an added reason for the reverence which is accorded to Fatima ☙.

Although she was so often busy with pregnancies and giving birth and rearing children, she took as much part as she could in the affairs of the growing Muslim community of Medina. Before her marriage, she acted as a sort of hostess to the poor and destitute *ahl as-suffa*. As soon as the Battle of 'Uhud was over, she went with other women to the battlefield and wept over the dead martyrs and took time to dress her father's wounds. At the Battle of the Trench, she played a major supportive role together with other women in preparing food during the long and difficult siege. In the place of her camp there stands a mosque named Masjid Fatima, one of the seven mosques where the Muslims stood guard and performed their devotions.

She also accompanied the Prophet ☙ when he made *'umra* in the sixth year AH after the Treaty of Hudaibiyya. In the following year, she and her sister Umm Kulthum, were among the mighty throng of Muslims who took part with the Prophet ☙ in the liberation of Mecca. It is said that on this occasion, both Fatima and Umm Kulthum visited the home and the grave of their mother Khadija ☙ and recalled memories of their childhood and memories of long struggles in the early years of the Prophet's mission.

In Ramadan of the tenth year just before he went on his Farewell Pilgrimage, the Prophet ☙ confided to her, as a secret not yet to be told to others: *"Jibril ☙ recited the Qur'an to me and I to him once every year, but this year he has recited it with me* twice. I cannot but think that my time has come." On his return from the Farewell Pilgrimage, the Prophet ﷺ did become seriously ill. His final days were spent in the apartment of his wife 'Aisha ؓ. When she came to visit him, 'Aisha ؓ would leave father and daughter together.

One day he ﷺ summoned her. When she came, he kissed her and whispered some words in her ear. She wept. Then again he whispered in her ear and she smiled. Lady 'Aisha ؓ saw and asked: *"You cry and you laugh at the same time, Fatima. What did the Messenger of Allah say to you?"* Fatima ؓ replied: *"He first told me that he would meet his Lord after a short while and so I cried. Then he said to me: 'Don't cry, for you will be the first of my household to join me.' So I laughed."* He also said to her then: *"Aren't you pleased that you are the First Lady (sayyidat an-nisa') of this Umma?"*

Not long afterwards the Prophet ﷺ entered the isthmus. She was grief-stricken and she would often be seen weeping profusely. One of the companions noted that he did not see her laugh after the death of her father. One morning, early in the month of Ramadan, just a few months after her noble father had entered the isthmus, she woke up looking unusually happy and full of mirth. In the afternoon of that day, it is said that she called Salma bint Umais ؓ who was looking after her. She asked for some water and had a bath. She then put on new clothes and perfumed herself. She then asked Salma ؓ to put her bed in the courtyard of the house. With her face looking to the heavens above, she asked for her husband 'Ali ؓ.

He was taken aback when he saw her lying in the middle of the courtyard and asked her what was wrong. She smiled and said: *"I have an appointment today with the Messenger of Allah ﷺ."* 'Ali ؓ cried and she tried to console him. She told him to look after their sons al-Hasan and al-Husain ؓ and advised that she should be buried without ceremony. She then turned and faced the *qibla*, closed her eyes, and slept. It was a sleep from which she did not awake. She was just twenty-nine years old.

AL-GHAZALI, ABU HAMID MUHAMMAD B. MUHAMMAD B. MUHAMMAD B. AHMAD, *Hujjat al-Islam* AT-TUSI ؓ (INVOCATION 21)

The *Proof of Islam* and Sufi adept born in Tabiran, near Tus (just north of present-day Mashhad, Iran), in 450/1058, he was the Imam of his time, nicknamed Shafi'i the Second for his legal virtuosity, he was a brilliant intellectual who first studied jurisprudence at Tus, and then travelled the Islamic world, to Baghdad, Damascus, Jerusalem, Cairo, Alexandria, Mecca and Medina, taking Sacred Knowledge from its masters, among them the *Imam of the Two Sanctuaries* Juwaini, with whom he studied until the Imam's death, becoming at his hands a scholar in Shafi'i law, logic, tenets of faith, debate, and in the rationalistic doctrine of the philosophical schools of his time, which he was later called upon to refute.

When Juwaini passed away, Ghazali debated the Imams and scholars of Baghdad in the presence of the vizier Nizam al-Mulk, who was so impressed that he appointed him to a teaching post at the Nizamiyya Madrasa in Baghdad, where word of his brilliance spread, and scholars journeyed to hear him. His worldly success was something of a mixed blessing, and in mid-career, after considerable reflection, he was gripped by an intense fear for his soul and his fate in the afterlife, and he resigned from his post, travelling first to Jerusalem and then to Damascus to purify his heart by following the way of Sufism.

In Damascus he lived in seclusion for some ten years, engaged in spiritual struggle and the remembrance of Allah, at the end of which he emerged to produce his masterpiece *ihya' 'ulum ad-din* (Giving Life to the Religious Sciences), a classic among the books of the Muslims about internalising godfearingness *[taqwa]* in one's dealings with Allah, illuminating the soul through obedience to Him, and the levels of believers' attainments therein. The work shows how deeply Ghazali personally realised what he wrote about, and his masterly treatment of hundreds of questions dealing with the inner life that no one had previously discussed or solved is a performance of sustained excellence that shows its author's well-disciplined legal intellect and profound appreciation of human psychology.

He also wrote nearly two hundred other works, on the theory of government, Sacred Law, refutation of philosophers, tenets of faith, Sufism, Qur'anic exegesis, scholastic theology, and bases of Islamic jurisprudence. He entered the isthmus in Tabiran in 505/1111.

AL-HAKIM AT-TIRMIDHI, ABU 'ABD ALLAH MUHAMMAD B. 'ALI B. AL-HASAN B. BASHIR ﵀ (INVOCATION 15)

An acclaimed *faqih* (jurist) and *muhaddith* (traditionist) of Khorasan, he is mostly remembered as one of the great early authors on Sufism. Information about his life and pursuits can be found in the works by Taj ad-Din as-Subki (*tabakat ash-shafi'iyya al-kubra*), Khatib al-Baghdadi (*tarikh baghdad*), Ibn Hajar al-Asqalani (*lisan al-mizan*), as-Sulami (*tabaqat as-sufiyya*) and others. adh-Dhahabi defended him from detractors by saying, *"He is a leader in Hadith."*

He was born in Tirmidh, Khorasan, in present day Uzbekistan. There is no consensus on his date of birth, which ranges from 135 AH to 205 AH. Likewise, his date of passing ranges from 255 AH to 320 AH. He is said to have lived well over 100 years. His father was a *muhaddith* and a *faqih* and was his first teacher. He read *ahadith* and specialised in Hanafi *fiqh*, which was dominant in the region. His education included the sciences, such as Greek natural science and philosophy. His subsequent reference to learning the use of the astrolabe, implying knowledge of astronomy and mathematics, has been given different interpretations. This pursuit of knowledge of various disciplines earned him the title *al-hakim*. His written works display on Sufism, *hadith, kalam, aqida* and *fiqh* prove his intellectual and spiritual prowess. He speaks about his life in his autobiography titled, *bad'u shani Abu Abd Allah* (The Beginning of Abu 'Abd Allah's Pursuit). He entered into rational disputation with the *mutakillimun* of his era and maintained a critical attitude of them. He had prominent teachers and luminous students.

His life can be divided into the following periods: (The first period) is his childhood up to seven. Though we do not have exact information about this part of his life, we have enough to know that he displayed intellectual prowess that prepared him for his future role. He worked hard with his early teachers, obtained knowledge on various sciences (particularly on theology) and prepared for a mystic spiritual life. (The second period) embraces his life from eight to twenty-eight, when he received knowledge from different Sheikhs. He travelled to various cities of learning and also to Mecca for pilgrimage. Some sources pointed to the fact that he paid much attention to learning *hadith* and problems of *fiqh* in this period of his life. (The third period) of his life is related to learning the Qur'an thoroughly. Beyond the outward, he dived deep into the oceans of the final revelation. The philosophic mystic work by al-Antahi *"Healing of Hearts"* had a great influence on him.

He wrote 62 treatises and 108 books. His works can be divided into six subjects: *tafsir* (Qura'nic exegesis), *ahadith* (Prophetic tradition), *fiqh* (jurisprudence), Arabic terminology, anthropology and Islamic mysticism. A contemporary scholar notes, *he is the first and, up until the time of Ibn 'Arabi, the only mystic author whose writings present a broad synthesis of mystic experience, anthropology, cosmology and Islamic theology... His system of thought is representative of an old Islamic theosophy which had not yet consciously assimilated elements from the Aristotelian-Neoplatonic philosophic tradition.*

Some of his sayings include: *The worst sin with Allah is that the slave speaks about something that Allah concealed for him.* On knowledge and action, he said: *What sorrow could be greater than that of a man whom Allah has granted knowledge, but he did not act upon it.* Regarding love of the lower world, he admonished the people of his time: *What a great difference there is between you and those people [of the past]; worldly wealth came to them but they fled from it, whereas the world turns its back on you and you go after it.*

AL-HASAN AL-BASRI ﷺ (INVOCATION 32)

One of the most important personages in the history of Islam, he was born in 642 CE, nine years after the passing of the Prophet ﷺ, in Medina to Yasir and Khaira, both freed slaves. He was raised within the inner circle of the Prophet's family. *Sayyiduna* 'Umar b. al-Khattab is said to have christened him *Hasan* and prayed for him when he was a child. He met more than 100 companions of the Prophet, 70 of whom had participated in the Battle of Badr. He went to Wadi al-Qura for studies. Anas b. Malik, a companion of the Prophet, was his tutor.

His family moved to Basra after the Battle of Siffin, an armed political clash between sects. Basra served both as a commercial port and as a military base. Military expeditions disembarked from Basra to the east, some of which al-Basri participated in. He accompanied Rabi' b. Ziyad, the commander of one such expedition, as his clerk. He also participated in another military expedition on Kabul.

After returning to Basra, he was a *Qadi* (Islamic judge) without pay for a while upon request of the governor, Sulaiman b. Harb. After quitting from the role, he began to preach—for which he had a natural talent. Though his sermons are not available in the text form today, authors of his time report that his style was a rhetoric masterpiece. He fluently spoke in philosophical depth. Some of his tropes and allusions are still remembered and used in Sufi orders. He mostly exhorted that a true Muslim should not only avoid sins but stay in continuous anxiety against the fact that death was certain, and nobody could be sure of their own destiny in the other world. This cautious mentality would lead to the foundation of asceticism and mysticism in Islam.

He was apolitical in his attitude towards power. He never supported the 'Umayyad dynasty; however, he never participated in revolts against their rule; but he opposed them in certain situations. For instance, he criticized Mu'awiyya—the founder and first caliph of the 'Umayyad dynasty—when he assigned Yazid, his son as his heir because he was incapable. He condemned Hajjaj, the cruel governor of the 'Umayyad. He was forced to hide for some time because of that condemnation. He thanked Allah after Hajjaj's death and prayed for his policies to be destroyed.

He offered an intense way of piety saying that the true Muslim should avoid the colour and taste of this world for the sake of the benefits to be collected in the other world. This otherworldly approach gathered masses around him. Once he preached, "Every *umma* has its own idols. This *umma's* idols are the gold and the silver." He always emphasized working toward the other world and doing nothing for this one. He embodied what he preached, so it had a great effect on all those around him. He taught many students.

According to him, a *munafiq* (the hypocrite) is capable of doing more harm to Islam than a *kafir* (the infidel). This is because Muslims do not believe in what the *kafir* does or says, but they could be cheated by a *munafiq*. In the free will-fate debate, he refused fatalism and defended that people were responsible for their actions, which caused some critics to believe that he was a Mu'tazili, a rationalist school of Islamic theology. In fact, he was on the strict path which the *ahl as-sunna wa l-jama'a* have walked on so far.

For many, he is one of the pioneers of Islamic asceticism and mysticism. Though some dispute, there is enough evidence to prove that he did indeed receive the *khirqa* from *Imam* 'Ali b. Abi Talib ﷺ. He was an important bridge between the companions of the Prophet ﷺ and the next generation. Amongst his companions was the unique Rabi'a al-'Adawiyya. He entered the isthmus in 110 AH (728/9). He had three children, one girl and two boys.

IBRAHIM AT-TAIMI ﷺ (AL-MUSABBA'AT AL-ASHR)

Counted amongst the *tabi'un* and regarded as one of the most distinguished amongst them, he is Ibrahim b. Muhammad b. Ishaq at-Taimi. *al-Khatib al-Baghdadi* said that he was a descendant of *Sayyiduna* Abu Bakr as-Siddiq ﷺ while Ibn Hajar al-Asqalani said that he was a descendent of 'Ubaid Allah b. Mu'ammar of the Quraishi tribe of Taim.

He said: *The worst sin with Allah is that the slave speaks about something that Allah concealed for him.* On knowledge and action, he said: *What sorrow could be greater than that of a man whom Allah has granted knowledge, but he did not act upon it.* Regarding love of the lower world, he admonished the people of his time: *What a great difference there is between you and those people [of the past]; worldly wealth came to them but they fled from it, whereas the world turns its back on you and you go after it.*

He used to ponder greatly on his state and eventual return to his Lord. He said: *I imagined myself in Paradise eating from its fruits, drinking from its rivers, roaming its valleys, and enjoying the pleasures. Then I imagined myself in the Hellfire eating from its bitter thorny fruits, drinking from its boiling pus, suffering at its chains, and screaming amongst its inhabitants. Then I asked myself: "What is your wish?" The response was: "I wish to be returned to the worldly life so that I could perform more acts of virtue." Then I addressed myself saying: "You are where you wish to be, so rush in performing the acts you wished to perform."*

His passing is an deep lesson in sacrifice and brotherhood. Hajjaj b. Yusuf had given orders for the arrest of Ibrahim an-Nakha'i. The person deputed to locate him ended up at Ibrahim at-Taimi's and told him that he had orders to arrest Ibrahim. He said, *I am Ibrahim,* (though he knew that the man wanted was Ibrahim an-Nakha'i). The person arrested him and took him to Hajjaj who imprisoned him in a place that neither received sunlight nor was protected from severe cold. Another person was enchained in the same fetters with him. His condition deteriorated. When his mother visited him, she could not recognise him till he spoke to her. He remained in this cell till his death therein. Hajjaj saw a dream that very night in which someone announced that a person had passed away that day who would go to Paradise. In the morning, Hajjaj made enquiries and was told that Ibrahim at-Taimi had passed away in prison. Hajjaj commented, *This was one of the dreams in which the devils attack (men).* Hajjaj then ordered that he must be duly buried. He entered the isthmus in 92 AH.

Nabi ILYAS ﷺ (INVOCATION 18)

Prophet Ilyas ﷺ is mentioned twice in the Qur'an (6:85 and 37:123-130). He drank the *Water of Life*[9] and his domain is the oceans and seas, though his influence extends beyond. Through

9 This Water springs from the Divine Name "*The Living*" *[al-Hayy]* and symbolises Knowledge of the Absolute. The one who drinks the Water of Life finds eternal life through *al-Hayy*.

his Word descended the *Wisdom of Intimacy [al-hikma al-inasiyya]*[10].

Scholars of *tasawwuf* are unanimous in their belief that both he and al-Khidr ﷺ (see below) are alive and give guidance to spiritual aspirants, with Allah's permission. They spend Ramadan each year in Jerusalem, observing the fast. They then make the pilgrimage to Mecca. After the pilgrimage, they clip each other's hair and depart with remembrance of Allah Most High.

JABIR B. 'ABD ALLAH, ABU 'ABD ALLAH AL-KHAZRAJI AS-SULAMI ﷺ (INVOCATION 39)

He was one of the Ansars who became Muslim before the *Hijra.* He was present at 'Aqaba with his father as a child. He did not take part in Badr and 'Uhud as his father did not permit him to do so. After his father was martyred in the latter, he took part in 19 battles with the Prophet ﷺ. He has related 1,540 *ahadith.* He entered the isthmus in Medina 74 AH

JUWAIRIYA BINT HARITH ﷺ (INVOCATION 7)

An honoured *umm al-mu'minin* (mother of the believers). She was the daughter of al-Harith, chief of the Banu Mustaliq. She was taken captive during the Muslims' successful campaign against the tribe. She was worried that once the Muslims realized who she was, they would demand an exorbitant ransom for her safe release. After the Muslims had returned to Medina with their booty and prisoners, she demanded to see the Prophet ﷺ hoping that he would help to prevent what she

10 ElSenossi, Ali. *The Language of the Future*. http://almirajsuficentre.org.au/qamus/.

feared. Seeing how beautiful she was, 'Aisha ﷺ was not keen on her seeing the Prophet ﷺ. But she persisted, and eventually she was permitted to see the Prophet ﷺ and was taken to him while he was with 'Aisha ﷺ. After she had finished speaking, the Prophet ﷺ thought for a moment, and then said, *"Shall I tell you what would be better than this?"*

He ﷺ then asked her to marry him, and she immediately accepted. Although she was young, beautiful and of noble lineage, the Prophet ﷺ was thinking of how to save her and all her tribe from an ignoble fate. By marrying her, the Banu Mustaliq would be able to enter Islam with honour, and with the humiliation of their recent defeat removed, so that it would no longer be felt necessary by them to embark on a war of vengeance that would have continued until one of the two parties had been annihilated. As soon as the marriage was announced, all the booty that had been taken from the Banu Mustaliq was returned, and all the captives were set free, for they were now the in-laws of the Prophet ﷺ. Thus 'Aisha ﷺ once said of her, *"I know of no woman who was more of a blessing to her people than Juwairiya bint al-Harith."* After they were married, the Prophet ﷺ changed her name, which was Barra, to Juwairiya.

The Prophet ﷺ married her in 5 AH when he was 58 years and she 20. She was married to the Prophet ﷺ for six years, and lived for another thirty-nine years after his passing. She entered the isthmus sometime between 57 and 59 AH (676–679) at the age of sixty-five. The *dhikr* she narrated (which is included in this work and whose details are in the notes) is her lasting legacy till the Day of Judgement.

KA'B B. AHBAR, ABU ISHAQ B. MATI' AL-HIMYARI ﷺ (INVOCATION 34)

He was known as *Rabbi Ka'b*. He was a Jewish convert of Yemen who became Muslim in the caliphate of *Sayyiduna* Abu Bakr or *Sayyiduna* 'Umar ﷺ. He was the oldest authority for Jewish-Muslim traditions in Islam and was considered trustworthy. He entered the isthmus in 32 or 34 AH (652/3 or 654/5).

AL-KHIDR, ABU L-'ABBAS BALYA B. MALIKAN ﷺ (INVOCATION 18)

Though his name does not appear in the Qur'an, nearly all the commentators agree that the mysterious person who Prophet Musa ﷺ meets in *surat al-kahf* is al-Khidr. Like Prophet Ilyas (see above), he too drank the *Water of Life* and his domain is the earth. He initiates the holy ones into the Great Mysteries. He was given "insight of the heart" which is bestowed knowledge from Allah's Presence.

Scholars of *tasawwuf* are unanimous in their belief that both he and Ilyas ﷺ are alive and give guidance to spiritual aspirants, with Allah's permission. They spend Ramadan each year in Jerusalem, observing the fast. They then make the pilgrimage to Mecca. After the pilgrimage, they clip each other's hair and depart with remembrance of Allah Most High.

MA'QIL B. YASAR AL-MAZNI ﷺ (INVOCATION 30)

A noble *sahabi*. He has narrated at least 19 *ahadith*. His sister was married to a man and then that man divorced her and remained away from her till her period of the *idda* expired. The former husband then demanded for her hand in marriage again. Ma'qil got angry and said, *He kept away from her when he could still retain her and now he demands her hand again?* Ma'qil disagreed to remarry her to him. Then Allah revealed: *When you have divorced women and they have fulfilled the term of their prescribed period, do not prevent them from marrying their [former] husbands.'* (2.232) The Prophet ﷺ sent for Ma'qil and recited to him (Allah's order). He yielded to Allah's order.

MA'RUF AL-KARKHI, ABU MAHFUZ B. FIRUZ (INVOCATION 5)

He was a celebrated Sufi of the Baghdad school. His parents are believed to have been Christians or Sabians. He received the *khirqa* from *Imam* 'Ali ar-Rida. Amongst his teachers is Bakr b. Khunais al-Kufi. He taught Sari as-Saqati, who was the teacher of al-Junaid. He was famous for his emphasis on the virtues of generosity and devotedness.

From an early age, he rejected, even when beaten for it at school, the doctrine of the Trinity and declared his conviction that God is One. Eventually, he ran away from home and his parents pined for him. They said in his absence that, so long as he came back to them, they would surely approve and accept whatever religion he chose for himself. Some years later, he did call at their door. He announced himself by name adding that he was now a Muslim. His parents promptly converted to Islam at his hands.

He practised the most severe asceticism in support of a perfect humility and devotion. He became widely renowned throughout the Islamic world for his piety but was especially revered in the city of Baghdad where he had settled and where he had many students. He entered the isthmus in 200 AH or 201 AH (815/6 or 816/7).

It is recorded that Muslims, Christians and even Jews mourned his passing. Perhaps it is evidence of what he had attained through his spiritual quest—a fullness in his love of God. He is remembered through a number of anecdotes illustrating (1) his humility; (2) his moral and spiritual insight; and (3) his transcendence of this world, the constraints of time and space.

MU'ADH B. JABAL ﷺ

A noble *sahabi,* he studied the Qur'an and the laws of Islam until he became one of the most learned amongst the companions in the religion. Wherever he went, people would refer to him for legal judgements on matters over which they differed. The Prophet ﷺ has said about him, *The most knowledgeable of my nation in matters of halal and haram is Mu'adh b. Jabal.*

Counted amongst the Ansar, he was from the Khazraj tribe of Medina. He became a Muslim at a young age at the hands of Mus'ab b. 'Umair ﷺ, whom the Prophet ﷺ had deputed to Yathrib (Medina) prior to the *hijra.* He was among the 70 who had taken the Pledge of 'Aqaba. At that time he was so young that he did not even have a strand of beard. When the Prophet ﷺ arrived in Medina, he kept his company as much as possible. At Badr he was only 20 years old and thereafter fought in every battle with the Prophet ﷺ. It was only in the Battle of Hunain that he was absent because the Prophet ﷺ had sent him to Mecca to teach Islam to the new Muslims.

Sometime after the Prophet ﷺ had returned to Medina, deputations of the kings of Yemen came to him announcing that they and the people of Yemen had become Muslims. They requested that some teachers should be with them to teach people Islam. For this task the Prophet ﷺ commissioned a group of competent missionaries and made him their leader. Before he departed for Yemen, the Prophet ﷺ put the following question to him: *According to what will you judge?* He replied: *According to the Book of Allah.* The Prophet ﷺ rejoined: *And if you find nothing therein?* He replied: *According to the Sunna of the Prophet of Allah.* The Prophet ﷺ rejoined again: *And if you find nothing therein?* He replied: *Then I will exert myself to form my own judgement.* The Prophet ﷺ was pleased with this reply and said: *Praise be to Allah who has guided the messenger of the Prophet to that which pleases the Prophet.*

The Prophet ﷺ personally walked for some distance alongside him as he rode out of the city. When it came to bid farewell, the Prophet ﷺ said to him, *O Mu'adh, perhaps you shall not meet me again after this year. Perhaps when you return you shall see only my mosque and my grave.* He wept upon hearing this as he knew in his heart that he was never to meet the Prophet ﷺ in this world again. A feeling of sadness and desolation overtook him as he parted from the Prophet ﷺ. The Prophet's words came to pass; the Prophet ﷺ left this realm before he returned from Yemen.

When Abu Ubaida b. Jarrah ؓ was afflicted by the plague, he appointed him as the governor of the Levant. A plague had gained rapid momentum and affected many people. He addressed the people saying he heard the Prophet ﷺ say, *You people will migrate to the Levant and you will conquer this land. Thereafter such a sickness will appear which will be like sores and boils. Allah Most High will bless you with martyrdom and purify your actions.*

He then made the following prayer, *O Allah, if Mu'adh really heard this from the Prophet ﷺ, then bless him and his family with this virtue.* The plague then entered his home and no one from his family was spared. When he saw the signs of the plague appearing on him, he smiled and said, *If someone had to give me red camels in exchange of this, it would not please me.*

A man began crying when he saw his condition. He asked him, *Why are you crying?* The man replied, *I am not crying over any worldly benefit which I acquired from you, rather I am crying at the loss of the 'ilm (knowledge) I used to gain from you.* He consoled him saying, *Don't cry over that. Look at Ibrahim ﷺ; he was born and brought up in places where there was no knowledge. Allah Most High blessed him with knowledge. After my demise, you should obtain knowledge from four: 'Abd Allah b. Mas'ud, Salman al-Farsi, 'Abd Allah b. Salam and Abu Darda ﷺ.*

He entered the isthmus in Jordan in 18 AH, at the age of 38. His son is buried close to him. Many visitors have commented on the beautiful fragrance that is present in the room where he is buried. Caretakers have insisted they have never applied anything there.

Nabi MUSA B. 'IMRAN ﷺ (INVOCATION 33)

The Prophet Moses son of Amram ﷺ—through whose Word descended the Wisdom of Sublimity *[al-hikmat al-'Uluwiyya]*—is the most frequently mentioned personage in the Qur'an at 136 times. The Qur'an states that he was sent by Allah to the Pharaoh of Egypt and his establishments, and to the Bani Isra'il for guidance and warning. His life is narrated and recounted more than that of any other prophet. His story is generally seen as a spiritual parallel to the life of the Prophet ﷺ, and Muslims consider many aspects of their lives to be shared. Islamic literature also describes a parallel between their believers and the incidents which occurred in their lifetimes. The exodus of the Israelites from Egypt is considered similar to the (migration) from Mecca made by the companions.

He is very important in Islam for having been given the revelation of the Torah. He was one of the many prophets that the Prophet ﷺ met during the nocturnal journey *[isra' mi'raj]*. He urged the Prophet ﷺ to request Allah for reduction in the number of obligatory daily prayers until only the five obligatory prayers remained. He is further revered in Islamic literature, which expands upon the incidents of his life and the miracles attributed to him in the Qur'an and *ahadith*, such as his direct conversation with Allah.

QABISA B. AL-MUKHARIQ, ABU BISHR B. 'ABD ALLAH B. SHADDAD AL-HILALI ؓ (INVOCATION 9)

A noble *sahabi*, he has narrated *ahadith* related to natural phenomena like the solar eclipse. No date is available for his passing.

AL-QUSHAIRI, ABU L-QASIM 'ABD AL-KARIM B. HUZAN AN-NAISABURI ؒ (INVOCATION 35)

(Imam) He was born in 376 AH (986 CE) into a privileged Arab family from among the Banu Qushair who had settled in the Khorasan Province. This region was widely known as a centre of Islamic civilization up to the 13th century. As a young man he received the education of a country squire of the time:

adab, the Arabic language, chivalry and weaponry *[isti'mal as-silah]*. It all changed when he journeyed to the city of Nishapur and was introduced to the Sufi Shaikh Abu 'Ali ad-Daqqaq. The latter became his master and teacher of the mystical ways. He later married the daughter of ad-Daqqaq, Fatima. After the death of his master, he became the successor of his master and father-in-law and became the leader of mystic assemblies in the madrasa that ad-Daqqaq had built in 1001 CE. This later became known as *al-Madrasa al-Qushairiyya* or "The School of the Qushairi family".

In later years he performed the pilgrimage in the company of Abu Muhammad al-Juwaini (d. 438/1047), the father of *Imam al-Haramain* al-Juwaini, as well as traveling to Baghdad and the Hejaz. During these travels he took *ahadith* from various prominent Hadith scholars. Upon his return he began teaching Hadith, which is something he is famous for. He returned to Baghdad where the Caliph al-Qa'im had him perform hadith teachings in his palace. After his return to Khorasan, political unrest in the region between the Hanafis and Ash'ari-Shafi'is in the city forced him to leave Nishapur, but he was eventually able to return and lived there until his passing in 1072/465, when the Seljuq vizier Nizam al-Mulk re-established the balance of power between the Hanafis and the Shafi'is. He left behind six sons and several daughters between Fatima and his second wife and was buried near *al-Madrasa al-Qushairiyya*, next to his father in-law.

Lata'if al-isharat bi tafsir al-Qur'an—a complete commentary of the Qur'an—is one of his famous works. He determined that there were four levels of meaning in the Qur'an. First, the *ibara* which is the meaning of the text meant for the mass of believers. Second, the *ishara*, only available to the spiritual elite and lying beyond the obvious verbal meaning. Third, the *lata'if*, subtleties in the text that were meant particularly for saints. And finally, the *haqa'iq*, which he said were only comprehensible to the prophets. This text placed him among the elite of the Sufis and is widely used as a standard of genuine, orthodox Sufi thought.

His wide renown is due mainly to his *ar-risala al-qushairiyya*, or "al-Qushairi's Epistle on Sufism". This text is essentially a reminder to the people of his era that Sufis had authentic ancestral tradition, as well as a defence of Sufism against the doubters who rose in that era. He repeatedly acknowledges his debt to, and admiration for, his Sufi master (ad-Daqqaq) throughout the work. The latter was instrumental in introducing him to another outstanding Sufi authority of Khorasan, Abu 'Abd ar-Rahman as-Sulami (412/1021), who is quoted on almost every page of the Risala. The work has sections where he discusses the creed of the Sufis, mentions important and influential Sufis from the past, and establishes fundamentals of Sufi terminology, giving his own interpretation of those Sufi terms. He finally goes through specific practices of Sufism and the techniques of those practices. This text has been used by many Sufi saints in later times as a standard, as is obvious from the many translations into numerous languages.

Imam al-'Arus SYED MUHAMMAD B. AHMAD LEBBAI

Known by the Arabic and Tamil epithets *Imam al-'Arus* and *Mappillai Lebbai 'Alim* respectively, he is Syed Muhammad b. Ahmad Lebbai b. Miran Lebbai b. Ahmad Sadaqah. He is a scion of a noble house, jurisconsult of the Shafi'i school, exponent of the Sunni creed, inheritor of the Qadiri mantle, Kayalite by birth and Kilakarian by migration—both being centres of Islam in South India.

He has penned in both prose and poetry at least 109 works on a multitude of subjects, of which most are extant. He was involved in constructing not less than 350 mosques, madrasas, maktabs and Sufi tekkes in South Asia. To recognise his immense contributions to religious upliftment and communal harmony in Sri Lanka, the Colombo Municipal Council renamed "Forbes Lane" in the Maradana suburb to "Imamul Aroos Mawatha".

The *Arusiyya* branch of the *Qadiriyya* spiritual path—widely followed in South India, Sri Lanka, the Middle East and Far East—is eponymously named after his Arabic epithet. His two sons, *sahib al-khalwa* Sayyid 'Abd al-Qadir and *sahib al-jalwa* Shah al-Hamid, were both savants and saints in their own right, with the latter becoming his successor. He is interred at the 'Arusiyya Tekke in Kilakarai, Tamil Nadu, India.

SHADDAD B. AWS, ABU 'ABD AR-RAHMAN (INVOCATION 25)

A revered *sahabi*, he was known to be an extremely tolerant person and would speak very little. He can be described in three words: eloquent, forbearing and wise. Abu ad-Darda' used to say that many people attain knowledge but do not have tolerance. Abu Ya'la i.e. Shaddad had both *ilm* (knowledge) and *hilm* (tolerance). He has narrated 50 *ahadith* on good deeds, morals and the Levant *[ash-sham]*. He is also known for his own statements which provide guidance.

Once he complained to the Prophet ﷺ about his straitened condition. The Prophet ﷺ made *du'a* for him and said, *Poverty will never become your lot. The Levant will be conquered and you will acquire booty in abundance. Your children will become the leaders of Bait al-Muqaddas.* This prophecy came to pass. After the conquest of the Levant, the booty was collected and an army of 500 men were delegated to transfer the goods to Medina so that the Caliph, *Sayyiduna* Abu Bakr ؓ, could see it with his own eyes. Shaddad was appointed the leader of the caravan.

He says, *As I reached Medina with the spoils of war, the people saw us from a distance and noticed the large caravan of people coming in. Abu Bakr enquired what the fuss was all about and he was informed that the Muslims were victorious and that Shaddad had arrived with the booty.* He first entered the mosque and performed two cycles, and thereafter made his way to the *rawda* of the Prophet ﷺ to give salutations *[salam].* Perhaps, at that moment, he thought of how he had once complained to the Prophet ﷺ regarding his poverty and that the prophecy of the Prophet ﷺ had indeed come true.

After the passing away of the Prophet ﷺ, he moved to Palestine. *Sayyiduna* 'Umar b. al-Khattab ؓ appointed him governor of Homs. After *Sayyiduna* 'Uthman b. 'Affan ؓ was killed, he isolated himself from the tribulations and devoted himself to worship. He entered the isthmus in Jerusalem in 58 AH, at the age of 55.

Nabi **SULAIMAN B. DAWUD** ؑ **(INVOCATION 2)**

The Prophet Solomon ؑ son of David ؑ—through whose Word descended the Wisdom of the Merciful Beatitude *[al-hikmat ar-rahmaniyya]*—was the Prophet-King of the Israelites; he was the third King of Jewish people and wise ruler for the nation. He is one of the elect of Allah; he was bestowed with many miraculous gifts, including the ability to speak with animals and jinn. He remained faithful to the one and only Creator and Sustainer and Cherisher throughout his life. He reigned justly over the whole of the Israelites and was blessed with a level of Kingship, the like of which was given to none after him and before him. He fulfilled all of His commandments, has been promised nearness to Allah in Paradise at the end of his life.

AS-SUYUTI, *Jalal ad-Din* 'ABD AR-RAHMAN B. ABU BAKR B. MUHAMMAD B. SABIQ AD-DIN AL-MISRI ASH-SHAFI'I AL-ASH'ARI ﵀ (INVOCATION 19)

(Imam) Jalal ad-Din as-Suyuti was an authoritative Imam *[mujtahid]* and renewer *[mujaddid]* of the tenth Islamic century. He was a Hadith Master, jurist, Sufi, philologist, and historian, who authored works in virtually every Islamic science. He was born to a Turkish mother and a father of Persian origin in 849 AH and entered the isthmus in 911 AH in Cairo where he had been raised as an orphan. He memorized the Qur'an at the age of eight, followed by several complete works of Sacred Law, fundamentals of jurisprudence and Arabic grammar. He then devoted his life to studying the Sacred Sciences under approximately 150 sheikhs. In the pursuit of knowledge, he travelled to Damascus, the Hejaz, Yemen, India and Morocco, as well as to centres of learning in Egypt such as Mahalla, Dumyat, and Fayyum.

He spent some time as the head teacher of Hadith at the Shaikhuniyya school in Cairo, at the recommendation of Imam Kamal ad-Din b. al-Humam. He then took up the same position at Baibarsiyya, but was dismissed due to complaints from other sheikhs whom he had replaced. After this, he retired into scholarly seclusion, and did not return to the field of teaching. Ibn Iyas, in *tarikh misr*, reveals that when he reached forty years of age, he abandoned the company of men for the solitude of the garden of al-Miqyas, by the side of the river Nile, where he avoided his former colleagues as though he had never known them. He was blessed with great success in his years of solitude, and made significant contributions in almost every field of Islamic knowledge. The editors of *dalil makhtutat as-suyuti* (Guide to as-Suyuti's Manuscripts) have listed 723 works to his name. Wealthy Muslims and princes would visit him with offers of money and gifts but he rejected them and also refused the Sultan many times when requested for his presence.

His chain of transmission in *tasawwuf* goes back to *Imam* 'Abd al-Qadir al-Jilani. He belonged to the *Shadhiliyya* path—a branch of the *Qadiriyya*—which he eulogized in his brief defence of *tasawwuf* entitled *tashyid al-haqiqa al-aliyya.* When one of his sheikhs, Burhan ad-Din Ibrahim b. 'Umar al-Biqai (d. 885), attacked Ibn 'Arabi in a tract entitled *tanbih al-ghabi ila takfir Ibn 'Arabi* (Warning to the Dolt That Ibn 'Arabi is an Apostate), he countered with a tract entitled *tanbih al-ghabi fi takhti'a Ibn 'Arabi* (Warning to the Dolt That Faults Ibn 'Arabi). In his reply, he states that he considers Ibn 'Arabi a *Friend of Allah* whose writings are forbidden to those who read them without first learning the technical terms used by the Sufis.

After a tremendously prolific life of scholarship, he entered isthmus at the age of sixty two. He was interred at Hawsh Qawsun in Cairo.

'UMAR B. AL-KHATTAB, ABU HAFS AL-QURASHI AL-'ADAWI ﵁

Born in Mecca in 577 CE, he was the second caliph. He was initially hostile towards Islam. Upon hearing that his sister had become Muslim, he went to her, questioning her about Islam, and demanding that she give him the parts of the Koran that she had. His sister refused, stating that he was unclean, and demanded that he wash before touching the parchment. Eventually he relented and, on receiving the Koran, he recited it, broke down, and accepted Islam. From that day forward he became one of the foremost companions of the Prophet Muhammad ﷺ.

His initial hostility was turned against those who opposed Islam and he openly prayed at the Ka'ba and protected others who did so too. Reflecting on these events, 'Abd Allah b. Mas'ud said: *'Umar's embracing Islam was our victory, his migration to Medina was our success, and his reign was a blessing from Allah. We didn't offer prayers in the masjid al-haram until 'Umar had accepted Islam. When he accepted Islam, the Quraish were compelled to let us pray in the Mosque.*

His reign as caliph saw a vast expansion of the Islamic empire and his following saying neatly sums his rule: *By Allah, he that is weakest among you shall be in my sight the strongest, until I have vindicated for him his rights; but him that is strongest will I treat as the weakest, until he complies with the laws.* Simplicity and duty were his guiding principles and impartiality and devotion the leading features of his administration. He had one mantle and one shirt, both conspicuous for their patchwork—a simple and symbolic attire adopted by later Sufis. He entered the isthmus as a martyr in 23 AH (644) in Medina after Abu Lu'lu al-Majusi stabbed him in his waist while he was performing the dawn prayer. After getting permission from Lady 'Aisha, he was interred by the side of the Prophet Muhammad ﷺ.

'UTHMAN B. 'AFFAN, ABU LAILA AL-QURASHI (INVOCATION 17)

Born in Taif in 576CE, he was the third caliph and twice son-in-law of the Prophet ﷺ, thus known as *dhu n-nurain* (possessor of the two lights). Upon becoming caliph, he led a simple life, despite a flourishing family business. Although offered a stipend from the public treasury, the *bait al-mal*, he never took any salary for his service as caliph. The compiling of the Qur'an into a *mushaf*—begun at the time of *Sayyiduna* Abu Bakr —was completed during his reign. He showed patience and endurance as leader of the Muslim community and made it his practice to free slaves every Friday, look after widows and orphans, and give extensively in charity.

He was a man of great modesty. The Prophet ﷺ said that even the angels are shy in his presence. Lady 'Aisha reports: *The Prophet ﷺ was lying down in his house with his thighs or his calves exposed. Abu Bakr asked permission to enter and was permitted while the Prophet ﷺ was in that position and he came in and spoke with him ﷺ. Then, 'Umar asked permission to enter. He was granted permission and came in and spoke with him ﷺ while in that position. Then, 'Uthman asked permission and the Prophet ﷺ sat up and straightened his clothing. He was then permitted and* came in and spoke with the Prophet ﷺ. After he had gone, I said: "Abu Bakr ؓ entered and you did not get up for him or worry about him. 'Umar ؓ came in and you did not get up for him nor worry about him. But when 'Uthman ؓ came in, you straightened out your clothing! The Prophet ﷺ said: "Should I not be shy of a man around whom the angels are shy?"

He was a virtuous man of truthful and respectful ways. The Prophet ﷺ informed him (and us) of two things regarding his future: (a) he would enter Paradise, and (b) he would be tested with a major calamity. In a poignant narration from his last days, he said: *They are threatening to kill me now... Why kill me? I heard the Messenger of Allah ﷺ say: "It is not lawful to kill a man who is a Muslim except for one of the three reasons: (a) Kufr (disbelief) after accepting Islam, (b) fornication after marriage, or (c) wrongfully killing someone, for which he may be killed." I swear by Allah, I have not committed fornication before or after the coming of Islam, nor did I ever want another religion for me instead of my religion since Allah gave guidance to me, nor have I killed anyone. So for what reason do you want to kill me?*

After an intense siege of his house by a group of rebels who sought his overthrow, he was assassinated in his house in Medina. It was three days before he was finally laid to rest at the Baqi' Graveyard in *Dhu l-Hijja* 35 AH (656)

ZAID B. THABIT ؓ (INVOCATION 3)

A noble *sahabi*, he was known as *katibun wahi* (one who writes down the revelations). He was also one of the top reciters [*qari'*] and memorisers [*hafiz*] of the Qur'an. He accepted Islam at the age of 10 or 11, when the Prophet ﷺ migrated to Medina.

He was too young to fight in the Battle of Badr; the Prophet ﷺ forbade him from fighting. He started crying and his mother was deeply saddened as well. When the Battle of 'Uhud came, he was again forbidden from participating. So his mother encouraged him to memorise the Qur'an instead. By the time the Prophet ﷺ returned from battle, he had already memorized 17 chapters of the Quran. His mother told the Prophet ﷺ, *O Messenger of Allah, this son of mine writes very well and is among the best of those who read. He reads the Qur'an just as you would read O Messenger of Allah.*

The Prophet ﷺ decided to test the young boy and found him better than the description his mother gave. The Prophet ﷺ said, *O Zaid, I want you to learn the Hebrew language, for we interact with the Jews and we want somebody trustworthy to communicate with them.* Just two weeks later, he returned and submitted, *O Messenger of Allah, I have learnt Hebrew and I have mastered it completely.* The Prophet ﷺ then asked him to learn the Syriac language—a dialect of Middle Aramaic. 17 days later, he mastered that language completely as well. After this, the Prophet ﷺ used to call him to write down the revelations as they descended from Jibril ؑ.

During the caliphate of *Sayyiduna* Abu Bakr ؓ he was assigned the role of authenticating and collating the oral and textual Qura'nic revelation into a single bounded volume. When he entered the isthmus, the people said, *By Allah, today we have buried so much of the knowledge the Prophet ﷺ bequeathed us.*

OBITUARY: SHAIKH DR THAIKA SHU'AIB ALIM

SHAIKH DR THAIKA SHUAIB B. AHMAD ABDUL QADIR *(SHAMS al-'Ulama')* b. Shahul Hamid *(Sahib al-Jalwah)* b. Sayyid Muhammad *(Imam al-'Arus)* was born in 1930 in Kilakarai—a historical town in the Coromandel Coast that is home to one of the oldest mosques in the world[11]. He hails from a distinguished family of saints and savants whose ancestors came from the Arab lands and settled in various coastal towns of South India.

His early education and development *[tarbiyyah]* was in his hometown, under the auspices of his noble father and Habib Muhammad Sadaqatullah[12] (renowned as *Pallak Waliyullah* or "the Palanquin Saint"). He then travelled extensively in India, South Asia, Middle East and North Africa where he sat with many *Awliya* and *'Ulama*—both privately and in institutions. He attained a Bachelor's degree in Sri Lanka and pursued his postgraduate studies in the USA where he attained a Masters, a Ph.D and a D.Litt.

He was fluent in Arabic, English, Malayalam, Persian, Tamil and Urdu. From Mevlana Rumi ﵀ to Shakespeare and from Arabic *Qasidas* to Urdu *Ghazals*, he had memorised hundreds of lines of poetry. He had a high command of the Tamil language

---

11 https://en.wikipedia.org/wiki/Palaiya_Jumma_Palli, http://www.heritageonline.in/kilakarai-the-oldest-mosque-in-india/

12 http://taqwa.sg/v/articles/the-palanquin-saint/

as attested to by his excelling in the examination conducted by the Thiruvaduthurai Adheenam in Tamil Nadu, India. His long association with countries in North Asia had also made him conversant in Cantonese and basic Japanese.

Professionally, he was based—at various points of his life—in Sri Lanka, Singapore (Malaya), Hong Kong, Thailand, Europe and the UAE. He began by working at a trading company before embarking on a wide array of businesses ranging from gemstones to mining. He used the prolonged stays in the various countries to engage in missionary *[da'wah]* activities and to work on his multi-decade spanning research on Arwi (or Arabic-Tamil).

Tamil Muslims of India, Sri Lanka and the world over are forever indebted to him for the recording of their rich history in an 824-page tome. It was a milestone work for which he earned many accolades and which has the unique honour of being released by the Presidents of 3 SAARC countries—India, Sri Lanka and Maldives. Prof Dr Torsten Tschacher of Berlin says about the work:

> There are some books that inspire you momentarily, by presenting a new idea that makes you reconsider the approach you are taking towards a topic, or that help you to formulate new questions. And then there are books to which you return again and again, for the wealth of information they present, so that whenever you open the book up, you discover something new or suddenly realise the importance of some fact that you had hitherto missed. (Dr Shu'ayb's) *Arabic, Arwi and Persian in Sarandib and Tamil Nadu* belongs to the latter kind of books.[13]

13 Excerpt from a Foreword by Prof Dr Torsten Tschacher for an upcoming reprint of Shaikh Dr Thaika Shuaib's *Arabic, Arwi and Persian in Sarandib and Tamil Nadu.*

In addition to his research work, he authored 5 major works and 8 minor treatises. He published 11 bilingual articles that addressed polemical issues that engulfed the Tamil Muslim community in the 80's and 90's. His arrangement of the 'Arusi–Qadiri liturgy *Ratib Jalaliyyah* has more than 100,000 copies in circulation while his devotional prayer book *al-Munjiyat* has had 6 prints of 37,000 copies since 2006.

In 1994, he was presented with the *National Award for Outstanding Arabic Scholar*—a first for a Tamil Muslim—by the 9th President of India, Dr Shankar Dayal Sharma. In 2016, the 7th President of Sri Lanka, Maithripala Sirisena, was the guest of honour at a function in Colombo to felicitate him for his services rendered to the Muslim community in Sri Lanka and for promotion of religious harmony in the country.

From 2013 to his passing in 2021, he was listed in *The 500 Most Influential Muslims* by Georgetown University's Prince Alwaleed Bin-Talal Center for Muslim-Christian Understanding and the Royal Islamic Strategic Studies Centre of Jordan. Up till his last breadth, he was the patron, founder, president and trustee of multiple institutions and associations in India, Sri Lanka and the Far East.

★ ★ ★

THE SHAIKH WAS AUTHORISED IN THE *QADIRIYYAH* SUFI PATH BY his father *Shaikh Thaika* Ahmad Abdul Qadir[14] (the *'Arusiyyah*

---

14 https://arusiqadiri.wordpress.com/02/02/2010/taika-ahmad-%e98%80%2abd-al-qadir/

branch) and *Shaikh Sayyid* 'Abdul Karim al-Kasnazan[15] (the *Kasnazaniyyah* branch). He was also vested with honorary and blessed mantles of the *Rifa'iyyah, Shadhiliyyah* and *Chishtiyyah.* Without making a show of his affiliations, he propagated only the *'Arusiyyah–Qadiriyyah* way.

After the passing of his father in 1976, he became responsible for the 'Arusi–Qadiri affiliated mosques, madrasas, tekkes *[zawiyah/khanqah]* and other organisations in South Asia and the Middle East. Whenever a construction, renovation or an upgrading work needed to be done for a mosque, madrasa or tekke building, he would be the first to contribute to the fundraising or completely pay for the expense.

His jovial personality, hand of largesse, breadth of knowledge, miracle working and making things easy for people endeared him to one and all. While he was lenient with others, he was always uncompromising on himself, ensuring that even the seemingly smallest *Sunnah* was established. He was steadfast in his adherence to the *Shari'ah* with absolutely no compromise on *Halal* and *Haram* and what is right and wrong.

He had the Prophetic quality of connecting with everyone at their level—be they saints or sinners, laity or leaders, Muslims or otherwise. For all his worldly achievements and honours, what really mattered and was of paramount importance to him was guiding the seekers *[salikin]* on the spiritual path and seeing his *muridin* and *muhibbin* reach the Goal.

His constant, ardent prayer was that his *muridin* reach the

---

15 http://kasnazanway.com/shaikhs/abd-al-karim-al-kasnazan/biography-of-shaikh-%ca%bfabd-al-karim-al-kasnazan/

Divine Presence, attain success in *dunya* and ultimate felicity in *akhirah*, partake in Allah's and the Prophet's ﷺ generosity, and realise Allah's and the Prophet's ﷺ love. This was his goal, his purpose and his meaning in life—every waking day.

⋆ ⋆ ⋆

THE SHAIKH LEFT *DAR AL-FANA'* FOR *DAR AL-BAQA'* JUST AFTER midnight on Tuesday, 15th of June, 2021 | 3rd *Dhu l-Qa'dah* 1442. His last words, as his *ruh* left his body, was invoking Allah by His Beautiful Name *Yā Wālī*. As he desired, he was interred by the feet of his forefathers رضي الله عنهم at the *'Arusiyyah Takyah* in Kilakarai, Tamil Nadu, India.

He has left a legacy that will be difficult to emulate and a vacuum that will be hard to fill. Much remains to be said and written about the Shaikh, his works, his philanthropy, his influence in the corridors of power, his impact across the strata of society and his charisms *[karamat]*. For now, we end with the words of the Prophet ﷺ:

ثَلَاثَةٌ لَا يَسْتَخِفُّ بِحَقِّهِمْ إِلَّا مُنَافِقٌ:
ذُو الشَّيْبَةِ فِي الْإِسْلَامِ، وَذُو الْعِلْمِ، وَإِمَامٌ مُقْسِطٌ.

There are three types of people which only a hypocrite treats lightly: someone who grew old in Islam; someone who possesses Islamic learning; and a just leader.[16]

16 Abu Dawud, Ibn Abi Shaiba, al-Bukhari in *al-Adab al-Mufrad*, al-Tabarani and al-Baihaqi.

The description in the *hadith* above fits him to the letter: he was 90 (93 *hijri*) years when he was veiled from *dunya*; he possessed sound Islamic learning; and he was a just leader for a community spanning the globe. Allah ﷻ be pleased with him and please him, sanctify his secret, and benefit us by him in both abodes. *Amin!*

NOTES & REFERENCES

[1] ALLAH MOST HIGH says: ❬*When you read the Qur'an, seek Allah's protection from Satan the rejected one.*❭ (*an-nahl*, 16:98)

Allah Most High mandates that protection be sought from the accursed Satan before reading the Qur'an. If it applies to the Qur'an, it certainly applies when reading any other invocation and supplication.

The *isti'adha* in this invocation is an encompassing one from the following *hadith*: Narrated Abu Sa'id al-Khudri ﷺ:

> *When the Messenger of Allah ﷺ got up to pray at night [for tahajjud prayer] he uttered the takbir and then said: "Glory be to You, O Allah," and "Praise be to You," and "Blessed is You name," and "Exalted is Your greatness," and "there is no god but You." He then said: "There is no god but Allah" three times; he then said: "Allah is altogether great" three times; then "I seek refuge in Allah, All-Hearing and All-Knowing from the accursed devil, from his evil suggestion [hamz], from his puffing up [nafkh], and from his spitting [nafth]" He then recited [the Qur'an].* Abu Dawud said: It is said that this tradition has been narrated by 'Ali b. 'Ali from al-Hasan omitting the name of the Companion of the Prophet ﷺ. The misunderstanding occurred on the part of Ja'far. (Abu Dawud's *Sunan:* 775)

Sayyiduna ash-Shaikh 'Abd al-Qadir al-Jilani ﷺ mentions in his *ghunya* the following two *ahadith* from the Prophet ﷺ regarding seeking refuge:

1. Whosoever prays once for refuge with Allah, Allah will keep him safe throughout the whole of the day in which he makes the plea.
2. Lock the doors of sinful disobedience by offering the prayer for refuge with Allah *[bi l-isti'adha]*, and open the doors of worshipful obedience by invoking the Name of Allah *[bi t-tasmiya]*.

He ﷺ further writes that five benefits accrue to the servant of Allah from seeking refuge *[isti'adha]* with Him, namely the following:

1. Firm and constant adherence to the true religion and to right guidance *[ath-thabat 'ala d-din wa l-huda]*
2. Salvation from the evil of [Satan] the damned and from trouble and distress *[as-salama mina l-a'in wa l-'ana]*
3. Gaining admittance to the impregnable fortress and proximity [of the Divine Protector] *[ad-dukhul fi l-hisn al-hasin wa z-zulfa]*
4. Attaining to the *secure station* (see 44:51) in the company of the Prophets, veracious, martyrs and righteous *[al-wusul ila l-maqami l-amini ma'a n-nabiyyina wa s-siddiqina wa sh-shuhada' wa s-salihin]*
5. Obtaining the help and support of the Lord of the earth and the heaven *[nail ma'unati rabbi l-ard wa s-sama']*

﴿فَإِذَا قَرَأْتَ الْقُرْآنَ فَاسْتَعِذْ بِاللَّهِ مِنَ الشَّيْطَانِ الرَّجِيمِ﴾ (٦١)النحل:٨٩

حَدَّثَنَا عَبْدُ السَّلَامِ بْنُ مُطَهَّرٍ، حَدَّثَنَا جَعْفَرٌ، عَنْ عَلِيِّ بْنِ عَلِيٍّ الرِّفَاعِيِّ، عَنْ أَبِي الْمُتَوَكِّلِ النَّاجِيِّ، عَنْ أَبِي سَعِيدٍ الْخُدْرِيِّ، قَالَ كَانَ رَسُولُ اللَّهِ ﷺ إِذَا قَامَ مِنَ اللَّيْلِ كَبَّرَ ثُمَّ يَقُولُ «سُبْحَانَكَ اللَّهُمَّ وَبِحَمْدِكَ وَتَبَارَكَ اسْمُكَ وَتَعَالَى جَدُّكَ وَلَا إِلَهَ غَيْرُكَ» ثُمَّ يَقُولُ «لَا إِلَهَ إِلَّا اللَّهُ» ثَلَاثًا ثُمَّ يَقُولُ «اللَّهُ أَكْبَرُ كَبِيرًا» ثَلَاثًا «أَعُوذُ بِاللَّهِ السَّمِيعِ الْعَلِيمِ مِنَ الشَّيْطَانِ الرَّجِيمِ مِنْ هَمْزِهِ وَنَفْخِهِ وَنَفْثِهِ» ثُمَّ يَقْرَأُ قَالَ أَبُو دَاوُدَ وَهَذَا الْحَدِيثُ يَقُولُونَ هُوَ عَنْ عَلِيِّ بْنِ عَلِيٍّ عَنِ الْحَسَنِ مُرْسَلاً الْوَهَمُ مِنْ جَعْفَرٍ. (سنن أبي داود: (٢)كتاب الصلاة:٥٨٣)

[2] ALLAH MOST HIGH says: ﴾*It is from Solomon, and it says, "In the name of Allah, the Universally Merciful, the Singularly Compassionate,*﴿ (*an-naml*, 27:30)

Abu al-Malih reported on the authority of a man ؓ: *I was riding on a mount behind the Prophet ﷺ. It stumbled. Thereupon I said: "May the devil perish!" He said: "Do not say, 'may the devil perish!' for when you say that, he will swell such that he will be like a house, and say: 'by my power'. But say, 'in the name of Allah' for when you say that, he will diminish such that he will be like a fly."* (Abu Dawud's *Sunan:* 4982 & Ahmad's *Musnad:* vol.5 pg.59 with a reliable chain; *majma' az-zawa'id:* vol.10 pg.132.)

After citing this *hadith, Hafiz* Ibn Kathir writes the following at the beginning of his monumental *tafsir* work: *This is the blessed effect of "bismillah". Therefore it is recommended at the beginning of every deed or speech.* This echoes the *hadith* of *Sayyiduna* Abu Huraira ؓ who reported that the Prophet ﷺ said: *Any matter of importance which is not begun with the remembrance of Allah and with basmala remains defective.*

By uttering the *basmala*, one acknowledges one's own utter weakness and total inability. Consequently, one's trust in the support and assistance of Allah strengthens. *Sayyiduna ash-Shaikh* 'Abd al-Qadir al-Jilani ؓ has an exhaustive section in his *ghunya* on the *basmala*. It is a monumental read. We relate two reports regarding the meaning of the words/letters that make up the *basmala*:

1. It is related that 'Uthman b. 'Affan asked the Messenger of Allah ﷺ about the interpretation of *"In the Name of Allah, the All-Merciful, Most Merciful."* He ﷺ said, "The *ba'* is the trial *[bala']* of Allah, His relief, brilliance and radiance *[baha']*. The *sin* is the splendour *[sana']* of Allah. The *mim* is the Kingdom *[mulk]* of Allah. As for *Allah*, there is no god but Him. *ar-Rahman* is kind to both the pious and impious of His creatures. *ar-Rahim* is kind only to the believers."

2. Ka'b al-Ahbar said, "The *ba'* is His radiance *[baha']*, the *sin* is His splendour *[sana']*, and there is nothing higher than it. The *mim* is His kingdom *[mulk]*, and He has power over all things and nothing is hard for Him."

﴿إِنَّهُ مِنْ سُلَيْمَانَ وَإِنَّهُ بِسْمِ اللَّهِ الرَّحْمَٰنِ الرَّحِيمِ﴾ (٧٢)النمل:٠٣

حَدَّثَنَا وَهْبُ بْنُ بَقِيَّةَ، عَنْ خَالِدٍ، - يَعْنِي ابْنَ عَبْدِ اللَّهِ - عَنْ خَالِدٍ، - يَعْنِي الْحَذَّاءَ - عَنْ أَبِي تَمِيمَةَ، عَنْ أَبِي الْمَلِيحِ، عَنْ رَجُلٍ، قَالَ كُنْتُ رَدِيفَ النَّبِيِّ ﷺ فَعَثَرَتْ دَابَّتُهُ فَقُلْتُ تَعِسَ الشَّيْطَانُ . فَقَالَ «لَا تَقُلْ تَعِسَ الشَّيْطَانُ فَإِنَّكَ إِذَا قُلْتَ ذَلِكَ تَعَاظَمَ حَتَّى يَكُونَ مِثْلَ الْبَيْتِ وَيَقُولَ بِقُوَّتِي وَلَكِنْ قُلْ بِسْمِ اللَّهِ فَإِنَّكَ إِذَا قُلْتَ ذَلِكَ تَصَاغَرَ حَتَّى يَكُونَ مِثْلَ الذُّبَابِ».(سنن أبي داود: (٣٤) كتاب الأدب:٠١٢)

[3] ALLAH MOST HIGH says: ❮*A Messenger has come to you from among yourselves. Your suffering distresses him: he is deeply concerned for you and full of kindness and mercy towards the believers · If they turn away, say: 'Allah is enough for me: there is no god but He; I put my trust in Him; He is the Lord of the Supreme Throne.'*❯ (*at-tawba*, 9:128-129)

Narrated Zaid b. Thabit: *Abu Bakr sent for me and said, "You used to write the Divine Revelations for Allah's Messenger ﷺ; so you should search for (the Qur'an and collect) it." I started searching for the Qur'an till I found the last two Verses of surat at-tawba with Abu Khuzaima al-Ansari and I could not find these Verses with anybody other than him. [They were]: "Verily there has come unto you an Apostle [Muhammad] from amongst yourselves. It grieves him that you should receive any injury or difficulty ..."* (9:128-129). (Bukhari's *Sahih:* 4989)

Among the bounties of these two verses is that they were the last verses revealed to the heart of the Prophet ﷺ. *Sayyiduna ash-Shaikh* 'Abd al-Qadir al-Jilani ؓ begins his greatest prayer upon the Prophet *[as-salat al-kubra]* with these verses. Abu al-Qasim al-Ghafiqi in his *fada'il al-qur'an fi ragha'ib al-qur'an* mentions from 'Abd al-Malik b. Habib a narration from Muhammad b. Bakkar: *The Messenger of Allah ﷺ said: "Whoever recites regularly ❮laqad ja'akum rasulun min anfusikum...❯ till the end of the sura, will not die of destruction, violence, fire, or falling of iron."*

Shaikh 'Abdullahi Dan Fodio, in his *ta'lim al-anam*, says: In this verse is an indication that his people in Mecca were thoroughly aware of his nobility *[sharafahu]* and kindness *[fadlahu]* towards them, his truthfulness *[sidqahu]*, integrity *[amanatahu]*, his sincere advice to them *[nasihatahu lahum]*, and his concern in guiding them. They were aware of the intensity of dislike for what distresses them in this world and the Hereafter and his compassion and mercy towards those who believe. For He honoured him by giving him two of His own names: the kind, the compassionate *[ra'uf, rahim]*.

Faqih Bello says that whoever recites these two verses seven times at night will not die or be killed by means of iron, metal or steel during that day or night. Nor will death come upon him suddenly while he is in a state of heedlessness. He also informed that these two verses are among the blessings and miracles of the Qur'an which causes longevity and old age without senility or being decrepit.

About this it has been reported that a Muslim scholar who regularly recited these two verses (that end *surat at-tawba*) everyday repeatedly lived to the ripe old age of one-hundred and twenty years with physical health and well-being. When he finally died, he was praying the two *sunna* prayers before *subh*; and Allah Most High took his spirit with ease while he was in prostration.

The above are but a small subset of the benefits to be accrued from these two glorious verses. There are far too many *experiential* benefits that many savants and saints have described from the faithful reading of these verses in the morning and evening and at other times. These verses are vital for every seeking believer.

﴿لَقَدْ جَآءَكُمْ رَسُوْلٌ مِّنْ اَنْفُسِكُمْ عَزِيْزٌ عَلَيْهِ مَا عَنِتُّمْ حَرِيْصٌ عَلَيْكُمْ بِالْمُؤْمِنِيْنَ رَءُوْفٌ رَّحِيْمٌ ۞ فَاِنْ تَوَلَّوْا فَقُلْ حَسْبِيَ اللّٰهُ لَآ اِلٰهَ اِلَّا هُوَ عَلَيْهِ تَوَكَّلْتُ وَهُوَ رَبُّ الْعَرْشِ الْعَظِيْمِ﴾ (٩)التوبة: ١٢٨-١٢٩

حَدَّثَنَا يَحْيَى بْنُ بُكَيْرٍ، حَدَّثَنَا اللَّيْثُ، عَنْ يُونُسَ، عَنِ ابْنِ شِهَابٍ، اَنَّ ابْنَ السَّبَّاقِ، قَالَ اِنَّ زَيْدَ بْنَ ثَابِتٍ قَالَ اَرْسَلَ اِلَيَّ اَبُوْ بَكْرٍ رضي الله عنه قَالَ اِنَّكَ كُنْتَ تَكْتُبُ الْوَحْيَ لِرَسُوْلِ اللّٰهِ ﷺ فَاتَّبِعِ الْقُرْاٰنَ. فَتَتَبَّعْتُ حَتّٰى وَجَدْتُ اٰخِرَ سُوْرَةِ التَّوْبَةِ اٰيَتَيْنِ مَعَ اَبِي خُزَيْمَةَ الْاَنْصَارِيِّ لَمْ اَجِدْهُمَا مَعَ اَحَدٍ غَيْرَهُ ﴿لَقَدْ جَآءَكُمْ رَسُوْلٌ مِنْ اَنْفُسِكُمْ عَزِيْزٌ عَلَيْهِ مَا عَنِتُّمْ﴾ اِلٰى اٰخِرِهِ.(صحيح البخاري: (٩٤) كتاب فضائل القرآن: ١١)

وذكر أبو القاسم الغافقي في فضائل القرآن في رغائب القرآن لعبد الملك بن حبيب من رواية محمد بن بكار أن رسول الله ﷺ قال: من لزم قراءة: لقد جاءكم رسول من أنفسكم... إلى آخر السورة لم يمت هدما ولا غرقاً ولا حرقاً ولا ضرباً بحديدة.

[4] ALLAH MOST HIGH says: ❴*If they turn away, say: 'Allah is enough for me: there is no god but He; I put my trust in Him; He is the Lord of the Supreme Throne.'*❵ (*at-tawba*, 9:129)

Abu ad-Darda' ﷺ said: *If anyone says seven times morning and evening; "Allah suffices me: there is no god but He; I put my trust in Him; He is the Lord of the Supreme Throne", Allah will be sufficient for him against anything which grieves him, whether he is true or false in [repeating] them.* (Abu Dawud's *Sunan:* 5081 in *mawquf* form, Ibn as-Sunni: 71)

﴿فَإِن تَوَلَّوْا فَقُلْ حَسْبِيَ اللَّهُ لَا إِلَٰهَ إِلَّا هُوَ عَلَيْهِ تَوَكَّلْتُ وَهُوَ رَبُّ الْعَرْشِ الْعَظِيمِ﴾ (٩)التوبة: ٩٢١

حَدَّثَنَا يَزِيدُ بْنُ مُحَمَّدٍ الدِّمَشْقِيُّ، حَدَّثَنَا عَبْدُ الرَّزَّاقِ بْنُ مُسْلِمٍ الدِّمَشْقِيُّ، - وَكَانَ مِنْ ثِقَاتِ الْمُسْلِمِينَ مِنَ الْمُتَعَبِّدِينَ - قَالَ حَدَّثَنَا مُدْرِكُ بْنُ سَعْدٍ - قَالَ يَزِيدُ شَيْخٌ ثِقَةٌ - عَنْ يُونُسَ بْنِ مَيْسَرَةَ بْنِ حَلْبَسٍ عَنْ أُمِّ الدَّرْدَاءِ عَنْ أَبِي الدَّرْدَاءِ رَضِيَ اللَّهُ عَنْهُ قَالَ مَنْ قَالَ إِذَا أَصْبَحَ وَإِذَا أَمْسَى حَسْبِيَ اللَّهُ لَا إِلَهَ إِلَّا هُوَ عَلَيْهِ تَوَكَّلْتُ وَهُوَ رَبُّ الْعَرْشِ الْعَظِيمِ سَبْعَ مَرَّاتٍ كَفَاهُ اللَّهُ مَا أَهَمَّهُ صَادِقًا كَانَ بِهَا أَوْ كَاذِبًا .(سنن أبي داود: (٣٤) كتاب الأدب:٣٠٩)

[5] Muhammad b. Hassan said: Ma'ruf al-Karkhi told me, *"Shall I not teach you ten words: five for this world and five for the next? He who supplicates Allah with these words finds Allah (Exalted is He) by them." I said, "Write them down for me." He said, "No, but I shall repeat them to you as Bakr b. Khunais did for me. [Say] God is enough for me in my religion…"* (*ihya' 'ulum ad-din:* Book IX)

قال محمد بن حسان؛ قال لي معروف الكرخي رحمه الله ألا أعلمك عشر كلمات خمس للدنيا وخمس للآخرة من دعا الله عز وجل بهن وجد الله تعالى عندهن: قلت: اكتبها لي قال لا. ولكن أرددها عليك كما رددها علي بكر بن خنيس رحمه الله حسبي الله لديني حسبي الله لدنياي حسبي الله الكريم لما أهمني حسبي الله الحليم القوي لمن بغى علي حسبي الله الشديد لمن كادني بسوء حسبي الله الرحيم عند الموت حسبي الله الرءوف عند المسألة في القبر حسبي الكريم عند الحساب حسبي الله اللطيف عند الميزان حسبي الله القدير عند الصراط حسبي الله لا إله إلا هو عليه توكلت وهو رب العرش العظيم» وقد روي عن أبي الدرداء أنه قال «من قال في كل يوم سبع مرات «فإن تولوا فقل حسبي الله لا إله إلا هو عليه توكلت وهو رب العرش العظيم» كفاه الله عز وجل ما أهمه من أمر آخرته صادقاً كان أو كاذباً». (إحياء علوم الدين: (٩) كتاب الأذكار والدعوات)

[6] ALLAH MOST HIGH says: ❴*So glory be to Allah when you reach evening & when you rise in the morning; and to Him be praise, in the heavens and on earth, and at eventide and at noontide; He brings out the living from the dead, and brings out the dead from the living; and He gives life to the earth after it is dead; and thus shall you be risen up again [from dust].*❵ (*ar-rum*, 30:17-19)

Narrated 'Abd Allah b. 'Abbas ﷺ: The Prophet ﷺ said: *If anyone says in the morning: "So glory be to Allah in the evening and in the morning; to Him is the praise in the heavens and the earth, and in the late evening and at noon … thus shall you be brought forth," he will get that day what he has missed; and if anyone repeats these words in the evening he will get that night what he has missed.* ar-Rabi' transmitted it from al-Laith. (Abu Dawud's *Sunan*: 5076, Ibn as-Sunni: 56:79, and others)

﴿فَسُبْحَانَ اللهِ حِيْنَ تُمْسُوْنَ وَحِيْنَ تُصْبِحُوْنَ ۞ وَلَهُ الْحَمْدُ فِي السَّمَاوَاتِ وَالْأَرْضِ وَعَشِيًّا وَحِيْنَ تُظْهِرُوْنَ ۞

يُخْرِجُ الْحَيَّ مِنَ الْمَيِّتِ وَيُخْرِجُ الْمَيِّتَ مِنَ الْحَيِّ وَيُحْيِي الْأَرْضَ بَعْدَ مَوْتِهَا ۚ وَكَذٰلِكَ تُخْرَجُوْنَ﴾ (٣٠)الروم: ١٧-١٩

حَدَّثَنَا اَحْمَدُ بْنُ سَعِيْدٍ الْهَمْدَانِيُّ، قَالَ اَخْبَرَنَا ح، وَحَدَّثَنَا الرَّبِيْعُ بْنُ سُلَيْمَانَ، قَالَ حَدَّثَنَا ابْنُ وَهْبٍ، قَالَ اَخْبَرَنِي اللَّيْثُ، عَنْ سَعِيْدِ بْنِ بَشِيْرٍ النَّجَّارِيِّ، عَنْ مُحَمَّدِ بْنِ عَبْدِ الرَّحْمٰنِ الْبَيْلَمَانِيِّ، - قَالَ الرَّبِيْعُ ابْنُ الْبَيْلَمَانِيِّ - عَنْ اَبِيْهِ، عَنِ ابْنِ عَبَّاسٍ، عَنْ رَسُوْلِ اللهِ ﷺ اَنَّهُ قَالَ »مَنْ قَالَ حِيْنَ يُصْبِحُ ﴿ فَسُبْحَانَ اللهِ حِيْنَ تُمْسُوْنَ وَحِيْنَ تُصْبِحُوْنَ ۝ وَلَهُ الْحَمْدُ فِي السَّمٰوٰتِ وَالْأَرْضِ وَعَشِيًّا وَحِيْنَ تُظْهِرُوْنَ﴾ اِلٰى ﴿ وَكَذٰلِكَ تُخْرَجُوْنَ﴾ اَدْرَكَ مَا فَاتَهُ فِيْ يَوْمِهِ ذٰلِكَ وَمَنْ قَالَهُنَّ حِيْنَ يُمْسِيْ اَدْرَكَ مَا فَاتَهُ فِيْ لَيْلَتِهِ« . قَالَ الرَّبِيْعُ عَنِ اللَّيْثِ . (سنن أبي داود: (٣٤) كتاب الأدب:٣٠٤)

[7] Juwairiya reported that the Messenger of Allah ﷺ came out from (her apartment) in the morning as she was busy in observing her dawn prayer in her place of worship. He came back in the forenoon and she was still sitting there. He (the Holy Prophet) said to her: *You have been in the same seat since I left you.* She said: *Yes.* Thereupon Allah's Apostle ﷺ said: *I recited four words three times after I left you and if these are to be weighed against what you have recited since morning these would outweigh them and (these words) are: "Hallowed be Allah and praise is due to Him according to the number of His creation and according to the pleasure of His Self and according to the weight of His Throne and according to the ink (used in recording) words (for His Praise)."* (Muslim's *Sahih:* 2726 a/b)

حَدَّثَنَا قُتَيْبَةُ بْنُ سَعِيْدٍ، وَعَمْرٌو النَّاقِدُ، وَابْنُ اَبِيْ عُمَرَ، - وَاللَّفْظُ لِابْنِ اَبِيْ عُمَرَ - قَالُوْا حَدَّثَنَا سُفْيَانُ، عَنْ مُحَمَّدِ بْنِ عَبْدِ الرَّحْمٰنِ، مَوْلٰى اٰلِ طَلْحَةَ عَنْ كُرَيْبٍ، عَنِ ابْنِ عَبَّاسٍ، عَنْ جُوَيْرِيَةَ، اَنَّ النَّبِيَّ ﷺ خَرَجَ مِنْ عِنْدِهَا بُكْرَةً حِيْنَ صَلَّى الصُّبْحَ وَهِيَ فِيْ مَسْجِدِهَا ثُمَّ رَجَعَ بَعْدَ اَنْ اَضْحٰى وَهِيَ جَالِسَةٌ فَقَالَ » مَا زِلْتِ عَلَى الْحَالِ الَّتِيْ فَارَقْتُكِ عَلَيْهَا «. قَالَتْ نَعَمْ. قَالَ النَّبِيُّ ﷺ » لَقَدْ قُلْتُ بَعْدَكِ اَرْبَعَ كَلِمَاتٍ ثَلَاثَ مَرَّاتٍ لَوْ وُزِنَتْ بِمَا قُلْتِ مُنْذُ الْيَوْمِ لَوَزَنَتْهُنَّ سُبْحَانَ اللهِ وَبِحَمْدِهِ عَدَدَ خَلْقِهِ وَرِضَا نَفْسِهِ وَزِنَةَ عَرْشِهِ وَمِدَادَ كَلِمَاتِهِ«. (صحيح مسلم: (٨٤) كتاب الذكر والدعاء والتوبة والاستغفار:١٠٦)

[8] There are two recitals here from the venerable *Imam* Abu Hanifa ﵀:

[A] *'Allama* Najm al-Ghaiti reports that *Imam* Abu Hanifa ﵀ said: *I saw Allah in my dreams ninety-nine times. I told myself, "If I see Allah the hundredth time, I will ask Him how creation can attain salvation on the Day of Resurrection." Then I saw Allah the hundredth time and asked, "O my Lord, honoured is Your Proximity, exalted is Your Praise and sanctified are Your Names. How can creation attain salvation on the Day of Resurrection?" Allah replied, "Whoever reads in the morning and evening, 'Glorified be He, who is Infinite, Eternal, ...' will be saved from my punishment."*— (*muqaddamat nur al-'idda* pg.4; *imdiyya*; and others)

ذكر العلامة نجم الغيطي أن الإمام أبا حنيفة رَضِيَ اللهُ عَنْهُ قال : رأيت الله في منامي تسعة وتسعون مرة ، وبعدها قلت لنفسي ، لو رأيت الله في المرة المائه ، سأسأل الله كيف تكون النجاة والخلاص للخلق يوم القيامة ؟ وبعدها رأيت الله في المرة المائة ، وهكذا سألته ؟ أي ربي تعالى جدك و تقدست أسماؤك : كيف يكون للخلق النجاة والخلاص يوم القيامة ؟ فقال الله تعالى من قرأ في الصباح والمساء «سبحان أبدى الأبد ،سبحان الواحد الأحد ، سبحان الفرد الصمد ، سبحان رافع السماء بغير عمد ، سبحان من سوى الأرض على ماء جمد ، سبحان من قسم الرزق ولم ينسى أحد ، سبحان الذى لم يتخذ صاحبة ولا ولد ، سبحان

الذى لم يلد ولم يولد ولم يكن له كفواً أحد « سينجو من عذابي . (مقدمة نور الإيضاح ، صفحة اربعة)

[B] *Imam al-'Arus* ﵁ states in his *Maghani* that *Imam* Abu Hanifa ﵁ said that this invocation should be recited once after every prayer for preservation of faith. A slightly different first part of this is reported from Abu Turab an-Nakshabi. It is also attributed to *Imam* ash-Sha'rani. For our purpose, once in the morning and evening with the above recital suffices, *insha' Allah.*

قال أبوتراب النخشبي :رأيت النبي ﷺألف مرة وكلما سألته أن يعلمني شيئا يكون فيه نجاتي لم يزد في كل مرة على هذه الكلمات اللهم أحيني على الإسلام والسنة، وتوفني على الإيمان والتوبة (النجوم الزاهرة للحبيب العلامة زين بن سميط)

[9] Qabisa b. al-Mukhariq ﵁ asked the Messenger of Allah ﷺ *Teach me some words whereby Allah helps me; I have reached old age, and so cannot do many things which I used to do.*—The Messenger of Allah ﷺ said *Concerning your life of this world, say three times ... when you say these words, you shall be safe from sorrow, black leprosy, white leprosy, and semi-paralysis. As for your Afterlife, say ...* —He ﷺ continued *Verily when a man persists in [invoking with] them and does not forget them on the Day of Rising, four doors of Heaven are opened for him and he may enter through whichever he likes.* (*ihya' 'ulum ad-din:* Book IX)

There are two *ahadith*—one from Ahmad's *musnad* and another from various other collections—from which these recitals are taken. The Arabic of the *ahadith* are appended below the quote from the *ihya'*.

دعاء قبيصة بن المخارق إذ قال لرسول الله ﷺ «علمني كلمات ينفعني الله عَزَّوَجَلَّ بها فقد كبر سني وعجزت عن أشياء كثيرة كنت أعملها فقال عليه السلام: أما لدنياك فإذا صليت الغداة فقل ثلاث مرات سبحان الله وبحمده سبحان الله العظيم لا حول ولا قوة إلا بالله العلي العظيم فإنك إذا قلتهن أمنت من الغم والجذام والبرص والفالج. وأما لآخرتك فقل: اللهم اهدني من عندك وأفض علي من فضلك وانشر علي من رحمتك وأنزل علي من بركاتك. ثم قال ﷺ: أما إنه إذا وافى بهن عبد يوم القيامة لم يدعهن فتح له أربعة أبواب من الجنة يدخل من أيها شاء. (إحياء علوم الدين: (٩) كتاب الأذكار والدعوات. حديث إن قبيصة بن المخارق قال لرسول الله ﷺ علمني كلمات ينفعني الله بها فقد كبرت سني وعجزت الحديث أخرجه ابن السني في اليوم والليلة من حديث ابن عباس وهو عند أحمد في المسند مختصرا من حديث قبيصة نفسه وفيه رجل لم يسم)

عن رَجُل مِنْ اَهْلِ الْبَصْرَةِ ، عَنْ قَبِيْصَةَ بْنِ الْمُخَارِقِ، قَالَ: «اَتَيْتُ رَسُوْلَ اللهِ ﷺ، فَقَالَ لِيْ: يَا قَبِيصَةُ مَا جَاءَ بِكَ؟ قُلْتُ : كَبِرَتْ سِنِّيْ ، وَرَقَّ عَظْمِيْ ، فَاَتَيْتُكَ لِتُعَلِّمَنِيْ مَا يَنْفَعُنِيْ اللهُ عَزَّ وَجَلَّ بِهِ ، قَالَ: يَا قَبِيْصَةُ ، مَا مَرَرْتَ بِحَجَرٍ، وَلَا شَجَرٍ ، وَلَا مَدَرٍ ، اِلَّا اسْتَغْفَرَ لَكَ، يَا قَبِيْصَةُ، إِذَا صَلَّيْتَ الْفَجْرَ ، فَقُلْ : سُبْحَانَ اللهِ الْعَظِيْمِ وَبِحَمْدِهِ ، تُعَافٰى مِنَ الْعَمٰى، وَالْجُذَامِ ، وَالْفَالِجِ ، يَا قَبِيصَةُ، قُلْ: اللّٰهُمَّ اِنِّيْ اَسْأَلُكَ مِمَّا عِنْدَكَ ، وَاَفِضْ عَلَيَّ مِنْ فَضْلِكَ ، وَانْشُرْ عَلَيَّ رَحْمَتَكَ ، وَاَنْزِلْ عَلَيَّ مِنْ بَرَكَاتِكَ. (رواه الإمام أحمد: ٢٠٦٠٢)

من طريق نَافِعِ بْنِ عَبْدِ اللهِ السُّلَمِيِّ ، عَنْ عَطَاءٍ ، عَنِ ابْنِ عَبَّاسٍ ، رَضِيَ اللهُ عَنْهُمَا قَالَ: « بَيْنَمَا نَحْنُ عِنْدَ رَسُولِ اللهِ ﷺ، اِذْ أَقْبَلَ شَيْخٌ يُقَالُ لَهُ قَبِيْصَةُ ، فَقَالَ لَهُ رَسُوْلُ اللهِ ﷺ : مَا جَاءَ بِكَ ، وَقَدْ كَبِرَتْ سِنُّكَ ، وَرَقَّ عَظْمُكَ ؟ فَقَالَ: يَا رَسُوْلَ اللهِ، كَبِرَتْ سِنِّيْ، وَرقَّ عَظْمِيْ، وَضَعُفَتْ قُوَّتِيْ، وَاقْتَرَبَ اَجَلِيْ . فَقَالَ: اَعِدْ عَلَيَّ قَوْلَكَ، فَاَعَادَ عَلَيْهِ، ثُمَّ قَالَ رَسُوْلُ اللهِ ﷺ : مَا بَقِيَ حَوْلَكَ شَجَرٌ، وَلَا حَجَرٌ، وَلَا مَدَرٌ، اِلَّا بَكٰى رَحْمَةً لِقَوْلِكَ ، فَهَاتِ حَاجَتَكَ ، فَقَدْ وَجَبَ حَقُّكَ؟ فَقَالَ: يَا رَسُوْلَ اللهِ، عَلِّمْنِيْ شَيْئًا يَنْفَعُنِيْ

اللّٰهُ بِهِ فِي الدُّنْيَا وَالْاٰخِرَةِ ، وَلَا تُكْثِرْ عَلَيَّ؛ فَاِنِّي شَيْخٌ نَسِيٌّ، قَالَ: اَمَّا لِدُنْيَاكَ، فَاِذَا صَلَّيْتَ الصُّبْحَ فَقُلْ بَعْدَ صَلَاةِ الصُّبْحِ : سُبْحَانَ اللّٰهِ الْعَظِيْمِ وَبِحَمْدِهِ ، وَلَا حَوْلَ وَلَا قُوَّةَ اِلَّا بِاللّٰهِ ، ثَلَاثَ مَرَّاتٍ، يُوَقِّيْكَ اللّٰهُ مِنْ بَلَايَا اَرْبَعٍ : مِنَ الْجُذَامِ ، وَالْجُنُوْنِ ، وَالْعَمٰى ، وَالْفَالِجِ فَاَمَّا لِاٰخِرَتِكَ ، فَقُلِ : اَللّٰهُمَّ اهْدِنِيْ مِنْ عِنْدِكَ ، وَاَفِضْ عَلَيَّ مِنْ فَضْلِكَ ، وَانْشُرْ عَلَيَّ مِنْ رَّحْمَتِكَ ، وَاَنْزِلْ عَلَيَّ مِنْ بَرَكَاتِكَ، فَقَالَهَا الشَّيْخُ ، وَعَقَدَ اَصَابِعَهُ الْاَرْبَعَ، فَقَالَ اَبُوْ بَكْرٍ، وَعُمَرُ: خَالُكَ هٰذَا يَا رَسُوْلَ اللّٰهِ ، مَا اَشَدَّ مَا ضَمَّ عَلٰى اَصَابِعِهِ الْاَرْبَعِ ، فَقَالَ رَسُوْلُ اللّٰهِ ﷺ : وَالَّذِي نَفْسِيْ بِيَدِهِ، لَئِنْ وَفّٰى بِهِنَّ يَوْمَ الْقِيَامَةِ لَمْ يَدَعْهُنَّ ، لَيُفْتَحَنَّ لَهُ اَرْبَعَةُ اَبْوَابٍ مِنَ الْجَنَّةِ ، يَدْخُلُ مِنْ اَيِّهَا شَاءَ. (الطبراني في «المعجم الكبير » (٩٤٠) ، وأبو نعيم في «المعرفة» (٥٧٤٢) ، وابن الأثير في «أسد الغابة» (٤/٣٦٦) ، وابن السني في «عمل اليوم والليلة» (١٣٣))

[10] Narrated Abu Bakra: ʿAbd ar-Rahman b. Abu Bakra said that he told his father: *O my father, I hear you supplicating every morning: "O Allah, grant me health in my body. O Allah, grant me good hearing. O Allah, grant me good eyesight. There is no god but Thou." You repeat them three times in the morning and three times in the evening.* His father said: *I heard the Messenger of Allah ﷺ using these words as a supplication and I like to follow his practice.* The transmitter, ʿAbbas, said in this version: *And you say: "O Allah, I seek refuge in Thee from infidelity and poverty. O Allah, I seek refuge in Thee from punishment in the grave. There is no god but Thee". You repeat them three times in the morning and three times in the evening, and use them as a supplication. I like to follow his practice.* He said: *The Messenger of Allah ﷺ said: "The supplications to be used by one who is distressed are: 'O Allah, Thy mercy is what I hope for. Do not abandon me to myself for an instant, but put all my affairs in good order for me. There is no god but Thou.'"* Some transmitters added more than others. (Abu Dawud's *Sunan:* 5090)

حَدَّثَنَا الْعَبَّاسُ بْنُ عَبْدِ الْعَظِيْمِ، وَمُحَمَّدُ بْنُ الْمُثَنّٰى، قَالَا حَدَّثَنَا عَبْدُ الْمَلِكِ بْنُ عَمْرٍو، عَنْ عَبْدِ الْجَلِيْلِ بْنِ عَطِيَّةَ، عَنْ جَعْفَرِ بْنِ مَيْمُوْنٍ، قَالَ حَدَّثَنِيْ عَبْدُ الرَّحْمٰنِ بْنُ اَبِيْ بَكْرَةَ، اَنَّهُ قَالَ لِاَبِيْهِ يَا اَبَةِ اِنِّيْ اَسْمَعُكَ تَدْعُوْ كُلَّ غَدَاةٍ اَللّٰهُمَّ عَافِنِيْ فِيْ بَدَنِيْ اَللّٰهُمَّ عَافِنِيْ فِيْ سَمْعِيْ اَللّٰهُمَّ عَافِنِيْ فِيْ بَصَرِيْ لَا اِلٰهَ اِلَّا اَنْتَ تُعِيْدُهَا ثَلَاثًا حِيْنَ تُصْبِحُ وَثَلَاثًا حِيْنَ تُمْسِيْ. فَقَالَ اِنِّيْ سَمِعْتُ رَسُوْلَ اللّٰهِ ﷺ يَدْعُوْ بِهِنَّ فَاَنَا اُحِبُّ اَنْ اَسْتَنَّ بِسُنَّتِهِ. قَالَ عَبَّاسٌ فِيْهِ وَتَقُوْلُ اَللّٰهُمَّ اِنِّيْ اَعُوْذُ بِكَ مِنَ الْكُفْرِ وَالْفَقْرِ اَللّٰهُمَّ اِنِّيْ اَعُوْذُ بِكَ مِنْ عَذَابِ الْقَبْرِ لَا اِلٰهَ اِلَّا اَنْتَ تُعِيْدُهَا ثَلَاثًا حِيْنَ تُصْبِحُ وَثَلَاثًا حِيْنَ تُمْسِيْ فَتَدْعُوْ بِهِنَّ فَاُحِبُّ اَنْ اَسْتَنَّ بِسُنَّتِهِ قَالَ وَقَالَ رَسُوْلُ اللّٰهِ ﷺ « دَعَوَاتُ الْمَكْرُوْبِ اَللّٰهُمَّ رَحْمَتَكَ اَرْجُوْ فَلَا تَكِلْنِيْ اِلٰى نَفْسِيْ طَرْفَةَ عَيْنٍ وَاَصْلِحْ لِيْ شَاْنِيْ كُلَّهُ لَا اِلٰهَ اِلَّا اَنْتَ ». وَبَعْضُهُمْ يَزِيْدُ عَلٰى صَاحِبِهِ .(سنن أبي داود: (٤٣) كتاب الأدب:٣١٨)

[11] Narrated Anas b. Malik ؓ: The Prophet ﷺ said: *If anyone says in the morning or in the evening: "O Allah, in the morning we call Thee, the bearers of Thy Throne, Thy angels and all Thy creatures to witness that Thou art Allah than Whom alone there is no god, and that Muhammad is Thy worshipful-servant and protected-messenger," Allah will emancipate his fourth from Hell; if anyone says twice, Allah will emancipate his half; if anyone says it thrice, Allah will emancipate three-fourth; and if he says four times, Allah will deliver him from Hell.* (Abu Dawud's *Sunan:* 5069)

ANOTHER: Narrated Anas b. Malik ؓ: the Prophet ﷺ said: *If anyone says in the morning: "O Allah, in the morning we call Thee, the bearers of Thy Throne, Thy angels and all Thy creatures to witness that Thou art Allah than Whom there is no god, Thou being alone and without a partner, and that Muhammad is Thy worshipful-servant and protected-messenger," Allah will forgive him any sins that he commits that day; and if he repeats them in the evening. Allah will forgive him any sins he commits that night.* (Abu Dawud's *Sunan:* 5078)

حَدَّثَنَا اَحْمَدُ بْنُ صَالِحٍ، حَدَّثَنَا مُحَمَّدُ بْنُ اَبِي فُدَيْكٍ، قَالَ اَخْبَرَنِي عَبْدُ الرَّحْمَنِ بْنُ عَبْدِ الْمَجِيْدِ، عَنْ هِشَامِ بْنِ الْغَازِ بْنِ رَبِيْعَةَ، عَنْ مَكْحُوْلٍ الدِّمَشْقِيِّ، عَنْ اَنَسِ بْنِ مَالِكٍ، اَنَّ رَسُوْلَ اللهِ ﷺ قَالَ «مَنْ قَالَ حِيْنَ يُصْبِحُ اَوْ يُمْسِي اللّٰهُمَّ اِنِّي اَصْبَحْتُ اُشْهِدُكَ وَاُشْهِدُ حَمَلَةَ عَرْشِكَ وَمَلاَئِكَتَكَ وَجَمِيْعَ خَلْقِكَ اَنَّكَ اَنْتَ اللهُ لَا اِلٰهَ اِلَّا اَنْتَ وَاَنَّ مُحَمَّدًا عَبْدُكَ وَرَسُوْلُكَ اَعْتَقَ اللهُ رُبْعَهُ مِنَ النَّارِ فَمَنْ قَالَهَا مَرَّتَيْنِ اَعْتَقَ اللهُ نِصْفَهُ وَمَنْ قَالَهَا ثَلَاثًا اَعْتَقَ اللهُ ثَلَاثَةَ اَرْبَاعِهِ فَاِنْ قَالَهَا أَرْبَعًا اَعْتَقَهُ اللهُ مِنَ النَّارِ».(سنن أبي داود: (٤٣)كتاب الأدب:٢٩٧)

حَدَّثَنَا عَمْرُو بْنُ عُثْمَانَ، حَدَّثَنَا بَقِيَّةُ، عَنْ مُسْلِمٍ، - يَعْنِي ابْنَ زِيَادٍ - قَالَ سَمِعْتُ اَنَسَ بْنَ مَالِكٍ، يَقُوْلُ قَالَ رَسُوْلُ اللهِ ﷺ «مَنْ قَالَ حِيْنَ يُصْبِحُ اللّٰهُمَّ اِنِّي اَصْبَحْتُ اُشْهِدُكَ وَاُشْهِدُ حَمَلَةَ عَرْشِكَ وَمَلاَئِكَتَكَ وَجَمِيْعَ خَلْقِكَ اَنَّكَ اَنْتَ اللهُ لَا اِلٰهَ اِلَّا اَنْتَ وَحْدَكَ لَا شَرِيْكَ لَكَ وَاَنَّ مُحَمَّدًا عَبْدُكَ وَرَسُوْلُكَ اِلَّا غُفِرَ لَهُ مَا اَصَابَ فِي يَوْمِهِ ذٰلِكَ مِنْ ذَنْبٍ وَاِنْ قَالَهَا حِيْنَ يُمْسِي غُفِرَ لَهُ مَا اَصَابَ تِلْكَ اللَّيْلَةَ».(سنن أبي داود: (٤٣) كتاب الأدب:٣٠٦)

[12] Abu Huraira ﷺ said, *In the morning, the Prophet ﷺ would say, "O Allah, We enter the morning by You and we enter the evening by You. We live by You and we die by You and to You is gathering." In the evening, he would say, "O Allah, we enter the evening by You and we enter the morning by You and we live by You and we die by You and to You is the return."* (Bukhari's *al-adab al-mufrad:* 1199)

ANOTHER: Abu Huraira ﷺ said, *The Messenger of Allah ﷺ used to teach his Companions, saying: "When one of you reached the morning, then let him say, 'O Allah, by You we enter the morning, and by You we enter the evening, and be You we live, and by You we died, and to You is the Return.' And when he reaches the evening let him say, 'O Allah, by You we enter the evening, and by You we enter the morning, and by You we live, and by You we die, and to You is the Resurrection.'"* (Tirmidhi's *Jami'*: 3391, Abu Dawud's *Sunan*: 5068, Ibn Maja's *Sunan*: 3868 and others. It was graded as *sahih* by Ibn Hajar as in *futuhat ar-rabbaniyyah*: 3/86. Some versions of the narration have *nushur* mentioned for both morn and eve.)

حَدَّثَنَا مُعَلًّى، قَالَ: حَدَّثَنَا وُهَيْبٌ، قَالَ: حَدَّثَنَا سُهَيْلُ بْنُ اَبِي صَالِحٍ، عَنْ اَبِيْهِ، عَنْ اَبِي هُرَيْرَةَ قَالَ: كَانَ النَّبِيُّ ﷺ اِذَا أَصْبَحَ قَالَ: اَللّٰهُمَّ بِكَ اَصْبَحْنَا، وَبِكَ اَمْسَيْنَا، وَبِكَ نَحْيَا، وَبِكَ نَمُوْتُ، وَاِلَيْكَ النُّشُوْرُ، وَاِذَا اَمْسَى قَالَ: اَللّٰهُمَّ بِكَ أَمْسَيْنَا، وَبِكَ اَصْبَحْنَا، وَبِكَ نَحْيَا، وَبِكَ نَمُوْتُ، وَاِلَيْكَ الْمَصِيْرُ. (الأدب المفرد: كتاب الصباح والمساء:١١٩٩)

حَدَّثَنَا عَلِيُّ بْنُ حُجْرٍ، حَدَّثَنَا عَبْدُ اللهِ بْنُ جَعْفَرٍ، اَخْبَرَنَا سُهَيْلُ بْنُ اَبِي صَالِحٍ، عَنْ اَبِيْهِ، عَنْ اَبِي هُرَيْرَةَ، قَالَ كَانَ رَسُوْلُ اللهِ ﷺ يُعَلِّمُ اَصْحَابَهُ يَقُوْلُ «اِذَا اَصْبَحَ اَحَدُكُمْ فَلْيَقُلِ اللّٰهُمَّ بِكَ اَصْبَحْنَا وَبِكَ اَمْسَيْنَا وَبِكَ نَحْيَا وَبِكَ نَمُوْتُ وَاِلَيْكَ الْمَصِيْرُ. وَاِذَا اَمْسَى فَلْيَقُلِ اللّٰهُمَّ بِكَ اَمْسَيْنَا وَبِكَ اَصْبَحْنَا وَبِكَ نَحْيَا وَبِكَ نَمُوْتُ وَاِلَيْكَ النُّشُوْرُ» . قَالَ اَبُوْ عِيْسٰى هٰذَا حَدِيْثٌ حَسَنٌ . (جامع الترمذي: (٤٨) كتاب الدعوات عن رسول الله ﷺ:٢٢)

[13] ALLAH MOST HIGH says: ﴾*Remember that He promised, "If you are thankful, I will give you more, but if you are thankless, My punishment is terrible indeed."*﴿
(*ibrahim*, 14:7)

Narrated 'Abd Allah b. Ghannam ﷺ: The Prophet ﷺ said: *If anyone says in the morning: "O Allah, whatever favour has come to me, it comes from Thee alone Who has no partner; to Thee praise is due and thanksgiving," he will have expressed full thanksgiving for the day; and if anyone says the same in the evening, he will have expressed full thanksgiving for the night.* (Abu Dawud's *Sunan:* 5073) The version here is recorded in an-Nasa'i and Ibn as-Sunni.

﴿وَاِذْ تَاَذَّنَ رَبُّكُمْ لَئِنْ شَكَرْتُمْ لَاَزِيْدَنَّكُمْ وَلَئِنْ كَفَرْتُمْ اِنَّ عَذَابِيْ لَشَدِيْدٌ﴾ (١٤)إبراهيم: ٧

حَدَّثَنَا اَحْمَدُ بْنُ صَالِحٍ، حَدَّثَنَا يَحْيَى بْنُ حَسَّانَ، وَإِسْمَاعِيلُ، قَالاَ حَدَّثَنَا سُلَيْمَانُ بْنُ بِلاَلٍ، عَنْ رَبِيعَةَ بْنِ اَبِي عَبْدِ الرَّحْمٰنِ، عَنْ عَبْدِ اللّٰهِ بْنِ عَنْبَسَةَ، عَنْ عَبْدِ اللّٰهِ بْنِ غَنَّامٍ الْبَيَاضِيِّ، اَنَّ رَسُوْلَ اللّٰهِ ﷺ قَالَ «مَنْ قَالَ حِيْنَ يُصْبِحُ اللّٰهُمَّ مَا اَصْبَحَ بِيْ مِنْ نِعْمَةٍ فَمِنْكَ وَحْدَكَ لاَ شَرِيْكَ لَكَ فَلَكَ الْحَمْدُ وَلَكَ الشُّكْرُ. فَقَدْ اَدّٰى شُكْرَ يَوْمِهِ وَمَنْ قَالَ مِثْلَ ذٰلِكَ حِيْنَ يُمْسِيْ فَقَدْ اَدّٰى شُكْرَ لَيْلَتِهِ (» .(سنن أبي داود: (۴۳) كتاب الأدب:۳۰۱)

عَنْ عَبْدِ اللّٰهِ بْنِ غَنَّامٍ رضي الله عنه اَنَّ رَسُوْلَ اللّٰهِ ﷺ قَالَ: مَنْ قَالَ حِيْنَ يُصْبِحُ: اَللّٰهُمَّ مَا اَصْبَحَ بِيْ مِنْ نِعْمَةٍ اَوْ بِاَحَدٍ مِنْ خَلْقِكَ، فَمِنْكَ وَحْدَكَ لاَ شَرِيْكَ لَكَ، فَلَكَ الْحَمْدُ وَلَكَ الشُّكْرُ، فَقَدْ اَدّٰى شُكْرَ ذٰلِكَ الْيَوْمَ. (النسائي: عمل اليوم والليلة، ابن السني: (عمل اليوم والليلة)

[14] Both these invocations are from *Sayyida* Fatima az-Zahra al-Batul:

[A] Summary: *Imam* 'Ali sent Lady Fatima to the Messenger of Allah ﷺ to ask for some food as they were starving. He ﷺ told her that a fire was not lit [to cook food] in his own house for the past thirty days. He then offered to give her some goats or to teach her five words which Jibril had taught him ﷺ. Those words are the ones in this invocation. (at-Tabarani's *kitab ad-du'a*: 1047)

حَدَّثَنَا مُحَمَّدُ بْنُ نُصَيْرٍ الْاَصْبَهَانِيُّ، حَدَّثَنَا اِسْمَاعِيلُ بْنُ عَمْرٍو الْبَجَلِيُّ، حَدَّثَنَا سُفْيَانُ الثَّوْرِيُّ عَنْ عَبْدَةَ بْنِ اَبِي لُبَابَةَ عَنْ سُوَيْدِ بْنِ غَفَلَةَ قَالَ اَصَابَتْ عَلِيًّا رضي الله عنه فَاقَةٌ فَقَالَ لِفَاطِمَةَ رضي الله عنها لَوْ اَتَيْتِ رَسُوْلَ اللّٰهِ ﷺ فَسَأَلْتِيهِ وَكَانَ عِنْدَ اُمِّ اَيْمَنَ رضي الله عنها فَدَقَّتِ الْبَابَ فَقَالَ النَّبِيُّ ﷺ لِاُمِّ اَيْمَنَ اِنَّ هٰذَا لَدَقُّ فَاطِمَةَ وَلَقَدْ اَتَتْنَا فِيْ سَاعَةٍ مَا عَوَّدَتْنَا اَنْ تَأْتِيَنَا فِيْ مِثْلِهَا فَقُوْمِيْ فَافْتَحِيْ لَهَا الْبَابَ قَالَتْ فَفَتَحْتُ لَهَا الْبَابَ فَقَالَ يَا فَاطِمَةُ لَقَدْ اَتَيْتِنَا فِيْ سَاعَةٍ مَا عَوَّدْتِنَا اَنْ تَأْتِيْنَا فِيْ مِثْلِهَا فَقَالَتْ يَا رَسُوْلَ اللّٰهِ هٰذِهِ الْمَلاَئِكَةُ طَعَامُهَا التَّسْبِيْحُ وَالتَّحْمِيْدُ وَالتَّمْجِيْدُ فَمَا طَعَامُنَا قَالَ وَالَّذِيْ بَعَثَنِيْ بِالْحَقِّ مَا اقْتُبِسَ فِيْ اٰلِ مُحَمَّدٍ نَارٌ مُنْذُ ثَلاثِيْنَ يَوْمًا وَقَدْ اَتَانَا اَعْنُزٌ فَاِنْ شِئْتِ اَمَرْتُ لَكِ بِخَمْسَةِ اَعْنُزٍ وَاِنْ شِئْتِ عَلَّمْتُكَ خَمْسَ كَلِمَاتٍ عَلَّمَنِيْهِنَّ جِبْرِيْلُ عليه السلام اٰنِفًا قَالَتْ بَلْ عَلِّمْنِيَ الْخَمْسَ كَلِمَاتِ الَّتِيْ عَلَّمَكَهُنَّ جِبْرِيْلُ عليه السلام قَالَ قُوْلِيْ يَا اَوَّلَ الْاَوَّلِيْنَ يَا اٰخِرَ الْاٰخِرِيْنَ ذَا الْقُوَّةِ الْمَتِيْنَ وَيَا رَاحِمَ الْمَسَاكِيْنِ وَيَا اَرْحَمَ الرَّاحِمِيْنَ قَالَ فَانْصَرَفَتْ حَتّٰى دَخَلَتْ عَلٰى عَلِيٍّ رضي الله عنهما فَقَالَتْ ذَهَبْتُ مِنْ عِنْدِكَ اِلَى الدُّنْيَا وَاَتَيْتُكَ بِالْاٰخِرَةِ قَالَ خَيْرًا يَأْتِيْكِ (خَيْرًا يَأْتِيْكِ. (الطبراني: الدعاء: ۳۱۹/۱)

[B] Anas b. Malik reports that the Messenger of Allah ﷺ once said to Lady Fatima to recite the following, morning and evening: *"O Living, O Self-Subsistent, by Your mercy I beseech for help. correct for me all my affairs and do not entrust me to my myself for the blink of an eye."* (an-Nasa'i's *as-sunan al-kubra*, Chapter: *Actions of the Day and Night*, al-Hakim's *Mustadrak*: 1/545 who said it was *sahih* according to the criterion of the two Shaikhs, al-Bazzar's *kashf al-astar*: 3107, Ibn as-Sunni: 48, al-Baihaqi's *shu'ab*. al-Haithami said in *az-zawaid* (10/117) that its narrators were *sahih* other than 'Uthman b. Mawhib who is trustworthy.)

عن أنس بن مالك رضي الله عنه قال : قال النبي ﷺ لفاطمة رضي الله عنها ما يمنعك أن تسمعي ما أوصيك به ، أو تقولي إذا أصبحت وإذا أمسيت : يا حي يا قيوم برحمتك أستغيث ، أصلح لي شأني كله ، ولا تكلني إلى نفسي طرفة عين. رواه النسائي في «السنن الكبرى» (147/6) وفي «عمل اليوم والليلة» (رق/46) ، والحاكم في «المستدرك» (730/1) ، والبيهقي في «الأسماء والصفات» (112) ، وغيرهم. ولفظه في بعض الروايات : (أن تقولي إذا أصبحت وإذا أمسيت) .

[15] There are two different invocations for the morning and the evening:

[A] (MORNING) al-Hakim at-Tirmidhi ؒ is reported to have said *I saw Allah repeatedly in my dream. I said to Him "O Lord, I fear the cessation of faith. So He ordered me to recite this supplication* 41 *times between the Sunna of Subh and Fard of Fajr. And it is this: ya Hayyu ya Qayyumu..."*

Imam al-'Arus ؒ states in his *Maghani* that (the first part of) at-Tirmidhi's invocation be recited thrice after *salat al-fajr* for preservation of faith. He also mentions an *ahl al-bait tawassul du'a* for the same purpose which is followed by the second part of at-Tirmidhi's invocation. For our intent and purpose, once in the morning suffices, *insha' Allah*.

حاشية إعانة الطالبين على حل ألفاظ فتح المعين لشرح قرة العين بمهمات الدين لأبي بكر ابن السيد محمد شطا الدمياطي: وعن الترمذي الحكيم قال : رأيت الله في المنام مرارا فقلت له يا رب إني أخاف زوال الإيمان فأمرني بهذا الدعاء بين سنة الصبح والفريضة إحدى وأربعين مرة وهو هذا : يا حي يا قيوم يا بديع السموات والأرض يا ذا الجلال والإكرام يا الله لا إله إلا أنت أسألك أن تحي قلبي بنور معرفتك يا الله يا الله يا الله يا أرحم الراحمين.

There is also a blessed *hadith* that has these very words, as part of a larger supplication, for a different purpose. It was narrated that Anas b. Malik ؓ said: *I was sitting with the Messenger of Allah* ﷺ *and a man was standing and praying. When he bowed, prostrated and recited the tashahhud, he supplicated, and in his supplication he said: "Allahumma inni as'aluka bi-anna lakal-hamd, lailaha illa ant, al-mannanu badi'us-samawati wal-ard, ya dhal-jalali wal-ikram! Ya hayyu ya qayyum! Inni as'aluka." (O Allah, indeed I ask You since all praise is due to You, there is none worthy of worship but You, the Bestower, the Creator of the heavens and earth, O Possessor of majesty and honour, O Ever-living, O-Eternal, I ask of You.) The Prophet* ﷺ *said: "Do you know what he has supplicated with?" They said: "Allah* ﷻ *and His Messenger know best." He said: "By the One in Whose Hand is my soul, he called upon Allah by His greatest Name, which, if He is called by it, He responds, and if He is asked by it, He gives."* (an-Nasa'i's *Sunan:* 1300)

اَخْبَرَنَا قُتَيْبَةُ، قَالَ حَدَّثَنَا خَلَفُ بْنُ خَلِيْفَةَ، عَنْ حَفْصِ بْنِ اَخِيْ، اَنَسٍ عَنْ اَنَسِ بْنِ مَالِكٍ، قَالَ كُنْتُ مَعَ رَسُوْلِ اللهِ ﷺ جَالِسًا - يَعْنِيْ - وَرَجُلٌ قَائِمٌ يُصَلِّيْ فَلَمَّا رَكَعَ وَسَجَدَ وَتَشَهَّدَ دَعَا فَقَالَ فِيْ دُعَائِهِ اللّٰهُمَّ اِنِّيْ اَسْاَلُكَ بِاَنَّ لَكَ الْحَمْدَ لَا اِلٰهَ اِلَّا اَنْتَ الْمَنَّانُ بَدِيْعُ السَّمٰوَاتِ وَالْاَرْضِ يَا ذَا الْجَلَالِ وَالْاِكْرَامِ يَا حَيُّ يَا قَيُّوْمُ اِنِّيْ اَسْاَلُكَ . فَقَالَ النَّبِيُّ ﷺ لِاَصْحَابِهِ » تَدْرُوْنَ بِمَا دَعَا « . قَالُوا اللّٰهُ وَرَسُوْلُهُ اَعْلَمُ . قَالَ » وَالَّذِيْ نَفْسِيْ بِيَدِهِ لَقَدْ دَعَا اللّٰهَ بِاسْمِهِ الْعَظِيْمِ الَّذِيْ اِذَا دُعِيَ بِهِ اَجَابَ وَاِذَا سُئِلَ بِهِ اَعْطٰى «

(سنن النسائي: (١٣) كتاب السهو : ١٢٢

[B] (EVENING) Summary of a lengthy narration from 'Abd Allah b. 'Amr b. al-'As ؓ found in the *mustadrak* of al-Hakim an-Naisaburi ؒ: Jibril ؑ came to the Prophet ﷺ and said, *I have brought you a gift.* The Prophet ﷺ asked, *What is this gift?* Jibril ؑ then recited this beautiful supplication. The Prophet ﷺ then asked, *What is the reward for one who recites this supplication?* Jibril ؑ replied, *If all of the angels of the seven heavens were to come together to describe it, they would not succeed in describing it fully till the Day of Judgement. Each of them would describe something that the others did not. Among its rewards is that Allah says about the reciter, 'I reward him equal to what I have created in the seven heavens, in Paradise, in the Throne ['arsh], in the Footstool [kursi], as well as equal to the number of drops of rain and the amount of water in the sea and the number of pebbles and grains of sand.' Among its rewards is that Allah will give him the reward of all creation. Amongst its rewards is that Allah will give him the reward of seventy Prophets who had reached Messengership. And there are more.*

Though aspersions have been cast on the above narration's chain, this exceptional *gift* has found a special place in devotional circles. For our intent and purpose, once in the evening suffices, *insha' Allah.*

حدث الحاكم أبو عبد الله محمد بن عبد الله الحافظ إملاء غرة صفر سنة سبع وتسعين وثلاث مائة أنبأ أبو العباس محمد بن أحمد المحبوبي بمرو ثنا أحمد بن عيسى الطرطوسي وحدثنا أحمد بن سلمان الفقيه ببغداد ثنا إسماعيل بن إسحاق القاضي وحدثنا محمد بن صالح بن هانئ ثنا الفضل بن محمد الشعراني قالوا ثنا إسماعيل بن أبي أويس ثنا أحمد بن محمد بن داود الصنعاني أخبرني أفلح بن كثير ثنا بن جريج عن عمرو بن شعيب عن أبيه عن جده قال نزل جبريل ؑ إلى النبي ﷺ في أحسن صورة لم ينزل في مثلها قط ضاحكا مستبشرا فقال السلام عليك يا محمد قال وعليك السلام يا جبريل قال إن الله بعثني إليك بهدية كنوز العرش أكرمك الله بهن قال وما تلك الهدية يا جبريل فقال جبريل قل يا من أظهر الجميل وستر القبيح يا من لا يؤاخذ بالجريرة ولا يهتك الستر يا عظيم العفو يا حسن التجاوز يا واسع المغفرة يا باسط اليدين بالرحمة يا صاحب كل نجوى ويا منتهى كل شكوى يا كريم الصفح يا عظيم المن يا مبتدىء النعم قبل استحقاقها يا ربنا ويا سيدنا ويا مولانا ويا غاية رغبتنا أسألك يا الله أن لا تشوي خلقي بالنار فقال رسول الله ﷺ فما ثواب هذه الكلمات ثم ذكر باقي الحديث بعد الدعاء بطوله هذا حديث صحيح الإسناد فإن رواته كلهم مدنيون ثقات وقد ذكرت فيما تقدم الخلاف بين أئمة الحديث في سماع شعيب بن محمد بن عبد الله بن عمرو من جده. (المستدرك على صحيحين ، كتاب الدعاء)

[16] Abu Huraira ؓ reported that a person came to Allah's Messenger ﷺ and said: *Allah's Messenger, I was stung by a scorpion during the night. Thereupon he said: Had you recited these words in the evening: "I seek refuge in the Perfect Word of Allah from the evil of what He created," it would not have done any harm to you.* (Muslim's *sahih:* 2708 b & 2709 a, Malik's *muwatta*: 2/127, Abu Dawud's *Sunan*: 3899; Ibn Maja's *sunan*: 3518. at-Tirmidhi: 3600 relates it and graded it *hasan* in his *Jami'* with the additional mention of three times.)

Khawla bint Hakim as-Sulamiyya ؓ reported: *I heard Allah's Messenger ﷺ as saying: When any one of you stays at a place, he should say: "I seek refuge in the Perfect Word of Allah from the evil of that He created." Nothing would then do him any harm until he moves from that place.* (Ibn Maja's *sunan*: 3547)

Ibn as-Sunni said in his book: *Say three times "I seek refuge in the Perfect Word of Allah from the evil of what He created," and you will not be harmed.*

قَالَ يَعْقُوبُ وَقَالَ الْقَعْقَاعُ بْنُ حَكِيمٍ عَنْ ذَكْوَانَ أَبِي صَالِحٍ، عَنْ أَبِي هُرَيْرَةَ، أَنَّهُ قَالَ جَاءَ رَجُلٌ إِلَى النَّبِيِّ ﷺ فَقَالَ يَا رَسُولَ اللهِ مَا لَقِيتُ مِنْ عَقْرَبٍ لَدَغَتْنِي الْبَارِحَةَ قَالَ « أَمَا لَوْ قُلْتَ حِينَ أَمْسَيْتَ أَعُوذُ بِكَلِمَاتِ اللهِ التَّامَّاتِ مِنْ شَرِّ مَا خَلَقَ لَمْ تَضُرَّكَ » . (صحيح مسلم: (٤٨) كتاب الذكر والدعاء والتوبة والإستغفار: ٧٣

وَحَدَّثَنَا هَارُونُ بْنُ مَعْرُوفٍ، وَأَبُو الطَّاهِرِ، كِلاَهُمَا عَنِ ابْنِ وَهْبٍ، - وَاللَّفْظُ لِهَارُونَ - حَدَّثَنَا عَبْدُ اللهِ بْنُ وَهْبٍ، قَالَ وَأَخْبَرَنَا عَمْرٌو، - وَهُوَ ابْنُ الْحَارِثِ - أَنَّ يَزِيدَ بْنَ أَبِي، حَبِيبٍ وَالْحَارِثَ بْنَ يَعْقُوبَ حَدَّثَاهُ عَنْ يَعْقُوبَ بْنِ عَبْدِ اللهِ بْنِ الأَشَجِّ، عَنْ بُسْرِ بْنِ سَعِيدٍ، عَنْ سَعْدِ بْنِ أَبِي وَقَّاصٍ، عَنْ خَوْلَةَ بِنْتِ حَكِيمٍ السُّلَمِيَّةِ، أَنَّهَا سَمِعَتْ رَسُولَ اللهِ ﷺ يَقُولُ « إِذَا نَزَلَ أَحَدُكُمْ مَنْزِلاً فَلْيَقُلْ أَعُوذُ بِكَلِمَاتِ اللهِ التَّامَّاتِ مِنْ شَرِّ مَا خَلَقَ . فَإِنَّهُ لاَ يَضُرُّهُ شَىْءٌ حَتَّى يَرْتَحِلَ مِنْهُ » . (سنن ابن ماجه: (٣١)باب الْفَزَعِ وَالأَرَقِ وَمَا يُتَعَوَّذُ مِنْهُ: ١١٢)

[17] Aban b. 'Uthman ؓ said: I heard 'Uthman b. 'Affan (his father) ؓ say: I heard the Messenger of Allah ﷺ say: *If anyone says three times: "In the Name of Allah, when Whose name is mentioned*

nothing on Earth or in Heaven can cause harm, and He is the All-Hearing, the All-Knowing," he will not suffer sudden affliction till the morning, and if anyone says this in the morning, he will not suffer sudden affliction till the evening. Aban was afflicted by some paralysis and when a man who heard the tradition began to look at him, he said to him: *Why are you looking at me? I swear by Allah, I did not tell a lie about 'Uthman, nor did 'Uthman tell a lie about the Prophet ﷺ, but that day when I was afflicted by it, I became angry and forgot to say them.* (Abu Dawud's *Sunan:* 5088, Tirmidhi's *Jami'* (3385) who said this *hadith* is *hasan sahih* and others)

It was narrated from Aban b. 'Uthman, from 'Uthman, that the Prophet ﷺ said: *He who says in the early part of his day or night three times: "In the Name of Allah, when Whose name is mentioned nothing on Earth or in Heaven can cause harm, and He is the All-Hearing, the All-Knowing," nothing will harm him in that day or that night.* (at-Tirmidhi's *jami'*:3385, Ahmad's *musnad:* 528, and others)

حَدَّثَنَا عَبْدُ اللهِ بْنُ مَسْلَمَةَ، حَدَّثَنَا اَبُو مَوْدُودٍ، عَمَّنْ سَمِعَ اَبَانَ بْنَ عُثْمَانَ، يَقُوْلُ سَمِعْتُ عُثْمَانَ - يَعْنِيْ ابْنَ عَفَّانَ - يَقُوْلُ سَمِعْتُ رَسُوْلَ اللهِ ﷺ يَقُوْلُ « مَنْ قَالَ بِسْمِ اللهِ الَّذِيْ لَا يَضُرُّ مَعَ اسْمِهِ شَيْءٌ فِي الْاَرْضِ وَلَا فِي السَّمَاءِ وَهُوَ السَّمِيْعُ الْعَلِيْمُ ثَلَاثَ مَرَّاتٍ لَمْ تُصِبْهُ فَجْأَةُ بَلَاءٍ حَتّٰى يُصْبِحَ وَمَنْ قَالَهَا حِيْنَ يُصْبِحُ ثَلَاثَ مَرَّاتٍ لَمْ تُصِبْهُ فَجْأَةُ بَلَاءٍ حَتّٰى يُمْسِيَ » . قَالَ فَاَصَابَ اَبَانَ بْنَ عُثْمَانَ الْفَالِجُ فَجَعَلَ الرَّجُلُ الَّذِيْ سَمِعَ مِنْهُ الْحَدِيْثَ يَنْظُرُ اِلَيْهِ فَقَالَ لَهُ مَا لَكَ تَنْظُرُ اِلَيَّ فَوَاللهِ مَا كَذَبْتُ عَلٰى عُثْمَانَ وَلَا كَذَبَ عُثْمَانُ عَلَى النَّبِيِّ ﷺ وَلٰكِنَّ الْيَوْمَ الَّذِيْ اَصَابَنِيْ فِيْهِ مَا اَصَابَنِيْ غَضِبْتُ فَنَسِيْتُ اَنْ اَقُوْلَهَا. (سنن أبي داود: (٤٣) كتاب الأدب:٣١٦)

حَدَّثَنَا عَبْدُ اللهِ، حَدَّثَنِيْ مُحَمَّدُ بْنُ إِسْحَاقَ الْمُسَيَّبِيُّ، حَدَّثَنَا اَنَسُ بْنُ عِيَاضٍ، عَنْ اَبِيْ مَوْدُوْدٍ، عَنْ مُحَمَّدِ بْنِ كَعْبٍ، عَنْ أَبَانَ بْنِ عُثْمَانَ، عَنْ عُثْمَانَ، اَنَّ النَّبِيَّ ﷺ قَالَ مَنْ قَالَ بِسْمِ اللهِ الَّذِيْ لَا يَضُرُّ مَعَ اسْمِهِ شَيْءٌ فِي الْاَرْضِ وَلَا فِي السَّمَاءِ وَهُوَ السَّمِيْعُ الْعَلِيْمُ ثَلَاثَ مَرَّاتٍ لَمْ تَفْجَأْهُ فَاجِئَةُ بَلَاءٍ حَتَّى اللَّيْلِ وَمَنْ قَالَهَا حِيْنَ يُمْسِيْ لَمْ تَفْجَأْهُ فَاجِئَةُ بَلَاءٍ حَتّٰى يُصْبِحَ اِنْ شَاءَ اللهُ. (مسند أحمد: (٤)مُسْنَدُ عُثْمَانَ بْنِ عَفَّانَ رضي الله عنه:١٢٠)

[18] It is said that whenever al-Khidr عليه السلام and Ilyas عليه السلام meet at each Hajj season, they never separate without uttering these words. He who mentions these words three times every morning is safe from conflagration, drowning, and burglary, if Allah wills. (*ihya' 'ulum ad-din:* Book IX)

يقال: إن الخضر وإلياس عليهما السلام إذا التقيا في كل موسم لم يفترقا إلا عن هذه الكلمات «بسم الله ما شاء الله لا قوة إلا بالله ما شاء الله كل نعمة من الله ما شاء الله الخير كله بيد الله ما شاء الله لا يصرف السوء إلا الله» فمن قالها ثلاث مرات إذا أصبح أمن من الحرق والغرق والسرق إن شاء الله تعالى. (إحياء علوم الدين: (٩) كتاب الأذكار والدعوات)

[19] *Imam* as-Suyuti رحمه الله once became very ill and could not get up from his bed. In this state, he saw a dream vision in which a most beautiful man came to him with others. The latter were initially in the form of heavenly birds before transforming into humans. They sat next to *Imam* as-Suyuti. The most beautiful man then said: *My son, read this du'a: bismillah, rabbiyallah, hasbiyallah* ... He read the *du'a* as instructed and was able to get up from his bed and perform *tahajjud* like he had not been ill at all. The most handsome man was none other than the Prophet ﷺ and the heavenly birds that had transformed into humans were *Sayyiduna* Hamza رضي الله عنه and the martyrs of Badr رضي الله عنهم. (*nuzhat al-basatin*)

al-Qadi Yusuf an-Nabhani رحمه الله in his *sa'adat ad-darain fi as-salati 'ala Sayyidi al-kawnain, Shaikh* 'Abd ar-Rahman as-Sufuri in his *nuzhat al-majalis wa muntakhab an-nasa'is* and others report that many Saints have reported that this invocation is a cure for illnesses, a solution for afflictions, a proven success over enemies, a remedy for witchcrafts and a solution for debts. Additionally, there is also an *athar* with these very words.

Imam al-Yafi'i relates a slightly different version in *mirat al-jinan* (1/57) from the *khalifa*: Mahdi al-'Abbasi from his father from his grandfather from Ibn 'Abbas ﷺ who attributed to the Prophet ﷺ that: *He who says in the morning and evening: Bismillahi wa billahi... will be protected and saved from fire, drowning and bad ending.*

وقال بعض الصالحين أصابني وجع شديد فرأيت النبي في المنام قد وضع يده على رأس وقال ... ثم قال استكثروا من هذه الكلمات فإن فيها شفاء من كل سقم وفرجا من كل كرب ونصرا على الأعداء.

حَدَّثَنَا مُحَمَّدُ بْنُ اَحْمَدَ بْنِ جَعْفَرِ الْكُوفِيّ، حَدَّثَنَا عِيسَى بْنُ حَمَّادٍ، اَخْبَرَنَا اللَّيْثُ عَنْ يَحْيَى بْنِ اَيُّوبَ بِهٰذَا الدُّعَاءِ اللّٰهُمَّ اِنِّيْ اَسْأَلُكَ بِمَعَاقِدِ الْعِزِّ مِنْ عَرْشِكَ وَبِسَعَةِ رَحْمَتِكَ مِنْ كِتَابِكَ وَبِمَا جَرٰى بِهِ قَلَمُكَ مِنْ عِلْمِكَ وَبِاسْمِكَ الْاَعْظَمِ وَجَدِّكَ الْاَكْبَرِ وَبِاَنَّكَ لَا اِلٰهَ اِلَّا اَنْتَ تَغْفِرَ لِيْ وَتَرْحَمَنِيْ مَا شَاءَ اللّٰهُ كَانَ وَمَا لَمْ يَشَأْ لَمْ يَكُنْ لَا حَوْلَ وَلَا قُوَّةَ اِلَّا بِاللّٰهِ مَا شَاءَ اللّٰهُ كَانَ وَمَا لَمْ يَشَأْ لَمْ يَكُنْ يَقُوْلُهُ فِيْ دُبُرِ صَلَاةِ الْعَصْرِ، وَاِذَا قَامَ، وَاِذَا قَعَدَ قَالَ بِسْمِ اللّٰهِ رَبِّيَ اللّٰهُ حَسْبِيَ اللّٰهُ تَوَكَّلْتُ عَلَى اللّٰهِ اعْتَصَمْتُ بِاللّٰهِ فَوَّضْتُ اَمْرِيْ اِلَى اللّٰهِ لَا حَوْلَ وَلَا قُوَّةَ اِلَّا بِاللّٰهِ اَللّٰهُمَّ اَنْتَ صَاحِبِيْ عِنْدَ كُلِّ شِدَّةٍ وَوَلِيِّ عِنْدَ كُلِّ نِعْمَةٍ وَكُلِّ كُرْبَةٍ. (مصالحة الإمام مسلم والإمام النسائي للدمياطي)

[20] 'Abd Allah b. Mas'ud ﷺ relates that a Bedouin once came to the Prophet ﷺ and said, *"I swear by Allah that I fear regarding my life, my progeny, my family, and my wealth."* The Messenger of Allah ﷺ said to him, *"Recite every morning and evening, 'bismillahi 'ala dini...'"* After some time the Prophet ﷺ inquired regarding his fears and he replied that his fears had all vanished. (Ibn Asakir's *Tarikh:* v.54, p.396. A similar, shorter version reported by Ibn Asakir with a *hasan* chain as in *jami as-saghir* (6140) and similar was reported by Ibn as-Sunni (51).)

ANOTHER: Ma'qal bin Yasar ﷺ narrates: *Once I expressed my fears to the Messenger of Allah ﷺ over five things in my life:* (1) *I feared that I would be misled or deviate from the Sirat al-Mustaqim,* (2) *the second was regarding my life; I feared harm or illness would befall me,* (3) *the third was about my children; that they would suffer religious or worldly harm,* (4) the *fourth was my wife; that she may suffer physical or spiritual harm, and* (5) *the fifth was over my wealth; should there occur a loss of income or property. After listening to my fears, the Messenger of Allah ﷺ taught me the following to be recited 3 times morning and evening, "bismillahi 'ala dini..."* (*kanz al-'ummal:* v.2, p.636)

عن ابن مسعود قال: أتى النبي ﷺ رجل فقال: يا رسول الله، والله إني لأخاف في نفسي وولدي وأهلي ومالي فقال له رسول الله ﷺ قل كلما أصبحت وإذا أمسيت: بسم الله على ديني ونفسي وولدي وأهلي ومالي، فقالهن الرجل، ثم أتى النبي ﷺ، فقال له رسول الله ﷺ: ما صنعت فيما كنت تجد؟ قال: والذي بعثك بالحق لقد ذهب ما كنت أجد. (تاريخ إبن عساكر، كنز العمال)

[21] This invocation appears with various wordings in multiple *ahadith* compendiums. (See: at-Tirmidhi's *Jami'*: 3389, Abu Dawud's *Sunan*: 5072 & 1529, Ibn Maja's *Sunan:* 3870, Ahmad, Tabarani, al-Hakim's *mustadrak*) an-Nawawi in *al-adhkar* mentions that it is desirable to combine between them. The version here—with the words *wa bi l-qur'ani imaman*—is one found in *Imam* al-Ghazali's *ihya' 'ulum ad-din* and so we have credited him for it.

BENEFIT: There are also *ahadith* which mention the virtue of reciting this invocation after the *adhan*. (See: Muslim: 386, at-Tirmidhi's *Jami'*: 210, Abu Dawud's *Sunan*: 525, an-Nasa'i's *Sunan*: 680, Ibn Maja's *Sunan:* 721)

قال ﷺ من قال حين يصبح رضيت بالله رباً وبالإسلام ديناً وبالقرآن إماماً وبمحمد ﷺ نبياً رسولاً كان حقاً على الله أن
(يرضيه يوم القيامة* وفي رواية من قال ذلك رضي الله عنه. (إحياء علوم الدين: كتاب الأذكار والدعوات
*حديث من قال حين يصبح رضيت بالله ربا الحديث أخرجه أبو داود والنسائي في اليوم والليلة والحاكم وقال صحيح الإسناد
من حديث خادم النبي ﷺ ورواه الترمذي من حديث ثوبان وحسنه وفيه نظر ففيه سعد بن المرزبان ضعيف جدا

[22] 'Abdullah b. Mas'ud ؓ reported that when it was evening, Allah's Messenger ﷺ used to supplicate with these words. There are three versions of the words, with slight variations, in *Sahih Muslim*:

"We entered upon evening and the whole Kingdom of Allah also entered upon evening and praise is due to Allah. There is no god but Allah, the One Who has no partner with Him." Hasan said that Zubaid reported to him that he memorised it from Ibrahim in these very words. *"His is the Sovereignty and Praise is due to Him, and He is Potent over everything. O Allah, I beg of Thee the good of this night and I seek refuge in Thee from the evil of this night and the evil which follows it. O Allah, I seek refuge in Thee from sloth, from the evil of vanity. O Allah, I seek refuge in Thee from torment in the Hell-Fire and from torment in the grave."*—(2723a)

"We have entered upon evening and so, too, the whole Kingdom of Allah has entered upon evening. Praise is due to Allah. There is no god but Allah, the One having no partner with Him." He (the narrator) said: I think that he also uttered (these words): *"His is the Sovereignty and to Him is praise due and He is Potent over everything. My Lord, I beg of Thee good that is in this night and good that follows it and I seek refuge in Thee from the evil that is in this night and from the evil of that which follows it. My Lord, I seek refuge in Thee from sloth, from the evil of vanity. My Lord, I seek refuge in Thee from torment of the Hell-Fire and from torment of the grave."* And when it was morning, he said like this: *"We entered upon morning and the whole Kingdom of Allah entered upon morning."*—(2723b)

"We have entered upon evening and so has the Kingdom of Allah entered upon evening; praise is due to Allah, there is no god but Allah the One, and there is no partner with Him. O Allah, I beg of Thee the blessing of this night and the blessing of that which lies in it. I seek refuge in Thee from the evil of it and what lies in it. O Allah, I seek refuge in Thee from sloth, from decrepitude, from the evil of vanity, from trial of the world, and from torment of the grave." Zubaid, through another chain of transmitters, has narrated on the authority of 'Abd Allah directly this addition: *"There is no god but Allah, the One, there is no partner with Him, His is the Sovereignty and to Him is praise due and He is Potent over everything."*—(2723c)

حَدَّثَنَا قُتَيْبَةُ بْنُ سَعِيدٍ، حَدَّثَنَا عَبْدُ الْوَاحِدِ بْنُ زِيَادٍ، عَنِ الْحَسَنِ بْنِ عُبَيْدِ اللَّهِ، حَدَّثَنَا إِبْرَاهِيمُ بْنُ سُوَيْدٍ النَّخَعِيُّ، حَدَّثَنَا عَبْدُ الرَّحْمَنِ بْنُ يَزِيدَ، عَنْ عَبْدِ اللَّهِ بْنِ مَسْعُودٍ، قَالَ كَانَ رَسُولُ اللَّهِ ﷺ إِذَا أَمْسَى قَالَ « أَمْسَيْنَا وَأَمْسَى الْمُلْكُ لِلَّهِ وَالْحَمْدُ لِلَّهِ لاَ إِلَهَ إِلاَّ اللَّهُ وَحْدَهُ لاَ شَرِيكَ لَهُ » . قَالَ الْحَسَنُ فَحَدَّثَنِي الزُّبَيْدُ أَنَّهُ حَفِظَ عَنْ إِبْرَاهِيمَ فِي هَذَا « لَهُ الْمُلْكُ وَلَهُ الْحَمْدُ وَهُوَ عَلَى كُلِّ شَىْءٍ قَدِيرٌ اللَّهُمَّ أَسْأَلُكَ خَيْرَ هَذِهِ اللَّيْلَةِ وَأَعُوذُ بِكَ مِنْ شَرِّ هَذِهِ اللَّيْلَةِ وَشَرِّ مَا بَعْدَهَا اللَّهُمَّ إِنِّي أَعُوذُ بِكَ مِنَ الْكَسَلِ وَسُوءِ الْكِبَرِ اللَّهُمَّ إِنِّي أَعُوذُ بِكَ مِنْ عَذَابٍ فِي النَّارِ وَعَذَابٍ فِي الْقَبْرِ » .(كتاب الذكر والدعاء والتوبة والاستغفار:١٠٠)

حَدَّثَنَا عُثْمَانُ بْنُ أَبِي شَيْبَةَ، حَدَّثَنَا جَرِيرٌ، عَنِ الْحَسَنِ بْنِ عُبَيْدِ اللَّهِ، عَنْ إِبْرَاهِيمَ، بْنِ سُوَيْدٍ عَنْ عَبْدِ الرَّحْمَنِ بْنِ يَزِيدَ، عَنْ عَبْدِ اللَّهِ، قَالَ كَانَ نَبِيُّ اللَّهِ ﷺ إِذَا أَمْسَى قَالَ « أَمْسَيْنَا وَأَمْسَى الْمُلْكُ لِلَّهِ وَالْحَمْدُ لِلَّهِ لاَ إِلَهَ إِلاَّ اللَّهُ وَحْدَهُ لاَ شَرِيكَ لَهُ » . قَالَ أُرَاهُ قَالَ فِيهِنَّ « لَهُ الْمُلْكُ وَلَهُ الْحَمْدُ وَهُوَ عَلَى كُلِّ شَىْءٍ قَدِيرٌ رَبِّ أَسْأَلُكَ خَيْرَ مَا فِي هَذِهِ اللَّيْلَةِ وَخَيْرَ مَا بَعْدَهَا وَأَعُوذُ بِكَ مِنْ شَرِّ مَا فِي هَذِهِ اللَّيْلَةِ وَشَرِّ مَا بَعْدَهَا رَبِّ أَعُوذُ بِكَ مِنَ الْكَسَلِ وَسُوءِ الْكِبَرِ رَبِّ أَعُوذُ بِكَ مِنْ عَذَابٍ فِي النَّارِ وَعَذَابٍ فِي الْقَبْرِ » وَإِذَا أَصْبَحَ قَالَ ذَلِكَ أَيْضًا « أَصْبَحْنَا وَأَصْبَحَ الْمُلْكُ لِلَّهِ » . (كتاب الذكر والدعاء والتوبة والاستغفار:١٠١).

حَدَّثَنَا أَبُو بَكْرِ بْنُ أَبِي شَيْبَةَ، حَدَّثَنَا حُسَيْنُ بْنُ عَلِيٍّ، عَنْ زَائِدَةَ، عَنِ الْحَسَنِ بْنِ، عُبَيْدِ اللَّهِ عَنْ إِبْرَاهِيمَ بْنِ سُوَيْدٍ، عَنْ عَبْدِ الرَّحْمَنِ بْنِ يَزِيدَ، عَنْ عَبْدِ اللَّهِ، قَالَ كَانَ رَسُولُ اللَّهِ ﷺ إِذَا أَمْسَى قَالَ » أَمْسَيْنَا وَأَمْسَى الْمُلْكُ لِلَّهِ وَالْحَمْدُ لِلَّهِ لاَ إِلَهَ إِلاَّ اللَّهُ وَحْدَهُ لاَ شَرِيكَ لَهُ اللَّهُمَّ إِنِّي أَسْأَلُكَ مِنْ خَيْرِ هَذِهِ اللَّيْلَةِ وَخَيْرِ مَا فِيهَا وَأَعُوذُ بِكَ مِنْ شَرِّهَا وَشَرِّ مَا فِيهَا اللَّهُمَّ إِنِّي أَعُوذُ بِكَ مِنَ الْكَسَلِ وَالْهَرَمِ وَسُوءِ الْكِبَرِ وَفِتْنَةِ الدُّنْيَا وَعَذَابِ الْقَبْرِ » . قَالَ الْحَسَنُ بْنُ عُبَيْدِ اللَّهِ وَزَادَنِي فِيهِ زُبَيْدٌ عَنْ إِبْرَاهِيمَ بْنِ سُوَيْدٍ عَنْ عَبْدِ الرَّحْمَنِ بْنِ يَزِيدَ عَنْ عَبْدِ اللَّهِ رَفَعَهُ أَنَّهُ قَالَ » لاَ إِلَهَ إِلاَّ اللَّهُ وَحْدَهُ لاَ شَرِيكَ لَهُ لَهُ الْمُلْكُ وَلَهُ الْحَمْدُ وَهُوَ عَلَى كُلِّ شَىْءٍ قَدِيرٌ (» . (كتاب الذكر والدعاء والتوبة والاستغفار:١٠٢

[23] Abu Huraira ؓ reported: Abu Bakr ؓ asked: *O Messenger of Allah, teach me some words so that I may recite them in the morning and in the evening.* The Messenger of Allah ﷺ said: Recite these words: *Allahumma fatira s-samawati wa l-ardi* ... The Messenger of Allah ﷺ added: *Recite these words in the morning and the evening and when you go to bed.* (Tirmidhi (3529); Abu Dawud (2392); Ibn as-Sunni (45); an-Nasai (11); al-Bukhari in *adab al-mufrad* (1202); an-Nawawi in *riyad as-salihin* (1454); al-Hakim (1/513) who graded its chain as *sahih* and adh-Dhahabi agreed)

وعنه أن أبا بكر الصديق رضي الله عنه قال: يا رسول الله مرني بكلمات أقولهن إذا أصبحت وإذا أمسيت، قال: قل: »اللهم فاطر السماوات والأرض عالم الغيب والشهادة، رب كل شيء ومليكه أشهد أن لا إله إلا أنت، أعوذ بك من شر نفسي وشر الشيطان وشركه» قال: »قلها إذا أصبحت، وإذا أمسيت، وإذا أخذت مضجعك». رواه أبو داود والترمذي وقال حديث حسن صحيح (سنن أبي داود: (٨) كتاب الوتر:١٤٠)

[24] Narrated Abu Sa'id al-Khudri ؓ: One day the Messenger of Allah ﷺ entered the mosque. He saw there a man from the Ansar called Abu Umama. He said: *What is the matter that I am seeing you sitting in the mosque when it is no time of prayer?* He said: *I am entangled in cares and debts, Messenger of Allah.* He replied: *Shall I not teach you words by which, when you say them, Allah will remove your care and settle your debt?* He said: *Why not, Messenger of Allah?* He said: *Say in the morn and eve: "O Allah, I seek refuge in Thee from care and grief, I seek refuge in Thee from incapacity and slackness, I seek refuge in Thee from cowardice and niggardliness, and I seek in Thee from being overcome by debt and being put in subjection by men."* He said: *When I did that Allah removed my care and settled my debt.* (Abu Dawud's *Sunan:* 1555)

حَدَّثَنَا اَحْمَدُ بْنُ عُبَيْدِ اللهِ الْغُدَانِيُّ، اَخْبَرَنَا غَسَّانُ بْنُ عَوْفٍ، اَخْبَرَنَا الْجُرَيْرِيُّ، عَنْ اَبِي نَضْرَةَ، عَنْ اَبِي سَعِيْدٍ الْخُدْرِيِّ، قَالَ دَخَلَ رَسُولُ اللهِ ﷺ ذَاتَ يَوْمٍ الْمَسْجِدَ فَاِذَا هُوَ بِرَجُلٍ مِنَ الْاَنْصَارِ يُقَالُ لَهُ اَبُوْ اُمَامَةَ فَقَالَ » يَا اَبَا اُمَامَةَ مَا لِيْ اَرَاكَ جَالِسًا فِي الْمَسْجِدِ فِيْ غَيْرِ وَقْتِ الصَّلاَةِ » . قَالَ هُمُوْمٌ لَزِمَتْنِيْ وَدُيُوْنٌ يَا رَسُوْلَ اللهِ . قَالَ » اَفَلاَ اُعَلِّمُكَ كَلاَمًا اِذَا اَنْتَ قُلْتَهُ اَذْهَبَ اللهُ عَزَّ وَجَلَّ هَمَّكَ وَقَضٰى عَنْكَ دَيْنَكَ » . قَالَ قُلْتُ بَلٰى يَا رَسُوْلَ اللهِ . قَالَ » قُلْ اِذَا اَصْبَحْتَ وَاِذَا اَمْسَيْتَ اللّٰهُمَّ اِنِّيْ اَعُوْذُ بِكَ مِنَ الْهَمِّ وَالْحَزَنِ وَاَعُوْذُ بِكَ مِنَ الْعَجْزِ وَالْكَسَلِ وَاَعُوْذُ بِكَ مِنَ الْجُبْنِ وَالْبُخْلِ وَاَعُوْذُ بِكَ مِنْ غَلَبَةِ الدَّيْنِ وَقَهْرِ الرِّجَالِ » . قَالَ (فَفَعَلْتُ ذٰلِكَ فَاَذْهَبَ اللهُ عَزَّ وَجَلَّ هَمِّيْ وَقَضٰى عَنِّيْ دَيْنِيْ. (سنن أبي داود: (٨) كتاب الوتر:١٤٠

[25] ALLAH MOST HIGH says: ❨*I said, "Ask forgiveness of your Lord: He is ever forgiving. He will send down abundant rain from the sky for you; He will give you wealth and sons; He will provide you with gardens and rivers."*❩ (*nuh*, 71:10-12)

﴾*And those who, having done something to be ashamed of, or wronged their own souls, earnestly bring Allah to mind, and ask for forgiveness for their sins,—and who can forgive sins except Allah?—and are never obstinate in persisting knowingly in (the wrong) they have done.*﴿ (al 'imran, 3:135)

Narrated Shaddad b. Aws ﵁: the Prophet ﷺ said, *the most superior way of asking for forgiveness from Allah is: "Allahumma anta Rabbi la ilaha illa anta, khalaqtani wa ana 'abduka, wa ana 'ala 'ahdika wa wa'dika mastata'tu, a'udhu bika min sharri ma sana'tu, abu'u laka bini'matika 'alayya, wa abu'u laka bidhanbi faghfir li fa innahu la yaghfiru adhdhunuba illa anta."* The Prophet ﷺ added, *if somebody recites it during the day with firm faith in it, and dies on the same day before the evening, he will be from the people of Paradise; and if somebody recites it at night with firm faith in it, and dies before the morning, he will be from the people of Paradise.* (Bukhari's *Sahih:* 6306, at-Tirmidhi's *Jami'*:3390, an-Nasa'i's *Sunan*: 8/279)

۞ يُرْسِلِ السَّمَآءَ عَلَيْكُمْ مِدْرَارًا ۞ فَقُلْتُ اسْتَغْفِرُوْا رَبَّكُمْ اِنَّهٗ كَانَ غَفَّارًا﴾
وَيُمْدِدْكُمْ بِاَمْوَالٍ وَبَنِيْنَ وَيَجْعَلْ لَكُمْ جَنّٰتٍ وَيَجْعَلْ لَّكُمْ اَنْهٰرًا﴾ (٧١)نوح:١٠-١٢

وَالَّذِيْنَ اِذَا فَعَلُوْا فَاحِشَةً اَوْ ظَلَمُوْا اَنْفُسَهُمْ ذَكَرُوا اللّٰهَ فَاسْتَغْفَرُوْا لِذُنُوْبِهِمْ﴾
وَمَنْ يَغْفِرُ الذُّنُوْبَ اِلَّا اللّٰهُ وَلَمْ يُصِرُّوا عَلٰى مَا فَعَلُوْا وَهُمْ يَعْلَمُوْنَ﴾ (٣)ال عمران:١٣٥

حَدَّثَنَا اَبُوْ مَعْمَرٍ، حَدَّثَنَا عَبْدُ الْوَارِثِ، حَدَّثَنَا الْحُسَيْنُ، حَدَّثَنَا عَبْدُ اللّٰهِ بْنُ بُرَيْدَةَ، عَنْ بُشَيْرِ بْنِ كَعْبٍ الْعَدَوِيِّ، قَالَ حَدَّثَنِيْ شَدَّادُ بْنُ اَوْسٍ ﵁ عَنِ النَّبِيِّ ﷺ » سَيِّدُ الْاِسْتِغْفَارِ اَنْ تَقُوْلَ اللّٰهُمَّ اَنْتَ رَبِّيْ، لَا اِلٰهَ اِلَّا اَنْتَ، خَلَقْتَنِيْ وَاَنَا عَبْدُكَ، وَاَنَا عَلٰى عَهْدِكَ وَوَعْدِكَ مَا اسْتَطَعْتُ، اَعُوْذُ بِكَ مِنْ شَرِّ مَا صَنَعْتُ، اَبُوْءُ لَكَ بِنِعْمَتِكَ عَلَيَّ وَاَبُوْءُ لَكَ بِذَنْبِيْ، فَاغْفِرْ لِيْ، فَاِنَّهُ لَا يَغْفِرُ الذُّنُوْبَ اِلَّا اَنْتَ «. قَالَ » وَمَنْ قَالَهَا مِنَ النَّهَارِ مُوْقِنًا بِهَا، فَمَاتَ مِنْ يَوْمِهِ قَبْلَ اَنْ يُمْسِيَ، فَهُوَ مِنْ اَهْلِ الْجَنَّةِ، وَمَنْ قَالَهَا مِنَ (اللَّيْلِ وَهُوَ مُوقِنٌ بِهَا، فَمَاتَ قَبْلَ اَنْ يُصْبِحَ، فَهُوَ مِنْ اَهْلِ الْجَنَّةِ «. (صحيح البخاري: (٨٠) كتاب الدعوات:٣

[26] Abu ad-Darda' ﵁ was told, *Your house has caught fire!* (for a fire had already broken out in his quarter). He said, *Allah will never do that!* He was told three times but he continued to say, *Allah will never do that!* Then someone came up to him and said, *O Abu ad-Darda', the fire went out when it came near your house!* He said, *I already knew that.* He was then told, *We do not know which of your two statements was more astonishing!* To which he said, *I heard the Messenger of Allah say, "If one says these words in the daytime or at night, nothing will hurt him." So I recited them. They are, "Allahumma anta Rabbi..."* (Ibn Asakir and ad-Dailami's *kanz al-ummal*: 2/163, at-Tabarani's *ad-Du'a*: 343, and Ibn as-Sunni: 56 & 57)

قيل لأبي الدرداء ﵁ : قد احترقت دارك - وكانت النار قد وقعت في محلته - فقال ما كان الله ليفعل ذلك، فقيل له ذلك ثلاثاً وهو يقول: ما كان الله ليفعل ذلك. ثم أتاه آت فقال: يا أبا الدرداء إن النار حين دنت من دارك طفئت، قال: قد علمت ذلك، فقيل له: ما ندري أي قوليك أعجب؟ قال: إني سمعت رسول الله ﷺ قال: من يقول هؤلاء الكلمات في ليل أو نهار لم يضره شيء وقد قلتهن وهي «اللهم أنت ربي لا إله إلا أنت عليك توكلت وأنت رب العرش العظيم ما شاء الله كان وما لم يشأ لم يكن لا حول ولا قوة إلا بالله العلي العظيم أعلم أن الله على كل شيء قدير وأن الله قد أحاط بكل شيء علماً وأحصى كل شيء عدداً. اللهم إني أعوذ بك من شر نفسي ومن شر كل دابة أنت آخذ بناصيتها ﴿إن ربي على صراط مستقيم﴾». (الطبراني، إبن السني)

[27] Anas b. Malik ؓ said the Messenger of Allah ﷺ would recite these prayers in the morning and evening: *Allahumma inni as'aluka min fuja'ati l-khair...* (Reported by Ibn as-Sunni (39). as-Suyuti graded it as *hasan* in *jami as-saghir*)

[28] Ibn 'Umar ؓ said: *The Messenger of Allah ﷺ would not leave these prayers in the evening and morning* '... (Reported by Abu Dawud (5074); an-Nasa'i (8/282); Ibn Hibban (3356 Mawarid) who graded it *Sahih*; al-Bukhari in *adab al-mufrad* and others. an-Nawawi said in al-*adhkar* (183) that its chains were *sahih*.

حَدَّثَنَا يَحْيَى بْنُ مُوسَى الْبَلْخِيُّ، حَدَّثَنَا وَكِيعٌ، ح وَحَدَّثَنَا عُثْمَانُ بْنُ أَبِي شَيْبَةَ، - الْمَعْنَى - حَدَّثَنَا ابْنُ نُمَيْرٍ، قَالاَ حَدَّثَنَا عُبَادَةُ بْنُ مُسْلِمٍ الْفَزَارِيُّ، عَنْ جُبَيْرِ بْنِ أَبِي سُلَيْمَانَ بْنِ جُبَيْرِ بْنِ مُطْعِمٍ، قَالَ سَمِعْتُ ابْنَ عُمَرَ، يَقُولُ لَمْ يَكُنْ رَسُولُ اللَّهِ ﷺ يَدَعُ هَؤُلاَءِ الدَّعَوَاتِ حِينَ يُمْسِي وَحِينَ يُصْبِحُ « اللَّهُمَّ إِنِّي أَسْأَلُكَ الْعَافِيَةَ فِي الدُّنْيَا وَالآخِرَةِ اللَّهُمَّ إِنِّي أَسْأَلُكَ الْعَفْوَ وَالْعَافِيَةَ فِي دِينِي وَدُنْيَاىَ وَأَهْلِي وَمَالِي اللَّهُمَّ اسْتُرْ عَوْرَتِي » . وَقَالَ عُثْمَانُ « عَوْرَاتِي وَآمِنْ رَوْعَاتِي اللَّهُمَّ احْفَظْنِي مِنْ بَيْنِ يَدَىَّ وَمِنْ خَلْفِي وَعَنْ يَمِينِي وَعَنْ شِمَالِي وَمِنْ فَوْقِي وَأَعُوذُ بِعَظَمَتِكَ أَنْ أُغْتَالَ مِنْ تَحْتِي » . قَالَ أَبُو دَاوُدَ قَالَ وَكِيعٌ يَعْنِي الْخَسْ.

[29] The Messenger of Allah ﷺ said to Lady 'Aisha ؓ, *You must use this perfect prayer whose use is general. Say, "Allahumma inni as'aluka min al-khairi kullihi..."* (Ahmad's *musnad:* 24590)

ANOTHER: It was narrated from 'Aisha that the Messenger of Allah ﷺ taught her this supplication: *"Allahumma inni as'aluka min al-khairi kullihi..."* (Ibn Maja's *Sunan:* 3846)

BENEFIT: *Imam al-'Arus* ؒ in his *maghani* recommends that this be recited once in the morning and once in the evening (together with the next *dhikr*).

حَدَّثَنَا مُحَمَّدُ بْنُ جَعْفَرٍ ، حَدَّثَنَا شُعْبَةُ ، عَنْ جَبْرِ بْنِ حَبِيبٍ ، عَنْ أُمِّ كُلْثُومٍ ، عَنْ عَائِشَةَ ، اَنَّ اَبَا بَكْرٍ دَخَلَ عَلَى رَسُوْلِ اللهِ ﷺ فَاَرَادَ اَنْ يُكَلِّمَهُ وَعَائِشَةُ تُصَلِّيْ ، فَقَالَ لَهَا رَسُوْلُ اللهِ ﷺ: عَلَيْكِ بِالْكَوَامِلِ ، اَوْ كَلِمَةً اُخْرٰى، فَلَمَّا انْصَرَفَتْ عَائِشَةُ سَأَلَتْهُ عَنْ ذٰلِكَ؟ فَقَالَ لَهَا : قُوْلِيْ: اَللّٰهُمَّ اِنِّيْ اَسْاَلُكَ مِنَ الْخَيْرِ كُلِّهِ عَاجِلِهِ وَاٰجِلِهِ مَا عَلِمْتُ مِنْهُ ، وَمَا لَمْ اَعْلَمْ ، وَاَعُوْذُ بِكَ مِنَ الشَّرِّ كُلِّهِ عَاجِلِهِ وَاٰجِلِهِ مَا عَلِمْتُ مِنْهُ ، وَمَا لَمْ اَعْلَمْ ، وَاَسْاَلُكَ الْجَنَّةَ وَمَا قَرَّبَ إِلَيْهَا مِنْ قَوْلٍ اَوْ عَمَلٍ ، وَاَعُوْذُ بِكَ مِنَ النَّارِ وَمَا قَرَّبَ اِلَيْهَا مِنْ قَوْلٍ اَوْ عَمَلٍ ، وَاَسْأَلُكَ مِنَ الْخَيْرِ مَا سَأَلَكَ عَبْدُكَ وَرَسُوْلُكَ مُحَمَّدٌ ﷺ وَاَسْتَعِيْذُكَ مِمَّا اسْتَعَاذَكَ مِنْهُ عَبْدُكَ وَرَسُوْلُكَ مُحَمَّدٌ ﷺ وَاَسْأَلُكَ مَا قَضَيْتَ لِيْ مِنْ اَمْرٍ اَنْ تَجْعَلَ عَاقِبَتَهُ رَشَدًا. حَدَّثَنَاهُ عَبْدُ الصَّمَدِ ، حَدَّثَنَا شُعْبَةُ ، حَدَّثَنَا جَبْرُ بْنُ حَبِيبٍ ، قَالَ : سَمِعْتُ اُمَّ كُلْثُوْمٍ بِنْتَ اَبِيْ بَكْرٍ ، تُحَدِّثُ : عَنْ عَائِشَةَ ، اَنَّ رَسُوْلَ اللهِ ﷺ قَالَ لَهَا : عَلَيْكِ بِالْجَوَامِعِ الْكَوَامِلِ فَذَكَرَ الْحَدِيثَ. حَدَّثَنَا عَفَّانُ ، حَدَّثَنَا حَمَّادُ بْنُ سَلَمَةَ، حَدَّثَنَا جَبْرُ بْنُ حَبِيبٍ ، عَنْ اُمِّ كُلْثُوْمٍ بِنْتِ اَبِيْ بَكْرٍ ، عَنْ عَائِشَةَ ، فَذَكَرَ نَحْوَهُ. (مسند أحمد: حَدِيثُ السَّيِّدَةِ عَائِشَةَ رَضِيَ اللهُ عَنْهَا: ٢٤٥٩٠)

حَدَّثَنَا اَبُوْ بَكْرِ بْنُ اَبِيْ شَيْبَةَ، حَدَّثَنَا عَفَّانُ، حَدَّثَنَا حَمَّادُ بْنُ سَلَمَةَ، اَخْبَرَنِيْ جَبْرُ بْنُ حَبِيبٍ، عَنْ اُمِّ كُلْثُوْمٍ بِنْتِ اَبِيْ بَكْرٍ، عَنْ عَائِشَةَ، اَنَّ رَسُوْلَ اللهِ ﷺ عَلَّمَهَا هٰذَا الدُّعَاءَ « اَللّٰهُمَّ اِنِّيْ اَسْاَلُكَ مِنَ الْخَيْرِ كُلِّهِ عَاجِلِهِ وَاٰجِلِهِ مَا عَلِمْتُ مِنْهُ وَمَا لَمْ اَعْلَمْ وَاَعُوْذُ بِكَ مِنَ الشَّرِّ كُلِّهِ عَاجِلِهِ وَاٰجِلِهِ مَا عَلِمْتُ مِنْهُ وَمَا لَمْ اَعْلَمْ اَللّٰهُمَّ اِنِّيْ اَسْاَلُكَ مِنْ خَيْرِ مَا سَاَلَكَ عَبْدُكَ وَنَبِيُّكَ وَاَعُوْذُ بِكَ مِنْ شَرِّ مَا عَاذَ بِهِ عَبْدُكَ وَنَبِيُّكَ اَللّٰهُمَّ اِنِّيْ اَسْاَلُكَ الْجَنَّةَ وَمَا قَرَّبَ اِلَيْهَا مِنْ قَوْلٍ اَوْ عَمَلٍ وَاَعُوْذُ بِكَ مِنَ النَّارِ وَمَا قَرَّبَ اِلَيْهَا مِنْ قَوْلٍ اَوْ عَمَلٍ وَاَسْاَلُكَ اَنْ تَجْعَلَ كُلَّ قَضَاءٍ قَضَيْتَهُ لِيْ خَيْرًا ». (سنن إبن ماجه: (٣٤) كتاب الدعاء:٢٠)

[30] Narrated Ma'qil b. Yasar ؓ: The Prophet ﷺ said: *Whoever says three times when he gets up in the morning: "a'udhu billahi s-sami al-'alim min ash-shaitani r-rajim" and he recites three verses from*

the end of Surat al-Hashr, Allah appoints seventy-thousand angels to say Salat upon him until the evening. If he dies on that day, he dies a martyr. The one who says it in the evening will have the same. (Tirmidhi's *jami'*: 2922, al-Baihaqi's *shuab al-iman* as in *kanz al-ummal*, ad-Darimi's *sunan*: 80, at-Tabarani's *al-kabir*. Tirmidhi said this *hadith* is *gharib* which we do not know except via this route.)

The Prophet ﷺ said: *"Whoever recites the last verses of al-Hashr during the day or night, and dies during that day or night, then Paradise is incumbent for him."* (al-Baihaqi's *shuab al-iman*: 2501, Ibn Adiyy's *al-kamil*: 3/318, as-Suyuti's *jami' as-saghir*: 1943)

Ibn 'Abbas narrated that the Prophet ﷺ said: *"The Great Names of Allah are in the last six verses of Surat al-Hashr."* (as-Suyuti's *jami' as-saghir*: 853)

Anas b. Malik narrated that the Prophet ﷺ advised a man to recite the last verse of *surat al-hashr* when he goes to bed. He ﷺ said: *"If you die, you will a martyr,"* or he said: *"you will be from the people of paradise."* (Ibn Sunni: 712)

Abu Umama narrated that the Prophet ﷺ said: *"If you die, you will a martyr,"* or he said: *"you will be from the people of paradise."* (Ibn Sunni: 712)

Anas b. Malik narrated that the Prophet ﷺ said: *"Whoever reads the last part of Surat al-Hashr, all his past and future sins will be forgiven."* (*al-khisal al-mukaffira*: 1/66)

BENEFIT: The Prophet ﷺ said to *Imam* 'Ali b. Abi Talib ؓ, *"O 'Ali, if you have headache, place your hand (on your head) and recite the last part of Surat al-Hashr."* (ash-shawkani's *al-fawa'id al-majmu'a*: 313). A similar narration from Ibn 'Abbas has been recorded by *Khatib* al-Baghdadi.

حَدَّثَنَا مَحْمُودُ بْنُ غَيْلَانَ، حَدَّثَنَا أَبُو أَحْمَدَ الزُّبَيْرِيُّ، حَدَّثَنَا خَالِدُ بْنُ طَهْمَانَ أَبُو الْعَلَاءِ الْخَفَّافُ، حَدَّثَنِي نَافِعُ بْنُ أَبِي نَافِعٍ، عَنْ مَعْقِلِ بْنِ يَسَارٍ، عَنِ النَّبِيِّ ﷺ قَالَ « مَنْ قَالَ حِينَ يُصْبِحُ ثَلَاثَ مَرَّاتٍ أَعُوذُ بِاللَّهِ السَّمِيعِ الْعَلِيمِ مِنَ الشَّيْطَانِ الرَّجِيمِ وَقَرَأَ ثَلَاثَ آيَاتٍ مِنْ آخِرِ سُورَةِ الْحَشْرِ وَكَّلَ اللَّهُ بِهِ سَبْعِينَ أَلْفَ مَلَكٍ يُصَلُّونَ عَلَيْهِ حَتَّى يُمْسِيَ وَإِنْ مَاتَ فِي ذَلِكَ الْيَوْمِ مَاتَ شَهِيدًا وَمَنْ قَالَهَا حِينَ يُمْسِي كَانَ بِتِلْكَ الْمَنْزِلَةِ » . قَالَ أَبُو عِيسَى هَذَا حَدِيثٌ غَرِيبٌ لَا نَعْرِفُهُ إِلَّا مِنْ هَذَا الْوَجْهِ . (جامع الترمذي: (٤٥) كتاب فضائل القرآن عنرسول الله ﷺ: ٣١٧٢)

[31] ALLAH MOST HIGH says: ﴾*Allah will find a way out for those who are mindful of Him, and will provide for them from an unexpected source; Allah will be enough for those who put their trust in Him. Allah achieves His purpose; Allah has set a due measure for everything.*﴿ (*at-talaq*, 65:2-3)

Abu Dharr al-Ghifari ؓ narrates the Messenger of Allah ﷺ says: *Indeed, I know a verse to which if the people held on it would be sufficient for them...* (Ahmad's *Musnad:* 21090, al-Hakim, al-Baihaqi, Ibn Marduya)

Ibn 'Abbas ؓ narrates the Messenger of Allah ﷺ says: *(After reciting the above verse) If the people were to apply this verse in their lives they would be free from all the doubt and distress of the world, the distress of death, and the distress of the Doomsday.* (Abu Nu'aim, Abu Ya'la)

This verse was revealed about 'Awf b. Malik al-Ashja'i whose son was imprisoned by the idolaters. He went to the Messenger of Allah ﷺ and complained to him about his poverty, saying: *The enemy has imprisoned my son and his mother is very distressed, what do you advise me to do?* The Prophet ﷺ said to him: *Be fearful of Allah and be patient. I also command you and your wife to often repeat 'there is no strength or might except by Allah'.* So he went home and said to his wife: *The Messenger of Allah ﷺ commanded both of us to often repeat 'there is no strength or might except by Allah'.* She said: *How good is that with which he has commanded us!* And they both started saying it straightaway. It happened that the enemy became distracted from their son and the latter led their sheep away and fled. He brought these sheep to his father; they were four thousand heads. This verse was revealed about this incident.

'Abd al-'Aziz b. 'Abdan informed us > Muhammad b. 'Abd Allah b. Nu'aim Abu l-Qasim al-Hasan b. Muhammad b. al-Husain as-Sakuni > 'Ubaid b. Kathir al-'Amiri > 'Abbad b. Ya'qub > Yahya b. Adam > Isra'il > 'Ammar b. Mu'awiyya > Salim b. Abi al-Ja'd > Jabir b. 'Abd Allah who said: *This verse was revealed about a man from Ashja'. This man was poor but had numerous children. He went to the Messenger of Allah ﷺ and asked him for help. The Prophet ﷺ told him: "Fear Allah and be patient!" The man went back to his companions and when they asked him about what the Prophet had given him, he said: "He did not give me anything; he simply said: Fear Allah and be patient." Not long after this, a son of this man, who had been captured by the enemy, brought him sheep. The man went to the Messenger of Allah ﷺ to ask him about what he should do with the sheep, and told him the full story. The Messenger of Allah ﷺ said to him: "Keep them, they are yours."* (al-Wahidi's *asbab an-nuzul:* 65:3)

Many savants have related from experience regarding the efficacy of these verses. Ahmed Hulusi writes in *The Power of Prayer: I personally have many experiences in regards to the benefits of this verse. Whoever is distressed or troubled, suffering from financial hardship or in a troublesome situation should recite this verse at least one thousand times a day, they will be delivered from that situation in no time. Anyone who is unemployed, in debt or is suffering family-related difficulties, in fact anyone who thinks they may be a victim of black magic, should definitely recite this verse for salvation and healing.* For the quick acceptance of *du'a,* one should recite the verses 500 or 250 times in one sitting and complete with *ya musabbiba l-asbab, sabbib,* three times. Allah Most High will accept the petition and remove the [financial] difficulty immediately, *Insha' Allah.*

وَمَن يَتَّقِ اللَّهَ يَجْعَل لَّهُ مَخْرَجًا ۞
وَيَرْزُقْهُ مِنْ حَيْثُ لَا يَحْتَسِبُ ۚ وَمَن يَتَوَكَّلْ عَلَى اللَّهِ فَهُوَ حَسْبُهُ ۚ
إِنَّ اللَّهَ بَالِغُ أَمْرِهِ ۚ قَدْ جَعَلَ اللَّهُ لِكُلِّ شَيْءٍ قَدْرًا﴾ (٦٥)الطلاق:٢-٣

حَدَّثَنَا يَزِيدُ ، حَدَّثَنَا كَهْمَسُ بْنُ الْحَسَنِ ، حَدَّثَنَا أَبُو السَّلِيلِ ، عَنْ أَبِي ذَرٍّ ، قَالَ : جَعَلَ رَسُولُ اللَّهِ ﷺ يَتْلُو عَلَيَّ هَذِهِ الْآيَةَ : ﴿وَمَنْ يَتَّقِ اللَّهَ يَجْعَلْ لَهُ مَخْرَجًا﴾ حَتَّى فَرَغَ مِنَ الْآيَةِ ، ثُمَّ قَالَ : يَا أَبَا ذَرٍّ لَوْ أَنَّ النَّاسَ كُلَّهُمْ أَخَذُوا بِهَا لَكَفَتْهُمْ قَالَ فَجَعَلَ يَتْلُوهَا ، وَيُرَدِّدُهَا عَلَيَّ حَتَّى نَعَسْتُ ، ثُمَّ قَالَ : يَا أَبَا ذَرٍّ ، كَيْفَ تَصْنَعُ إِنْ أُخْرِجْتَ مِنَ الْمَدِينَةِ ؟ قَالَ : قُلْتُ : إِلَى السَّعَةِ وَالدَّعَةِ ، أَنْطَلِقُ حَتَّى أَكُونَ حَمَامَةً مِنْ حَمَامِ مَكَّةَ . قَالَ : كَيْفَ تَصْنَعُ إِنْ أُخْرِجْتَ مِنْ مَكَّةَ ؟ قَالَ : قُلْتُ : إِلَى السَّعَةِ وَالدَّعَةِ ، إِلَى الشَّامِ وَالْأَرْضِ الْمُقَدَّسَةِ . قَالَ : كَيْفَ تَصْنَعُ إِنْ أُخْرِجْتَ مِنَ الشَّامِ ؟ قَالَ : قُلْتُ : إِذَنْ وَالَّذِي بَعَثَكَ بِالْحَقِّ أَضَعَ سَيْفِي عَلَى عَاتِقِي . قَالَ : أَوَ خَيْرٌ مِنْ ذَلِكَ ؟ قَالَ : قُلْتُ : أَوَخَيْرٌ مِنْ ذَلِكَ ؟ قَالَ : تَسْمَعُ وَتُطِيعُ وَإِنْ كَانَ عَبْدًا حَبَشِيًّا. (مسند أحمد: مسند الأنصاري:٢١٠٩٠)

[32] ALLAH MOST HIGH says: ﴾*And indeed, those who disbelieve would almost make you slip with their [malignant] eyes [of hatred & envy] when they hear the Qur'an and they say, "Indeed, he is mad," but truly it is nothing other than a Reminder to the entire cosmos.*﴿ (*al-qalam,* 68:51-52)

This verse was revealed when the disbelievers wanted to give the *evil eye* to the Messenger of Allah ﷺ. Some people from the Quraish looked once at him and said: *We have never seen anyone like him or like his proofs.* The Banu Asad were renowned for their evil eye. A fat camel or cow would pass by one of them and, after giving it the evil eye, he would say to his slave-girl: *O girl, take a large basket and a silver coin and bring us some of the meat of this!* The camel or cow would fall dead straight after that and would then be hamstrung. Said al-Kalbi: *There was a man from the Arabs who used to abstain from food for two or three days and then raise part of his tent, upon the passing by of cattle, and say: "There are no grazing camels or sheep today better than these", and the cattle would not proceed far before some of them would fall dead. The disbelievers requested this man to give the evil eye to the Messenger of Allah ﷺ but Allah, exalted is He, protected His Prophet and* revealed this verse". (al-Wahidi's *asbab an-nuzul*: 68:51)

In a poignant section of the *mathnawi*, Mevlana Jalaluddin Rumi mentions rhythmically the disastrous effects of the evil eye and prescribes this verse as a protection against it: *For [even] a mountain slips [from its foundations] at the [evil] eye of the wicked: read and mark in the Qur'an [the words] "they cause thee to stumble (68:51)" From [their] looking [at him], Ahmad, [who was] like a mountain, slipped in the middle of the road, without mud and without rain. He remained in astonishment, saying, "Wherefore is this slipping? I do not think that this occurrence is empty [of meaning]," Until the Verse [of the Qur'an] came and made him aware that this had happened to him in consequence of the evil eye and enmity [of the unbelievers]. [God said to the Prophet], "Had it been anyone except thee, he would at once have been annihilated: he would have become the prey of the [evil] eye and in thrall to destruction; but there came [from Me] a protection, sweeping along [majestically], and thy slipping was [only] for a sign."*

Take a warning, look on that mountain, and do not expose thy [petty] leaf [to destruction], O thou who art less than a straw. "O Messenger of Allah, some persons in that assembly [of the unbelievers] smite with their [evil] eye the vultures [flying aloft]. By their looks the head of the lion of the jungle is cloven asunder, so that the lion makes moan. He [such a one] casts on a camel an eye like death, and then sends a slave after it, saying, 'Go, buy some of the fat of this camel': he [the slave] sees the camel fallen dead on the road. (He sees) mortally stricken by disease the camel that used to vie with a horse in speed; for, without any doubt, from envy and [the effect of] the evil eye the celestial sphere would alter its course and revolution."

The water is hidden and the water-wheel is visible, yet as regards [the wheel's] revolution the water is the source of action. The remedy of the evil eye is the good eye: it makes the evil eye naught beneath its kick. [Divine] mercy has the precedence [over Divine wrath]: it [the good eye] is [derived] from [Divine] mercy, [while] the evil eye is the product of [Divine] wrath and execration. (mathnawi: 5:495-510)

Hasan al-Basri reports that it is recommended to recite the above verses to ward off the effects of evil eye. (Zamakhshari's *al-kashshaf*: vol.3/4 p.1279) These two verses may be recited and blown on the person afflicted by the evil eye, and the ill effect will be dispelled, *insha' Allah*.

﴿وَإِن يَكَادُ الَّذِينَ كَفَرُوا لَيُزْلِقُونَكَ بِأَبْصَارِهِمْ لَمَّا سَمِعُوا الذِّكْرَ وَيَقُولُونَ إِنَّهُ لَمَجْنُونٌ A وَمَا هُوَ إِلَّا ذِكْرٌ لِّلْعَالَمِينَ﴾ (٦٨) القلم: ٥١-٥٢

حَدَّثَنَا أَحْمَدُ بْنُ عُبَيْدِ اللهِ الْغُدَانِيُّ، أَخْبَرَنَا غَسَّانُ بْنُ عَوْفٍ، أَخْبَرَنَا الْجُرَيْرِيُّ، عَنْ أَبِي نَضْرَةَ، عَنْ أَبِي سَعِيدٍ الْخُدْرِيِّ، قَالَ دَخَلَ رَسُولُ اللهِ ﷺ ذَاتَ يَوْمٍ الْمَسْجِدَ فَإِذَا هُوَ بِرَجُلٍ مِنَ الْأَنْصَارِ يُقَالُ لَهُ أَبُو أُمَامَةَ فَقَالَ: « يَا أَبَا أُمَامَةَ مَا لِي أَرَاكَ جَالِسًا فِي الْمَسْجِدِ فِي غَيْرِ وَقْتِ الصَّلَاةِ » . قَالَ هُمُومٌ لَزِمَتْنِي وَدُيُونٌ يَا رَسُولَ اللهِ . قَالَ : « أَفَلَا أُعَلِّمُكَ كَلَامًا إِذَا أَنْتَ قُلْتَهُ أَذْهَبَ اللهُ عَزَّ وَجَلَّ هَمَّكَ وَقَضَى عَنْكَ دَيْنَكَ » . قَالَ قُلْتُ بَلَى يَا رَسُولَ اللهِ . قَالَ : « قُلْ إِذَا أَصْبَحْتَ وَإِذَا أَمْسَيْتَ اللَّهُمَّ إِنِّي أَعُوذُ بِكَ مِنَ الْهَمِّ وَالْحَزَنِ وَأَعُوذُ بِكَ مِنَ الْعَجْزِ وَالْكَسَلِ وَأَعُوذُ بِكَ مِنَ الْجُبْنِ وَالْبُخْلِ وَأَعُوذُ بِكَ مِنْ غَلَبَةِ الدَّيْنِ وَقَهْرِ الرِّجَالِ » . قَالَ (فَفَعَلْتُ ذَلِكَ فَأَذْهَبَ اللهُ عَزَّ وَجَلَّ هَمِّي وَقَضَى عَنِّي دَيْنِي. (سنن أبي داود: (٨) كتاب الوتر: ١٤٠٠)

[33] In this verse, the extraordinary fortitude of Prophet Musa ؑ at the Great Contest is made clear. Facing 70 (or more) of the kingdom's topmost sorcerers who were most skilled in the dark arts of *sihr*, there was a slight trepidation in his heart (TaHa:67) when the sorcerers' 70 staffs turned into 70 wriggling snakes. At that moment when his courage wavered, he turned to none but Allah who renewed his strength and confidence, and inspired him to say: *what you have brought is only 'magic'*.

Herein lies the crucial lesson and critical importance of this particular verse in repelling witchcraft and sorcery: the illusory power only lasts for as long as one forgets that it is an illusory power. The moment one remembers it is fake and calls it out, the spell and its power is broken, *bi idhni Llah.* It is for this reason that this verse has been experientially seen to be an antidote for even the most severe cases of witchcraft and sorcery. Reciting this verse in these Last Days *[akhir zaman]* is an immunisation against the forces of evil, *insha' Allah.*

[34] Ka'b b. Ahbar ﵁ is reported to have said, *Seven verses from the book of Allah, if I were to recite it, I would not care if the sky fell upon the earth, I will be protected.* (*al-maslak al-qarib li kulli salikin munib*)

In the Nusantara, these are known as *ayat tujuh.* It is said that whoever reads these verses or bears it on them, Allah Most High will save them from all torment, even if it were as big as Mount Uhud. Reciting them once in the morning and evening is a protection against all evil, *insha' Allah.* As we are fast approaching the time of Dajjal—the anti-Christ—these verses have been included for added potency in our shield against his delusions, harm and evil.

قال كعب الأحبار: سبع آيات من كتاب الله تعالى إذا قرأتهن لا أبالي ولو انطبقت السماء على الأرض لنجوت: ﴿قُل لَّن يُّصِيْبَنَا اِلَّا مَا كَتَبَ اللّٰهُ لَنَا هُوَ مَوْلٰنَا وَعَلَى اللّٰهِ فَلْيَتَوَكَّلِ الْمُؤْمِنُوْنَ﴾ (التوبة:٥١) ﴿وَاِنْ يَّمْسَسْكَ اللّٰهُ بِضُرٍّ فَلَا كَاشِفَ لَهٗ اِلَّا هُوَ وَاِن يُّرِدْكَ بِخَيْرٍ فَلَا رَآدَّ لِفَضْلِهٖ يُصِيبُ بِهٖ مَنْ يَّشَآءُ مِنْ عِبَادِهٖ وَهُوَ الْغَفُوْرُ الرَّحِيْمُ﴾ (يونس:١٠٧) ﴿وَمَا مِن دَآبَّةٍ فِى الْاَرْضِ اِلَّا عَلَى اللّٰهِ رِزْقُهَا وَيَعْلَمُ مُسْتَقَرَّهَا وَمُسْتَوْدَعَهَا كُلٌّ فِيْ كِتَابٍ مُّبِيْنٍ﴾ (هود:٦) ﴿اِنِّيْ تَوَكَّلْتُ عَلَى اللّٰهِ رَبِّيْ وَرَبِّكُمْ مَّا مِن دَآبَّةٍ اِلَّا هُوَ اٰخِذٌ بِنَاصِيَتِهَا اِنَّ رَبِّيْ عَلٰى صِرَاطٍ مُّسْتَقِيْمٍ﴾ (هود:٥٦) ﴿وَكَاَيِّنْ مِّنْ دَابَّةٍ لَا تَحْمِلُ رِزْقَهَا اللّٰهُ يَرْزُقُهَا وَاِيَّاكُمْ وَهُوَ السَّمِيْعُ الْعَلِيْمُ﴾ (العنكبوت:٦٠) ﴿مَا يَفْتَحِ اللّٰهُ لِلنَّاسِ مِن رَّحْمَةٍ فَلَا مُمْسِكَ لَهَا وَمَا يُمْسِكْ فَلَا مُرْسِلَ لَهٗ مِنْۢ بَعْدِهٖ وَهُوَ الْعَزِيْزُ الْحَكِيْمُ﴾ (فاطر:٢) ﴿وَلَئِنْ سَاَلْتَهُمْ مَّنْ خَلَقَ السَّمٰوٰتِ وَالْاَرْضَ لَيَقُوْلُنَّ اللّٰهُ قُلْ اَفَرَاَيْتُمْ مَّا تَدْعُوْنَ مِنْ دُوْنِ اللّٰهِ اِنْ اَرَادَنِيَ اللّٰهُ بِضُرٍّ هَلْ هُنَّ كَاشِفَاتُ ضُرِّهٖ اَوْ اَرَادَنِيْ بِرَحْمَةٍ هَلْ هُنَّ مُمْسِكَاتُ رَحْمَتِهٖ قُلْ حَسْبِيَ اللّٰهُ عَلَيْهِ يَتَوَكَّلُ الْمُتَوَكِّلُوْنَ﴾ (الزمر:٣٨)
(المسلك القريب لكل سالك منيب)

[35] *Imam* Abu al-Qasim al-Qushairi's son was once very ill. He was inspired in a dream to collate and compile these six verses as a means for a healing cure. There are two versions of the dream and they are given in the Arabic text. Regular recital of these verses will protect one from diseases, *insha' Allah.* As new viruses, illnesses and diseases are being discovered at an alarming rate, these verses have been included for added strength in our protection against viral pandemics, debilitating illnesses and crippling diseases.

قال الامام أبو القاسم القشيري ﵀: مرض ولدي مرضا شديدا ، فرأيت رسول الله ﷺ في المنام فقال: ماجاء بك ؟ قلت: حال ولدي، فقال لي: وأين أنت من آيات الشفاء ؟ فقلت: لاأعرفها، فاستيقظ من نومه وبدأ يتلو القرآن، فما مرّ بآية فيها شفاء إلا وجمعها، وإذا هي في ست سور من القرآن، بقول الامام رحمه الله: فكتبتها في قدح ومحوتها بماء وسقيتها ولدي فكأنما نشط من عقال ،.وهي: أعوذ بالله من الشيطان الرجيم ﴿وننزل من القرآن ما هو شفاء ورحمة للمؤمنين﴾ ﴿ويشف صدور قوم مؤمنين﴾ ﴿قل هو للذين آمنوا هدى وشفاء﴾ ﴿يخرج من بطونها شراب مختلف ألوانه فيه شفاء للناس﴾ ﴿وإذا مرضت فهو يشفين﴾ ﴿وشفاء لما في الصدور﴾
فقد ذكر الألوسي هذا الخبر في كتابه روح المعاني، ولكنه ذكر أنه رأى ربه في المنام وليس الرسول ﷺ، ذكر ذلك عند قوله تعالى: وَنُنَزِّلُ مِنَ الْقُرْآنِ مَا هُوَ شِفَاءٌ وَرَحْمَةٌ لِلْمُؤْمِنِينَ {الإسراء: ٢٨}. قال: وآيات الشفاء ست وهي: وَيَشْفِ صُدُورَ قَوْمٍ

مُؤْمِنِينَ {التوبة: ٤١}. وَشِفَاءٌ لِمَا فِي الصُّدُورِ {يونس: ٥٧}. فيه شِفَاءٌ لِلنَّاسِ {النحل: ٦٩}. وَنُنَزِّلُ مِنَ الْقُرْآنِ مَا هُوَ شِفَاءٌ وَرَحْمَةٌ لِلْمُؤْمِنِينَ {الإسراء: ٢٨}. قُلْ هُوَ لِلَّذِينَ آمَنُوا هُدًى وَشِفَاءٌ {فصلت: ٤٤}.

قال السبكي: وقد جربت كثيراً، وعن القشيري أنه مرض له ولد أيس من حياته فرأى الله تعالى في منامه فشكى له سبحانه ذلك فقال له: اجمع آيات الشفاء واقرأها عليه أو اكتبها في إناء واسقه ما محيت به، ففعل فشفاه الله تعالى.

قال الصفوري ورأيت في طبقات ابن السيف مرض ولد للإمام أبي القاسم القشيري مرضا شديداً قال والده ﷺ فرأيت الحق ﷻ في المنام فشكوت ذلك إليه فقال سبحانه اقرأ عليه آيات الشفاء واكتبها في ناء واسقه ففعل ذلك فعوفي الولد وآيات الشفاء ست ويشف صدور قوم مؤمنين وشفاء لما في الصدور فيه شفاء للناس وننزل من القرآن ما هو شفاء ورحمة للمؤمنين وإذا مرضت فهو يشفين هو للذين آمنوا هدى وشفاء. (نزهة المجالس ومنتخب النفائس)

[36] *Sayyiduna ash-Shaikh* 'Abd al-Qadir al-Jilani ؓ has presented this noble *wazifa* for recitation every morning and evening, three times. In so doing, no harm will befall the reciter, by the leave of Allah. (*fuyudat rabbaniyya* p.42)

ولسيّدنا الشّيخ عبد القادر الجيلاني ﷺ وأرضاه هذه الوظيفة الشريفة تقرأ في كل صباح ومساء (ثلاث مرات) لا يضره شيء بإذن الله تعالى ، وهو... (الفيوضات الرّبّانية في المآثر والاوراد القادرية: ٤٢)

[37] Two different *daqa'iq* are presented for morning and evening:

[A] MORNING: *Sayyiduna ash-Shaikh* 'Abd al-Qadir al-Jilani ؓ has said *anyone who is constant in this daqa'iq, six times daily (or seven according to another report), he will behold countless marvels. The preconditions are truthfulness [sidq], sincere devotion [ikhlas], bond of connection [rabita], and complete dedication of one's heart [tawajjuh al-qalb]*.—(*fuyudat rabbaniyya* p.98)

At first sight, this appears to be a mysterious invocation. A closer look reveals a pattern: it mentions five *lata'if* or "subtle spiritual centres" viz. *qalb, qalab, sirr, 'aql* and *ruh*; five personages from the Story of Moses viz. *Sayyiduna Musa* ؑ, *Sayyiduna Harun* ؑ, *Sayyiduna Khidr* ؑ, Fir'awn and Haman; and two enemies of man viz. *nafs* and *hawa*. It also mentions *'irfan* or Gnosis. Discussing these terms and personages, and the reasoning behind their mention and arrangement as done by *Sayyiduna ash-Shaikh* 'Abd al-Qadir al-Jilani ؓ is beyond the scope of this work.

ولسيّدنا الشّيخ عبد القادر الجيلاني ﷺ من دقائقه ذكرها في الغنية من داوم على قراءتها كلّ يوم (ست مرات) وفي رواية (سبع مرات) رأى من العجائب ما لا يحصى الصدق والاخلاص والرابطة وتوجه القلب شرط ، وهي ... (الفيوضات الرّبّانية في المآثر والاوراد القادرية:٩٨)

[B] EVENING: This is a uniquely powerful invocation attributed to *Sayyiduna ash-Shaikh* 'Abd al-Qadir al-Jilani ؓ. Known simply as the *forty kaf* or *chehel kaf*, its popularity extends from Senegal to Singapore. Consequently, multiple versions with slight variations exist. The version presented here is the one for which the author has been given *ijaza* for. It is regrettable that some who do not understand it take it to be a tongue twister or, worse, mock it.

Its meaning, in essence, is a reminder to one's self about being sufficed with Allah Most High. An additional couplet with fifteen more *kafs* has been added (making it a total of fifty-five *kafs*).

The benefits from its recitation are tremendous and have been experientially witnessed Different ways of reciting it have been prescribed by the *masha'ikh*. For our intent and purpose, once a day in the evening suffices.

[38] Two different *ahzab* are presented for morning and evening:
[A] MORNING: This is from the spiritual bequests of *Sayyiduna ash-Shaikh* 'Abd al-Qadir al-Jilani ﵁. It is known as *wird al-ishraq* and should be recited at sunrise. In it one seeks to enter into the safety, security and sanctuary of Allah's protecting mercy by washing away one's claim to any power or strength. An apt end to the morning invocations and begin the day, *insha' Allah.*

ورد الإشراق يقرأ عند الإشراق لسيّدنا الشّيخ عبد القادر الجيلاني ﵁
(الفيوضات الرّبّانيّة في المآثر والاوراد القادريّة: ٩٢)

[B] EVENING: A short yet highly potent *hizb* from the corpus of *Sayyiduna ash-Shaikh* 'Abd al-Qadir al-Jilani ﵁. In this, Allah Most High is entreated by expressing one's abject spiritual poverty, utter hopelessness and absolute neediness. A fitting climax to the invocations in the evening and begin the night, *insha' Allah.*

ورد الحزب الصغير لسيّدنا الشّيخ عبد القادر الجيلاني ﵁ (الفيوضات الرّبّانيّة في المآثر والاوراد القادريّة: ٩٠)

[39] ALLAH MOST HIGH says: ﴿*Allah and His angels whelm in blessings the Prophet. O you of faith! Ask blessings on him and salute him with a worthy salutation.*﴾ (*al-ahzab*, 33:56)

BENEFIT: An esoteric interpretation of the above *ayat* is: ﴿*Verily, Allah and His angels establish a felt connection [yusalluna 'ala] with the Prophet. O you who take the step of faith, establish a felt connection with him [sallu 'alayhi] and give yourselves up [to him] in utter self-surrender [sallimu tasliman].*﴾

Anas b. Malik reported that the Prophet ﷺ said: *If anyone invokes blessing on me once, Allah invokes blessing on him ten times and removes ten wrongdoings from him.* (Bukhari's *al-adab al-mufrad:* 643) The Prophet ﷺ also said: *He who invokes blessings upon me ten times in the morning & ten times in the evening, my intercession will reach him on the Day of Resurrection.* (at-Tabarani reports with two chains one of which is good and whose narrators have been declared trustworthy. See *majma az-zawaid*: 10/120. *Hafiz* ad-Dimyati relates in *al-matjar ar-rabih fi thawab al-'amal as-salih.*)

There are countless permutations of *salawat* upon the Prophet ﷺ—both from the *ahadith* and from the inspired compositions of the *awliya'* and *salihun*. Some of these are specifically mentioned for mornings and evenings while others are general for all times. A selection from both types has been included. The primary *salawat* in this *adhkar*—for both morning and evening—is a particularly poignant 3-*salawat* set that is also found in the first *hizb* of *Imam* al-Jazuli's *dala'il al-khairat*. Regarding this *salawat*, we have the following report from *Sayyiduna* Jabir b. 'Abd Allah ﵁:

> Jabir b. 'Abd Allah reports that the Messenger of Allah ﷺ said: *Whosoever reaches the morning and evening and says, "O Allah, Lord of the praiseworthy one ﷺ, whelm in blessings the praiseworthy one ﷺ and family of the praiseworthy one ﷺ, and reward the praiseworthy one as befits him." tires out 70 angels writing good deeds for one thousand mornings. Nothing remains of the rights of his Prophet Muhammad ﷺ that he has not fulfilled, his parents are forgiven, and he is gathered [in the hereafter] with Muhammad ﷺ and the family of Muhammad ﷺ.* (Suyuti's *al-hawi li l-fatawi: akhir al-'ujaza az-zarnabiyya fi l-sulala az-zainabiyya*)
>
> BENEFIT: at-Tabarani reports that Ibn 'Abbas ﵁ narrated that the Prophet ﷺ said: *Whoever says: 'May Allah reward our Prophet Muhammad with that which he is worth on our behalf', he would put 70 angels in difficulty in writing its reward.* (*al-mu'jam al-kabir:* 11509. See also: *targhib:* vol.2 pg.504, *majma'az-zawaid:* vol.10 pg.163 & *al-qawl al-badi':* pg. 116.)

[A] MORNING: *durud fathiyya.* Preceding the above *salawat* for the morning is a set of 17-*salat* and *salam* upon the Prophet ﷺ known as *durud fathiyya.* The *Muhaddith* Shah Waliyullah Dehlavi ؒ said about this, *"After completing the morning [subh] prayers recite this [durud] fathiyya.* 1,400 *people have become perfect Awliya' by the blessing [baraka] of reciting this." Imam* Yusuf an-Nabhani ؒ relates the same in his *sa'adat ad-da'arain.*

[B] EVENING: *durud ruhiyya.* Likewise for the evening, preceding the above *salawat* from *Sayyiduna* Jabir ؓ is a 13-*salat* set known as (amongst other names) *durud ruhiyya.* It is equivalent to one thousand *salawat*; reciting it once is equal to reciting the *dala'il al-khairat* completely. Several savants and saints have reported that reciting it daily brings about purification of the heart. The benefits to be accrued by the body and soul are immense; life in this world and the hereafter will be exalted, *insha' Allah.*

BENEFIT: Reciting it three times at a graveyard will relief the inhabitants from the torment of the graves for eighty years; reciting it four times will relief the inhabitants from the torment of the graves till Judgement Day. The one who recites this twenty-four times and "gifts" it to his parents will be deemed to have discharged his duties to them; such parents will be visited by a thousand angels. Allah and His Messenger know best.

﴿إِنَّ اللهَ وَمَلٰئِكَتَهُ يُصَلُّوْنَ عَلَى النَّبِيِّ يَآ اَيُّهَا الَّذِيْنَ اٰمَنُوْا صَلُّوْا عَلَيْهِ وَسَلِّمُوْا تَسْلِيْمًا﴾ (٣٣)الأحزاب:٥٦

حَدَّثَنَا اَبُوْ نُعَيْمٍ، قَالَ: حَدَّثَنَا يُوْنُسُ بْنُ اَبِيْ اِسْحَاقَ، عَنْ بُرَيْدِ بْنِ اَبِيْ مَرْيَمَ، سَمِعْتُ اَنَسَ بْنَ مَالِكٍ، عَنِ النَّبِيِّ ﷺ قَالَ: مَنْ صَلّٰى عَلَيَّ وَاحِدَةً صَلَّى اللّٰهُ عَلَيْهِ عَشْرًا، وَحَطَّ عَنْهُ عَشْرَ خَطِيْئَاتٍ.(الأدب المفرد: (١٣) كتاب الدعاء: ٤٠)

قال جابر بن عبد الله عن النبي ﷺ أنه قال : «من أصبح وأمسى قال : اللهم يا رب محمد صل على محمد ، وآل محمد ، واجز محمدا ﷺ ما هو أهله أتعب سبعين كاتبا ألف صباح ولم يبق لنبيه محمد ﷺ حق أداه وغفر لوالديه وحشر مع محمد وآل محمد » .

(الحاوي للفتاوي: آخر العجاجة الزرنبية في السلالة الزينبية)

40 The *adhkar* is concluded with verse 10:10—the exalted *Prayer of the People of Paradise. Imam* al-Qurtubi says that along with this, one should also add the last verses of *surat saffat* (37:180-182) [in a *du'a*] i.e.

﴿سُبْحَانَ رَبِّكَ رَبِّ الْعِزَّةِ عَمَّا يَصِفُوْنَ A وَسَلَامٌ عَلَى الْمُرْسَلِيْنَ A وَالْحَمْدُ لِلّٰهِ رَبِّ الْعَالَمِيْنَ﴾

Regarding the last verses of *surat saffat,* the Messenger of Allah ﷺ said: *Whosoever desires to receive a large amount of reward on the Day of Qiyama should recite the following (i.e. last verses of surat saffat) at the end of a gathering when he intends to stand up.* (Recorded by *Imam* Ibn Abi Hatim in his *Tafsir*, with a *sahih* chain that is *mursal* i.e. broken after the *tabi'i.* See also *Tafsir* Ibn Kathir, *Surat Saffat*, 180-182 & *nata'ij al-afkar*, vol.2 pg.306. Abu Muhammad al-Baghawi records in his *Tafsir* a narration from *Imam* 'Ali b. Abi Talib ؓ).

BENEFIT: It is the practice of our *masha'ikh* to recite the last verses of *surat saffat* three times at the end of *du'a.*

THE TEN SEVENS BEFORE SUNRISE & BEFORE SUNSET
[al-musabba'at al-'ashr qabla tulu' ash-shams wa qabla al-ghurub]

41 (Some) Virtues of <u>surat al-fatiha</u>:

(1) Anas b. Malik ؓ reported: The Prophet ﷺ was on a journey and he descended from his riding animal as a man among his companions was walking by his side. The Prophet turned to him and he said, *"Shall I not tell you of the greatest of the Quran?"* The Prophet recited to him, *"All praise is due to Allah, the Lord of the worlds,"* (1:1) meaning *surat al-Fatiha*.

(2) Ibn 'Abbas ؓ reported: While the Angel Gabriel was sitting with the Prophet ﷺ he heard a creaking noise above him. Gabriel raised his head and he said, *"This is a door of heaven that has been opened today and it has never been opened before today."* Then an angel descended from it, and Gabriel said, *"This angel descended to the earth today and he has never descended until today."* The angel greeted him with peace and he said, *"Rejoice in two lights you have been given, which were not given to any prophet before you: the opening of the Book, Surat al-Fatiha, and the last verses of Surat al-Baqara. You will never recite a letter from them but that you will be given."*—Muslim (806)

(3) Ubayy b. Ka'b ؓ reported: the Messenger of Allah ﷺ asked, *"How do you recite in prayer?"* Ubayy said, *"I recite the foundation of the Book, Surat al-Fatiha."* The Prophet said, *"By the One in whose hand is my soul, nothing like it has been revealed in the Torah, nor the Gospel, nor the Psalms, nor the Furqan. Verily, they are the seven oft-repeated verses and the great Qur'an given to me."*—Tirmidhi (2875)

(4) Ata' reported: Abu Huraira ؓ said, *"In every prayer is a recitation. Prayers that were recited aloud by the Prophet ﷺ we have recited aloud to you, and what he recited silently we have kept silent with you. Whoever recites the foundation of the Book, Surat al-Fatiha, has done enough, but to recite more is better."*—al-Bukhari (738) and Muslim (396)

(5) Abu Huraira ؓ reported: The Prophet ﷺ said, *"Allah Almighty said: I have divided prayer between Myself and My servant into two halves, and My servant shall have what he has asked for. When the servant says, 'All praise is due to Allah the Lord of the worlds,' Allah says: My servant has praised Me. When he says, 'The Gracious, the Merciful,' Allah says: My servant has exalted Me. When he says, 'The Master of the Day of Judgment,' Allah says: My servant has glorified Me and my servant has submitted to Me. When he says, 'You alone we worship, You alone we ask for help,' Allah says: This is between Me and My servant, and My servant will have what he has asked for. When he says, 'Guide us to the straight path, the path of those whom you have favoured, not those who went astray,' Allah says: This is for My servant, and My servant will have what he has asked for."*—Muslim (395)

42 (Some) Virtues of the <u>mu'awwidhatain—surat al-falaq & surat an-nass</u>:

(1) 'Uqba b. 'Amir ؓ reported: The Messenger of Allah ﷺ *"Have you not seen the verses Allah revealed to me in the night? No one has seen the likes of them, 'Say: I seek refuge in the Lord of the people,'* (114:1) *and, 'Say; I seek refuge in the Lord of the daybreak.'"* (113:1)—Muslim (814)

(2) Ibn 'Abis al-Juhani ؓ reported: The Messenger of Allah ﷺ said to him, *"O Ibn 'Abis, shall I not tell you about the best way to seek refuge for those who seek it?"* He said, *"Of course, O Messenger of Allah."* The Prophet said, *"These two chapters: Say, I seek refuge in the Lord of the daybreak* (113:1) *and, Say, I seek refuge in the Lord of the people* (114:1)."—an-Nasa'i (5432)

(3) Abu Sa'id ؓ reported: The Messenger of Allah ﷺ would seek refuge from jinn and

the evil eye of man, until the two chapters of refuge were revealed, *al-Falaq* and *an-Nass*. After they were revealed, he held to both of them and left everything else.—at-Tirmidhi (2058)

(4) 'Uqba b. 'Amir reported ﷺ: The Messenger of Allah ﷺ commanded me to recite the two chapters of refuge, *al-Falaq* and *an-Nass*, at the end of every prayer.—at-Tirmidhi (2903)

(5) 'Aisha ﷺ reported: The Messenger of Allah ﷺ when anyone from his family was sick, he would blow over them with the two chapters of refuge. When he was sick with the illness in which he died, I blew over him and wiped himself with his hands, as they had greater blessings than my hand.—Muslim (2192)

(6) 'Aisha ﷺ reported: When the Messenger of Allah ﷺ would lie down for sleep, he would blow into his hands, recite the two chapters of refuge, *al-Falaq* and *an-Nass*, and he would wipe his hands over his body.—al-Bukhari (5960)

(7) 'Abd Allah b. Khubaib ﷺ reported: The Messenger of Allah ﷺ said, *"Speak."* I said, *"What should I say?"* The Prophet said, *"Say: He is Allah, the One,* (112:1) *and the two chapters of refuge, al-Falaq and an-Nass, every evening and morning three times. They will be enough for you against everything."*—at-Tirmidhi (3575)

[43] See above.

[44] (Some) Virtues of *surat al-ikhlas:*

(1) Anas b. Malik ﷺ reported: A man said, *"O Messenger of Allah, I love this chapter, 'Say: He is Allah, the One,'"* (112:1). The Messenger of Allah ﷺ said, *"Your love for it will admit you into Paradise."*—al-Bukhari (742)

(2) Abu Huraira ﷺ reported: I met with the Prophet ﷺ and he heard a man reciting the verses, *"Say: He is Allah, the One, the Eternal Refuge,"* (112:1-2). The Prophet said, *"It is necessary for him."* I said, *"What is necessary?"* The Prophet said, *"Paradise."*—at-Tirmidhi (2897)

(3) Buraida b. al-Husaib ﷺ reported: The Prophet ﷺ heard a man supplicating, saying, *"O Allah, I ask you by my testimony that you are Allah, there is no God but you, the One, the Eternal Refuge, who does not give birth and was not born, and to whom no one is equal,"* (112:1-4). The Prophet said, *"By the One in whose hand is my soul, he has asked Allah by His greatest name, for which He answers when called upon and He gives when asked."*—at-Tirmidhi (3475)

(4) Abu Sa'id al-Khudri ﷺ reported: A man heard another man reciting, *"Say, He is Allah, the One,"* (112:1) again and again. The next morning he came to the Messenger of Allah ﷺ and told him about it, as if he thought it was not enough to recite. The Prophet said, *"By the one in whose hand is my soul, it is equal to a third of the Quran."*—al-Bukhari (4726)

(5) Mu'adh b. Anas ﷺ reported: The Prophet ﷺ said, *"Whoever recites the chapter ten times completely, 'He is Allah, the One'* (112:1), *Allah will build a palace for him in Paradise."*—Ahmad (15183)

(6) 'Abd Allah b. Khubaib ﷺ reported: The Messenger of Allah ﷺ said, *"Speak."* I said, *"What should I say?"* The Prophet said, *"Say: He is Allah, the One,* (112:1) *and the two chapters of refuge, al-Falaq and an-Nass, every evening and morning three times. They will be enough for you against everything."*—at-Tirmidhi (3575)

45 (Some) Virtues of *surat al-kafirun*:
   (1) 'Abd Allah b. 'Umar ؓ reported: The Messenger of Allah ﷺ said, *"The chapter, 'Say: He is Allah the One,' (112:1) is equal to one-third of the Quran. The chapter, 'Say: O unbelievers,' (109:1) is equal to one-fourth of the Quran."* Ibn 'Umar said, *"The Prophet would recite either of them in his two cycles before dawn prayer."*—al-mu'jam al-kabir (13319)

46 (Some) Virtues of *ayat al-kursi*:
   (1) Ubayy b. Ka'b ؓ reported: The Messenger of Allah ﷺ said, *"O Abu Mundhir, do you know which verse in the book of Allah with you is greatest?"* I recited the verse of the throne, *"Allah, there is no God but him, the Living, the Sustainer,"* (2:255). The Prophet struck me on the chest and he said, *"By Allah, Abu Mundhir, rejoice in this knowledge!"*—Muslim (810)

   (2) Abu Huraira ؓ reported: The Messenger of Allah ﷺ entrusted me to protect the charity of Ramadan. Someone came to me and began taking from the food. I took hold of him and I said, *"I will certainly take you to the Messenger of Allah!"* Abu Huraira told the story to the Prophet and he said, *"The man told me that when I go to bed, I should recite the verse of the throne. Allah would appoint a protector with me and no devil would come near to me until morning."* The Prophet said, *"He told you the truth, although he is a liar. That was Satan."*—al-Bukhari (4723)

   (3) Abu Umama ؓ reported: The Messenger of Allah ﷺ said, *"Whoever recites the 'verse of the Throne' (ayat al-kursi) after every prescribed prayer, there will be nothing standing between him and his entry into Paradise but death."*—al-mu'jam al-kabir (7406)

47 (Some) Virtues of *tasbih, tahmid, tahlil, takbir & hawqala*:
   (1) 'Abd Allah b. Abi Awfa ؓ reported: A man came to the Prophet ﷺ and he said, *"I cannot memorize anything from the Qur'an, so teach me what will suffice me."* The Prophet said, *"Say: Glory be to Allah, all praise is due to Allah, there is no God but Allah, Allah is the greatest, and there is no power or might but in Allah the Exalted, the Almighty."* The man said, *"O Messenger of Allah, these words are for Allah, but what is for me?"* The Prophet ﷺ said, *"Say: O Allah, have mercy on me, provide for me, forgive me, and guide me."*—Abu Dawud (832)

   (2) Samurah b. Jundab ؓ reported: The Messenger of Allah ﷺ said, *"The most beloved words to Allah are four: glory be to Allah, praise be to Allah, there is no god but Allah, and Allah is the greatest. There is no harm in starting with any of them."*—Muslim (2137)

   (3) Abu Huraira ؓ reported: The Messenger of Allah ﷺ said, *"The best words are four: glory be to Allah, praise be to Allah, there is no god but Allah, and Allah is the greatest."*—Ibn Khuzaima (1142)

   (4) Talha ؓ reported: The Messenger of Allah ﷺ said, *"There is no one better to Allah than a believer who lives long to glorify Him, exalt Him, and declare His oneness."*—Ahmad (1401)

   (5) Abu Sa'id ؓ reported: The Prophet ﷺ said, *"If the servant glorifies Allah, Allah Almighty says: Record for my servant an abundance of my mercy. If the servant praises Allah, Allah Almighty says: Record for my servant an abundance of my mercy. If the servant declares there is no God but Allah, Allah Almighty says: Record for my servant an abundance of my love."*—ad-du'a li-Tabarani (1582)

   (6) 'Aisha ؓ reported: The Prophet ﷺ said, *"Verily, every human being among the children of Adam was created with three hundred and sixty joints. Whoever exalts Allah, praises*

Allah, declares Allah is one, glorifies Allah, removes a rock from the roads of people, or a thorn, or a bone from the roads of people, and enjoins good and forbids evil by the number of those joints, he will walk on that day delivering himself from the Hellfire."—Muslim (1007)

[48] (Some) Virtues of <u>salat 'ala n-nabi</u> ﷺ:
   (1) Abu Huraira ؓ reported that the Messenger of Allah ﷺ said, *"Whoever sends prayers upon me once, Allah will send ten prayers upon him."*— Muslim and Tirmidhi

   (2) 'Abd Allah b. Amr ؓ said, *"Whoever sends one prayer upon the Prophet ﷺ, Allah Most High and His angels will send blessings upon him seventy times in return."*—Ahmad

   (3) Anas b. Malik ؓ reported that the Messenger of Allah ﷺ said, *"Whoever sends prayers upon me once, Allah will send ten prayers upon him, ten of his sins will be effaced, and his rank will be raised ten ranks [in Paradise]."* —an-Nasa'i and Ibn Hibban

   (4) 'Ali b. Abi Talib ؓ reported that the Messenger of Allah ﷺ said, *"Whoever sends one prayer upon me, Allah will record for him the reward of a qirat, and a qirat is equivalent to the mountain of 'Uhud."*—musannaf 'abd ar-razzaq

   (5) Abu Bakr as-Siddiq ؓ reported, *"I heard the Messenger of Allah ﷺ say, 'Whoever sends prayers upon me, I shall certainly be his intercessor on the Day of Rising.'"*—Abu Hafs b. Shahin

   (6) Ibn 'Umar ؓ reported that the Messenger of Allah ﷺ said: *"Adorn your gatherings by sending prayers upon me because your prayers upon me will be a light for you on the Day of Judgment."*—musnad al-firdaws

   (7) 'Abd Allah b. Busr ؓ reported the Messenger of Allah ﷺ said, *"Every supplication is barred [from reaching Allah] unless the first of it includes the praise of Allah, Majestic and Sublime is He, and prayers upon the Prophet ﷺ, because only when this is included, and then one supplicates, will his supplications be accepted."*—an-Nasa'i

   (8) 'Abd Allah b. Jarrad ؓ reported, *"Once I was with the Prophet ﷺ and he told us: 'Perform Hajj, for it is greater in reward than participating in twenty military campaigns in the path of Allah. And indeed, sending prayers upon me is equal to all of that (in reward).'"*—musnad al-firdaws

   (9) Anas b. Malik ؓ reported that the Messenger of Allah ﷺ said, *"Send prayers upon me because your prayers upon me will be an expiation for you and a means of purification. Whoever sends one prayer upon me, Allah will send ten prayers upon him."*— al-qawl ad-dadi' and at-Targhib Abu l-Qasim at-Taimi

  (10) Abu Huraira ؓ reported that the Messenger of Allah ﷺ said, *"Send prayers upon me because your prayers upon me will purify you."*—Ibn Abi Shaiba

  (11) Abu Huraira ؓ reported the Messenger of Allah ﷺ said, *"Whoever fears forgetfulness, let him send copious prayers upon the Prophet ﷺ."*—Ibn Bashkuwal and as-Sakhawi

  (12) al-Harith ؓ reported: 'Ali ؓ said, *"Every supplication is veiled until one sends blessings upon Muhammad and the family of Muhammad, peace and blessings be upon him."*—al-mu'jam al-awsat (721)

  (13) Anas b. Malik ؓ reported: "I was standing in front of the Messenger of Allah ﷺ and he said: *'Whoever sends blessings upon me on Friday eighty times, Allah will forgive him the sins of eighty years.'* It was said: *'How may we send blessings upon you, O Messenger of Allah?'* He said: *'Say: "O Allah, send blessings upon Muhammad, Your slave, Your*

Messenger and Your Prophet, the ummi Prophet" and count it as one.'"—tarikh baghdad (13/464)

⁴⁹ (Some) Virtues of *istighfar*:
  (1) 'Ali b. Abi Talib ؓ reported: The Messenger of Allah ﷺ said, *"Verily, your Lord is delighted when His servant says: Lord, forgive my sins, for none forgives sins besides You."*—at-Tirmidhi (3446)

  (2) 'Abd Allah b. Busr ؓ reported: The Prophet ﷺ said, *"Blessed is he who finds many prayers for forgiveness in his record."*—Ibn Maja (3818)

  (3) Ibn 'Abbas ؓ reported: The Messenger of Allah ﷺ said, *"Whoever increases his prayers for forgiveness, Allah will grant him relief from every worry, a way out from every hardship, and provide for him in ways he does not expect."*—Ahmad (2234)

  (4) Az-Zubair ؓ reported: The Messenger of Allah ﷺ said, *"Whoever would love to be pleased with his record, let him increase seeking forgiveness on it."*—shu'ab al-iman (639)

  (5) Salam b. Miskin reported: Qatada ؓ said, *"Verily, this Quran tells you about your diseases and your cures. As for your diseases, they are your sins. As for your cures, it is seeking the forgiveness of Allah."*—shu'ab al-iman (6643)

  (6) 'Uqba b. 'Amir ؓ reported: A man came to the Messenger of Allah ﷺ and he said, *"O Messenger of Allah, one of us has committed a sin."* The Prophet said, *"It will be written against him."* The man said, *"Then he has sought forgiveness and repented."* The Prophet said, *"He will be forgiven and his repentance accepted."* The man said, *"Then he returns to committing a sin."* The Prophet said, *"It will be written against him."* The man said, *"Then he has sought forgiveness and repented."* The Prophet said, *"He will be forgiven and his repentance accepted. Allah will not tire of forgiveness unless you are tired of asking."*—al-mu'jam al-awsat (8918)

  (7) Abu Huraira ؓ reported: The Messenger of Allah ﷺ said, *"Verily, Allah Almighty will raise the status of his righteous servants in Paradise and they will say: O Lord, what is this? Allah will say: This is due to your child seeking forgiveness for you."*—Ahmad (10611)

  (8) 'Ubadah b. as-Samit ؓ reported: The Messenger of Allah ﷺ said, *"Whoever seeks forgiveness for the believing men and women, Allah will record a good deed for him by each man and woman."*—musnad ash-shamiyin (2118)

  (9) Abu Nu'aim reported: ar-Rabia' b. Khuthaim ؓ said to his companions, *"Do you know the disease, the cure, and the healing?"* They said no. ar-Rabia' said, *"The disease is sin, the cure is to seek forgiveness from Allah, and the healing is to repent and then not repeat it."*—hilyat al-awliya' (1722)

⁵⁰ (Some) Virtues of *du'a*:
  (1) Anas b. Malik ؓ reported: The Prophet ﷺ said, *"Supplication is the essence of worship."*—at-Tirmidhi (3371)

  (2) Abu Huraira ؓ reported: The Messenger of Allah ﷺ said, *"Allah says: I am as My servant expects of Me, and I am with him when he calls upon Me."*—Muslim (2675)

  (3) Abu Huraira ؓ reported: The Messenger of Allah ﷺ said, *"Whoever never asks from Allah, He will be angry with him."*—at-Tirmidhi (3373)

  (4) Abu Huraira ؓ reported: The Messenger of Allah ﷺ said, *"No Muslim sets his face towards Allah Almighty in some matter but that he will be given a response, whether it comes quickly or is stored for later."*—Ahmad (9785)

(5) 'Abd Allah b. Amr ﷺ reported: The Messenger of Allah ﷺ said, *"The hearts are vessels and some have greater capacity than others. When you ask from Allah Almighty, O people, then ask Him while you are convinced He will answer. Verily, Allah does not answer the supplication of a servant from behind an unmindful heart."*—Ahmad (6655)

(6) 'Abd Allah ﷺ reported: The Messenger of Allah ﷺ said, *"Ask Allah for His favour. Verily, Allah Almighty loves to be asked and among the best acts of worship is to wait in expectation of relief."*—at-Tirmidhi (3571)

(7) Abu Huraira ﷺ reported: The Messenger of Allah ﷺ said, *"When one of you calls upon Allah, let him hope for the greatest of things. Verily, nothing has any greatness over Allah."*—Ibn Hibban (896)

(8) Anas b. Malik ﷺ reported: The Messenger of Allah ﷺ said, *"Verily, Allah is merciful, conscientious, and generous. He would be shy for His servant to raise his hands to Him and then not place any goodness in either of them."*—*al-mustadrak 'ala sahihain* (1832)

(9) Anas b. Malik ﷺ reported: The Messenger of Allah ﷺ said, *"Do not become frustrated with supplication, for no one was ever ruined by supplication."*—Ibn Hibban (878)

(10) 'Aisha ﷺ reported: The Messenger of Allah ﷺ said, *"No worldly precaution is enough against the divine decree. Supplication benefits by what is sent down and what is not sent down. Verily, a supplication will confront a trial and they both fight each other until the Day of Resurrection."*—*al-mu'jam al-awsat* (2568)

(11) Anas b. Malik ﷺ reported: The Messenger of Allah ﷺ said, *"The servant will continue to be upon goodness as long as he is not impatient."* They said, *"O Messenger of Allah, how is he impatient?"* The Prophet said, *"He says: I have supplicated to my Lord and he did not answer me."*—Ahmad (12596)

تمت وبالخير عمت

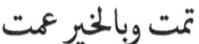

www.ingramcontent.com/pod-product-compliance
Lightning Source LLC
Chambersburg PA
CBHW030434010526
44118CB00011B/628
* 9 7 8 1 0 8 8 0 4 2 5 1 9 *